FamilyFun
Home

Polka-dot Nightstand,
page 84

FamilyFun Home

By Deanna F. Cook
and the experts at
FamilyFun magazine

DISNEY
EDITIONS

This book is dedicated to
the readers of *FamilyFun* magazine

Printed in Hong Kong
For information, address Disney Editions, 114 Fifth Avenue, New York, NY 10011-5690.

The activities and photographs in this book
were previously published in *FamilyFun* magazine.

FamilyFun magazine is a division of Disney Publishing Worldwide.
To order a subscription, call 800-289-4849.

FamilyFun Magazine
BOOK EDITORS: Deanna F. Cook and Alexandra Kennedy
MANAGING EDITOR: Barbara Findlen
ASSISTANT EDITOR: Grace Ganssle
CONTRIBUTING WRITER: Catherine Newman
COPY EDITOR: Paula Noonan
EDITORIAL ASSISTANTS: Jean Graham, Heather Johnson, and Julia Lynch
PICTURE EDITOR: Mark Mantegna
CONTRIBUTING EDITORS: Jonathan Adolph, Dawn Chipman, Ann Hallock,
Gregory Lauzon, and Cindy A. Littlefield
PRODUCTION EDITORS: Jennifer Mayer and Dana Stiepock
TECHNOLOGY COORDINATOR: Tom Lepper

Impress, Inc.
CREATIVE DIRECTOR: Hans Teensma
DESIGN DIRECTOR: Carolyn Eckert
PROJECTS DIRECTOR: Lisa Newman
ART ASSOCIATE: Jen Darcy

The staffs of **FamilyFun** and **Impress, Inc.,**
conceived and produced *FamilyFun Home* at
244 Main Street, Northampton, MA 01060

In collaboration with
Disney Editions, 114 Fifth Avenue, New York, NY 10011-5690.

Library of Congress Cataloging-in-Publication Data on file.

First Edition
1 3 5 7 9 10 8 6 4 2

ISBN 0-7868-5399-9

Acknowledgments

FamilyFun Contributors

Special thanks to the following *FamilyFun* magazine writers for their wonderful home ideas: Rani Arbo, Kevin Ayer, Lynne Bertrand, Tom Birdseye, Heidi Illingworth Boyd, Barry Brenesal, Marie E. Cecchini, Ronnie Citron-Fink, Kent Hicks, Susan Lapinski, Fred Levine, Shoshana Marchand, Sam Mead, Charlotte Meryman, Leslie Garisto Pfaff, Jodi Picoult, Janine Pouliot, Curtis Rist, Ronnie Rom, Barbara Rowley, Anthony Schmitz, Debra Judge Silber, Maryellen Sullivan, Stephen R. Swinburne, Nicole Wise, Lynn Zimmerman.

FamilyFun Readers

Special thanks also to the following *FamilyFun* readers who shared their family success stories: Traci Baker, Tamara Barnett, Tanya Beeler, Colleen Biondo, Janet Brewer, Janet Bricault, Cynthia Bruch, Connie Cannon, Debbe Carson, Lynn Clemens, Clare Collins, Stephanie Curley, Cyndi Dabney, Richard Dahle, Amy Davis, Sue Davis, Kandi Derrick, Mary Diller, Kim Donahue, Jimmy and Laura Dyke, Debbie Emery, Annette Entin, Marquesa Fedastion, Susan Fields, Julie Filbeck, Terri Finnegan, Richard Flanagan, Missy Foran, Carol Forsyth, Melissa France, Krista Gafkjen, Deb Garbenis, Liz Gasper, Joi Giacopuzzi-Steven, Robin Giese, Gale Goeman, Suzanne Grocki, Linda Hardy, Tamarah Henderson, Eva Hensbergen, Tracey Herburger, Rebecca Herschkopf, Mary Hess-Quinones, Penny Huffman, Angela Judd, Tish Keating-Skaronea, Hannah J. Keeley, Sue Kellner, Beth Kelley, Chevelle Kelly, Renee Kirchner, Kari Kjesbo, Julia Konopasek, Amy Laidlaw, Karen Langford, Cheryl LaVecchia, Marsha Lieberman, Bobbi Lemme, Carlo Leto, Susan Lill, Tammy Lindsay, Linda Ludwig, Birdie Lynn, Kelly Malone, Dee Martin, Angela Mathis, Caitlin McCoy, Krystyna McPhall, Theresa Medoff, Catherine Meliezer, Beth Moberg-Wolff, Melanie Osley, Beth Parks, Debbie Pazdziorny, Janine S. Pouliot, Beth Powanda, Jane Quinlan, Jeanie Ransom, Dehorah Rieflin, Anne Robinson, Cheryl Robinson, Amy Rodrigueze, Liz Ruff, Sandy Russell, Lisa Schmidt, Lynn Schumaker, Terrie Shortsleeve, Ann Cameron Siegal, Julie Slover, Becky Sprague, Therese Stenzel, Ellen Thomas, Margaret Tindol, David Vining, Vicki Watson, Angi Watters, Tara Yerkie, Lori Zobel.

FamilyFun Staff

With gratitude to the staff of *FamilyFun*'s art and editorial departments, who directed all of the original work. In addition to the book staff credited on the previous page, we'd like to acknowledge the following staff members: Douglas Bantz, Nicole Blasenak, Jodi Butler, Terry Carr, Moira Greto, Michael Grinley, Ginger Barr Heafey, Heather Humble, Melanie Jolicoeur, Elaine Kehoe, Laura MacKay, Adrienne Stolarz, Mike Trotman, Ellen Harter Wall, Sandra L. Wickland, and Katharine Whittemore.

About the Editors of *FamilyFun Home*

Deanna F. Cook, Creative Development Director of *FamilyFun* magazine, is the editor of the *FamilyFun* book series, which includes *FamilyFun Boredom Busters* and *FamilyFun Cookbook,* from Disney Editions, and the author of *The Kids' Multicultural Cookbook* and *Kids' Pumpkin Projects,* from Williamson. She lives in an 1890 house in Florence, Massachusetts, with her husband, Doug, and her two daughters, Ella and Maisie.

Alexandra Kennedy is the VP, Editorial Director of *FamilyFun* magazine and *Disney Magazine.* She and her husband, James Haug, and their two sons, Jack and Nicky, share a home with too many pets in Northampton, Massachusetts.

Special thanks to all the photographers, stylists, and models for their excellent work, which first appeared in *FamilyFun* magazine.

This book would not have been possible without the help of Disney Editions, especially of Duryan Bhagat, Janet Castiglione, Wendy Lefkon, Jill Newman, and Jody Revenson.

Contents

Collection Containers, page 96

Ready-to-wear, page 73

6 Workspaces **101** Keep your family organized with our creative and practical systems for home offices, craft areas, and laundry rooms ~ *Family Communication . . . 103* ✦ *Home Office . . . 108* ✦ *Craft Area . . . 116* ✦ *Laundry Solutions . . . 120*

7 Storage Spaces **125** Discover storage solutions that are easy and convenient for your entryway, basement, attic, or garage ~ *Entryway . . . 127* ✦ *Basement . . . 134* ✦ *Garage . . . 138*

8 Backyard Projects **141** With our step-by-step instructions, you can surprise your child with his very own picnic table, sandbox, or secret playhouse ~ *Porches & Patios . . . 143* ✦ *Play Zones . . . 149* ✦ *Backyard Forts . . . 161* ✦ *Backyard Birds . . . 172*

9 Gardening With Kids **179** Garden projects your kids will dig, from growing a sunflower fort to planting a butterfly garden ~ *Vegetable Gardening . . . 181* ✦ *Flower Gardening . . . 187* ✦ *Planting Trees . . . 195* ✦ *Water Gardening . . . 197* ✦ *Garden Crafts . . . 200*

CHAPTER ONE

Welcome Home

Tips for making your home a place where everyone in the family can relax and thrive

Our Massachusetts home is much more than the four walls around us — it is the place where my husband, Doug, and I are raising a family. Under our roof, we cook, play, work, celebrate, learn, and entertain with our girls, Maisie, two, and Ella, five. And whether we are decorating or organizing, we are always trying to create a place where all four of us — the kids and the parents — feel right at home.

It is in this family-friendly spirit that I present this book, *FamilyFun Home*. The creative ideas and practical solutions come from real families — the contributors, readers, and staff members of *FamilyFun* magazine. Over the years, we've learned that the secret to a successful home lies in the details — those little clutter-busting tips, toy storage strategies, and decorating ideas that make a home a

Ella and Deanna in their family kitchen

smoother-running — and therefore more fun — place to live.

As you'll see, the home solutions run the gamut but feature two essential keys to success: they're kid-friendly and they're easy. Take, for example, the Robinson family, whose ingenious way of displaying kids' art (page 50) also beautified their stairwell. Or the Spragues, who used a basketball hoop to encourage their kids to slam-dunk their laundry (page 72). Or the Filbecks, whose visual toy storage system (page 97) made a matching game out of putting away stray Legos and Barbies.

So whether your family lives in a two-bedroom city apartment or a sprawling old farmhouse, we're sure you'll find these ideas easy to adapt to your own home and family. They certainly have found a welcome place in my home.

— *Deanna F. Cook*

The Family-friendly Home

We've all had the feeling of walking into a home and knowing instantly that kids are welcome. It's not just the visible signs of children — the toys, the books, the plastic flotilla in the bathtub. Rather, it's the thoughtful adjustments made to honor the littler members of the household: hooks for coats hung at a kid's height, say, or a small table set up for craft projects. Such houses not only work for kids — they make sense for parents too. After all, that low hook means one less coat to pick up off the floor, and with a project table, you can actually eat at the kitchen table. By recognizing the way families really live, the ideas presented in this book can help make your house the haven you always hoped it would be.

Set up your home with the kids in mind. Simple things, such as step stools, colorfully labeled toy boxes, and self-serve snack stations, can make kids feel welcome in your home. As you know, when you're busy, you want kids to be able to help themselves: to a nutritious treat, an on-the-spot art activity, or some just-my-size cleaning supplies. Size up your home, then scale it down to accommodate your own not-yet-grown set.

Make your home comfortable for everyone. For a family with kids, the perfect home should be a safe harbor in a busy, chaotic world. Ask yourself, what is the feeling you want your house to evoke? Then, as you set up your rooms, think about creating a warm, inviting atmosphere. Set up a cozy chair by a sunny window, play music on your family room stereo, grow a pretty flower garden in your backyard. With a bit of imagination, you can create a place which you will always be happy to come home to — and which you may never want to leave.

Make lasting memories. When your kids look back at their childhoods, many of their most distinct and treasured memories will center around the family home. You might consider this as you organize their bedrooms, landscape your backyard, or even put out such finishing touches as candles on the table. Be sure to take pictures of your rooms and yard so your kids will remember their childhood home.

FAMILYFUN SUCCESS STORY
Greetings from Our House

"Our children enjoy participating in recording our telephone answering machine message. Each week, one of us chooses from a fishbowl a card with a song, story, or funny joke written on it. Then, we gather around to record the new message. We even change greetings to fit holidays, such as Christmas, Valentine's Day, and Halloween."

— **Richard Flanagan**
Charlotte, North Carolina

Personalizing Your Home

In a family home, the rooms under the roof should reflect — and showcase — the lively children who live there. One family we know has even worked this message right into the front door. On the jamb is a growth chart showing the ages and various heights of the home's three kids. Throughout this book, we offer dozens of projects that help you personalize your rooms and walls — and create a place you are proud to call home.

Display your kids' artwork and family photographs. Frame your kids' best artwork — watercolors, drawings, and crayon self-portraits — and prominently display them in your home. While you're at it, hang photographs of your children and favorite family vacation snapshots. Not only will these personalized pictures beautify your rooms, but they will also boost your children's self-esteem in the process.

Let your kids be interior decorators. You don't have to give them a roller and a can of paint (although you could! — see pages 76–80 for our inexpensive do-it-yourself wall-decorating ideas), but do give the kids a say in decorating the house — or at least their own bedrooms. Thoughout the book, look for our Decorate It and Kid-friendly Project tags.

Make it homemade. Whether it's a tire swing in the backyard or a light switch in your bedroom, your family will treasure it more (and save money) if you make it yourselves. Over the years we've been lucky enough to receive ideas from *FamilyFun* readers, and in the pages that follow we share a number of their home decorations.

Let your kids leave their mark. Smudgy handprints on the wall probably drive you crazy, but a wall printed with your kids' hands might be just the thing to personalize your basement. Consider hand-painted tablecloths, room signs made by the children, and clay-sculpted drawer knobs as you decorate. These unique details can add the perfect touch of family to your home.

FAMILYFUN SUCCESS STORY
Suburban Barn Raising

"It all started when our neighbors were putting in a second driveway and carport — a really major undertaking — while a bunch of us looked on, as often happened in our neighborhood. A friend of theirs, a former contractor, noticed us standing around and put us to work. We knew nothing about what we were doing — all of us were in big rubber boots, sliding around in the cement — but with a little supervision, and everyone working together, we got the project done.

"Soon after, the neighbors volunteered to help us with our next big task, painting our house. Thus our neighborhood's informal Home Improvement Coop was born: several families working together in the backyard. Next time, we'll all tackle another family's project. The work gets finished in a fraction of the time it would have taken a single family, the kids have fun, and we always celebrate our accomplishments with a neighborhood barbecue. Everybody wins."

— **Renee Kirchner**
Carrollton, Texas

Welcoming Guests

Sharing your home with guests, whether they're visiting family, friends from out of town, or even a handful of your children's buddies, can be a wonderful experience. Kids love the break from routine — doubling up with a sibling for the night, getting to stay up late, or delighting to find another friendly face at the breakfast table — plus, it's a great opportunity to foster their natural graciousness. Even at a young age, children can learn that the secret to welcoming guests isn't having a well-appointed guest room, a closet full of white towels, or an endless schedule of thrilling activities. It's the little things — a carefully made bed, a jar of wildflowers on the dresser, a warm greeting — that say "Our house is your house. Welcome!"

Make a welcome basket. Fill a basket with glad-to-see-you goodies, as shown above. Include rainy-day reading matter, snacks, and activity gifts (bubbles, watercolor paints and paper, or a deck of cards). To really roll out the red carpet, add a box of mints and a vase of fresh flowers picked from your backyard.

Offer a "Fun Book." For visitors unfamiliar with the lay of the land (and the location of the local pizza joint), pack a vacation's worth of hometown essentials — maps, restaurant menus, and pamphlets for area attractions — into one portable notebook. That way they can venture out on their own with ease when the rigors of daily life keep their hosts too busy to escort them.

Design a "Do Not Disturb" sign. Offer your guests this practical amenity: a doorknob sign that communicates their waking or sleeping preferences. Start with a craft foam door hanger (available at craft stores) or cut your own, then use puffy paint to write "We are sleeping in today" on one side, and "Please wake us for breakfast" on the other.

FAMILY KEEPSAKE
Household Guest Book

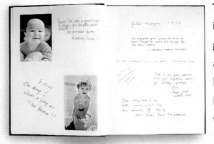

Take a cue from professional innkeepers and invite your guests to record their names and memories in a guest book. Next visit, you can all look back on your time together. We chose an 8½- by 11-inch hardbound sketch-book with acid-free paper to help preserve photos, but art supply and craft stores offer a variety of sketchbooks and scrapbooks that would work as well. Keep a cup of colored markers nearby, and include mementos such as children's drawings, pressed flowers, and ticket stubs.

For mounting, consider using a restickable glue stick, which allows you to reposition items without destroying the pages.

FamilyFun **Home**

Living Creatively Indoors and Out

How can you make your home a place that nurtures the creative spirit in your kids? Try thinking of your home as not only a place to live, but also as a classroom, an art station, or a nature center. A bird feeder hung near a window may inspire your budding naturalists; an easel set up in the kitchen will allow young Monets to paint while you get dinner on the table; a cozy, well-lit corner might encourage a Harry Potter reading marathon. Here are some other creative ideas:

Encourage open-ended play. Our play stations will foster imaginative play — and entertain your kids for hours. Indoors, you might set up our play kitchen on page 23 for pretend cooking sessions, or create our closet on page 116 for impromptu art projects. Out of doors, you might build a tepee or a fort for secret hideaway games, or make your own sandbox (see page 148–151).

Remember, learning begins at home. Some of your child's most memorable learning experiences take place when your family is at home. Helping to measure the ingredients for a favorite cookie recipe, your child starts getting the scoop on fractions. Watching sunflowers sprout in the garden, she discovers the thrill of scientific observation. While these everyday learning moments often seem to come about by chance, you can set up your home to make learning almost automatic.

Make time for free time at home. Try to carve out a little time every day for your kids to "do nothing" at home. If your house is set up for free play, you'll be amazed at how quickly quiet time turns into an egg-carton art project, or a tree-climbing adventure, or a daydreaming session in their rooms.

FAMILYFUN SUCCESS STORY
The Fun Zone

Tara Yerkie of Hartly, Delaware, realized that changing her family's too-much-TV habits meant changing her home. So she turned their little-used dining room into a special area where her kids, Aaron, 11, and Brandon, seven, could get creative. She filled a bunch of bookshelves with all the kids' books, games, and puzzles. She added a radio with a cassette deck for audio books. Tara also brought in cabinets with drawers for craft supplies and put a plastic tablecloth over the dining room table. The Yerkies' fun zone was born. Oh, and one other thing: she canceled their cable TV service. In a few days, the house was a different place, geared toward activities, not toward vegging out in front of the TV.

Making Chores Fun

Housework — when you have kids — is like bailing water. It's a steady stream of papers, clothes, dishes, and toys that rushes in faster than you can possibly toss it back out. Nothing is ever tidy, really. But if you can get the kids to chip in, there might be hope for you to have a somewhat neat house. In the pages that follow, you'll find lots of ideas — chore charts and maintenance-free storage solutions that make it fun and easy for kids to clean up after themselves.

Make chores a family affair. Kids crave your time and attention, in whatever form it takes. You might be surprised to find that an hour spent weeding the garden with your daughter affords her a low-key opportunity to share a secret or two about her life. And a laughter-filled afternoon spent bagging leaves as a family might make a memory to treasure.

Turn work into a game. You might simply put on a song and let your kids dance around the living room as they put away their toys. Or you could play a real game: try making Bingo cards, with a different chore in every square. The first child to complete a row of chores wins — a treat, maybe, or a video rental. A blacked-out card could mean a night out with Mom or Dad.

Offer an incentive. This means different things to different families: words of praise or encouragement, stickers on a chart, pretend money to be cashed in for treats, or even real cash. Some families distinguish between cleaning up after yourself (a basic responsibility) and a treat-earning chore like vacuuming or doing yard work.

Create a routine and stick to it. Finding a workable arrangement takes creativity, faith, and a lot of trial and error. But once you settle on a system that works for your family, try to stay committed.

FAMILYFUN SUCCESS STORY

Chore for Hire System

Stephanie Curley of North Attleboro, Massachusetts, uses friendly, economic competition to prompt Alex, age eight, and Michael, six, to do chores. Instead of assigning specific jobs, she posts a list of available chores and their wages (putting away laundry = 25 cents or vacuuming = a dollar). To choose a chore — and they can opt to do none — the kids simply write in their initials. On payday, Stephanie totals each boy's earnings and gives him his due. Putting the choice in their hands has not only cut down on grumbling, she reports, but has also motivated Alex and Michael to do more. As the initials start filling in, each boy vies for the tasks that will make him the week's top breadwinner.

FamilyFun **Home**

Controlling Clutter

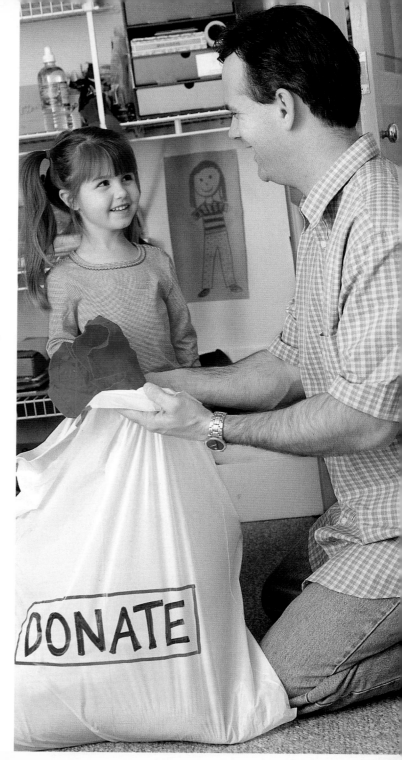

Legos. **Work sheets.** Soccer cleats. It's one of the paradoxes of family life: nobody can ever find the things they need, and yet there are things everywhere — underfoot, under the bed, on every tabletop. Our paradoxical solution? Less stuff means more stuff. The more clutter you clear away, the easier it will be for your family to find and use the things you actually need. So clutter, beware! There's nowhere to hide.

Maintain control. Determine your worst clutter zones — inside the front door, maybe, or the kitchen counter. Then develop a system for managing incoming items (perhaps a cubby for each family member, see page 127) and stick with it. Make sure your kids understand the strategy, and solicit their help in implementing it.

Save selectively. Do you need to keep all of your children's artwork? Hold onto every catalog? Store outgrown toys and clothes in the garage? Wherever stuff is accumulating, ask yourself why, and whether you can live without it.

Do more, bring home less. It may seem like clutter multiplies while you're not looking — but the truth is that things end up in our homes because we buy them, keep them, or collect them. Encourage your family to do activities that don't entail acquisition: visit a museum, take a bike ride or a hike, or build a sand castle at the beach.

FAMILYFUN SUCCESS STORY
The Great Cleanup

When it comes to clutter busting, our favorite container is the trash bag. This doesn't have to mean sending all your stuff to the dump — while bagging up what you no longer use, keep an eye out for items that are still in good condition and separate them for donation or to give to a friend with younger children. Give the rest of the junk the old heave-ho, though! On cleanup day, turn trash collecting into a scavenger hunt, and see how quickly you can fill a bag. Here are some trash-worthy (or recycling center) items:

- Jigsaw puzzles with missing pieces
- Ancient sports equipment
- Expired medicine and sunscreen
- Anything that has been broken — and not fixed — for over a year
- Dried-out or used-up art supplies
- Old schoolwork that nobody wants saved
- Way-past-their-prime yard toys
- Torn or stained children's clothing

CHAPTER TWO

Kid-friendly Kitchens & Baths

Bring new order, and more fun, to the hardest-working rooms in the house

When it comes to actual living, the kitchen beats the living room hands down. It is part command center, part gathering hall, part conference room, and part comfort station, not to mention the place where we do most of our eating, art projects, homework, and partying. Too often, however, kitchens present barriers to the littlest users ("I can't reach it, Mommy!"), thwarting both their growing independence and their desire to be helpful. So how can we make it the kind of space the whole family can enjoy?

For starters, we need to impose some order: kitchens attract not just people, but also all the clutter they bring with them. Plus, we have to adapt the kitchen to make it easy to navigate for all family members. To that end, we've cooked up some bright ideas to keep disarray at bay and make the kitchen a welcoming place — from a kids' Lunch Packing Station (page 25) to the latest in homemade fridge magnets (page 32).

Tiger Step Stool, page 41

Like the kitchen, the bathroom has more than one purpose. Sure, it's the room where you go to get clean, but it's also the room that kids play for hours in the suds and the one you struggle to keep neat. Our tubful of ideas for bathroom toys and tidyness will keep water babies of all ages happy. From soapy solutions (page 35) to traffic-control tips for those busy mornings (page 34), we've got the rub-a-dub-dub on wash-up fun.

Follow these tips to make your kitchen and bathroom user-friendly for everyone from parents to toddlers.

Remember the little people. Invest in a lightweight stool and store it somewhere obvious — by the kitchen or bathroom sink — so that kids can get to it easily. Designate one of your lower kitchen cabinets for the littlest kids. Stock it with cups, bowls, and other items they'll need.

Label everything. Mark drawers and cabinets with their contents so kids know where to find things (and where to put them away!). This is also a motivating way to jump-start young readers (bet you they learn to spell c-o-o-k-i-e-s in a week).

Encourage good habits. Make it easy for kids to help, and they'll be more inclined to chip in. Guarantee success with reasonable goals and accessible supplies: a handy sponge might remind your kids to wipe up; cutlery in a totable tray makes setting the table a snap.

Remember safety first. The kitchen and bathroom present a number of hazards for kids: hot stoves, sharp knives, slippery tubs, and cleaning supplies are among them. As soon as possible, teach kids about safety, and take obvious precautions by keeping dangerous substances out of kids' reach and by supervising the bathing activities of little ones.

Family Kitchen Essentials

Want happy kids in your kitchen? Think of everything on their level — from size to safety.

- Buy plastic bins in a variety of colors and assign one to each family member. Anything cluttering up valuable space (counter, table, or floor) gets whisked into the appropriate bin for disposal or redirection by its owner at some later date.
- Keep a stool or stepladder handy for little helpers (for a fun design, see the Tiger Step Stool on page 41).
- Give up a drawer or cabinet to your kids' toys and art supplies; this will keep clutter out of the rest of your kitchen, and it will welcome (and entertain) kids when they wander in seeking your company.
- Remember that the kitchen is prime hangout real estate. Keep a space clear for homework — an island with a stool pulled up, maybe, or part of a kitchen table. Set up a low table and chairs for littler kids who want to be a part of things (page 21).
- Remember basic safety rules: knives out of reach, the handles of cooking pots turned away, dangerous gadgets kept high up. Be sure to talk to your kids about where danger lurks in the kitchen: heat, blades, glass, and electricity are the main culprits.

Kids in the Kitchen

DO-IT-YOURSELF

The Chalkboard Nook

Turn the side of a kitchen island or an open stretch of wall into a doodling nook by hanging a chalkboard at your kids' height. While you're busy cooking, kids can draw or leave funny jokes and messages to one another. They might even jot down an inspirational poem or saying, or they can write out the evening's menu for the rest of the family to peruse while waiting.

HELPING HANDS

Think Small

Providing a selection of kid-size tools is an inviting way to say, "Wanna help?" Whether it's a junior set of cooking utensils kept in a special drawer or a toy broom and dustpan hung within a kid's reach, the gear lets a child experience the satisfaction of pitching in.

KID-FRIENDLY TIP

Set Up a Snack Station

Even before the last meal's dishes have dried, the cry comes: "I'm hungry!" Let the kids cure their own snack attacks by placing some plastic dishes and snacks in a designated self-service area. Gather the items together and put them in a lower cabinet or on a low shelf in the refrigerator so the kids can easily reach them. Add a few rules if you need to — such as no eating an hour before dinner. Keep a dish towel or a roll of paper towels down low as well for self-service cleanup.

Onion-print Apron

A budding chef needs an apron, of course. Spruce one up with colorful spirals stamped from onions. And while you're at it, why not make a couple of matching place mats?

MATERIALS

- **Onion**
- **Kitchen knife**
- **Plain apron (available at craft supply stores; wash before painting)**
- **Fabric paint**
- **Paintbrush**
- **Scrap paper**

Cut an onion in half, making sure the cut surfaces are as level as possible to create flat stamps. Press the two halves, cut side down, on a paper towel to draw out any excess moisture. Next, brush a thin, even layer of fabric

paint across the cut surface of one half (you can save the other half for another color) and have your child practice stamping the onion on scrap paper to see how many impressions he can make before brushing on more paint. If the fabric paint seems too thick, dilute it with a little water (this will make your stamp pattern more defined). Once your child has mastered the technique, he's ready to print directly on the apron. Let the finished designs dry completely and refer to the paint manufacturer's directions before washing the apron.

Onion-print Place Mats To make the place mats pictured on page 27, follow the directions above, but print on solid-colored cloth place mats.

TIPS AND TECHNIQUES

Cooking With Kids

1. Start young. Invite the kids into the kitchen as early as you can so they get accustomed to its sights and smells. Give them small projects to do — rinse asparagus in their toy kitchen, tear lettuce into pieces, or make guacamole by mashing avocados in a ziplock bag. If they help make the meal, they may be more inclined to eat it.

2. Create a space for little chefs. Set up a low table or use an island or a pull-out shelf with a tall stool. Reserve a drawer in the kitchen and stock it with kid-size tools — mini rolling pin, whisk, baking sheet, plastic picnic knives, an apron, etc.

3. Set up rules. Teach kids safe cooking habits from the get-go. Some basics: wash hands, wear an apron, tie hair back, never touch a hot stove, and always help clean up.

4. Teach kids where food comes from. Grow a vegetable garden, visit a neighborhood bakery, and take your kids to a local dairy farm to see (and maybe help) cows get milked.

5. Keep a file of kid-friendly recipes. Start a recipe file specifically for chefs in training. Once they start collecting their favorite dishes, they might even participate in dinner planning and preparation.

6. Assemble a kids' baking kit. Fill a large mixing bowl with goodies for learning to bake — including a homemade certificate from Mom or Dad promising an after-school session of baking lessons (see photo above).

FamilyFun Home

Kid-size Kitchen Table

Transform a small wooden table into a kid-size beach paradise, and your kids will sit happily through their meals. Plus, it doubles as a cozy art spot for kids to work at while dinner prep is underway.

MATERIALS

Paints

1 quart water-based primer

(We used semigloss interior latex paints by Crayola, except where noted)

1 quart Sky Blue (light blue)

1 quart Cerulean (dark blue)

1 quart Halloween orange

1 quart School Bus Yellow

1 quart Red

1 quart White

Other supplies

Sandpaper, if necessary

Unfinished kids' table and chair set

2-inch-wide foam wedge brush

1½- to 2-inch-wide polyester paintbrush

Low-tack painter's masking tape

1 roll repositionable medium adhesive Con-Tact paper

Plastic lid, 3-inch diameter

1-inch-wide polyester paintbrush

Large plate for sun's center

½-inch-wide detail paintbrush

Plastic lid, 2½-inch diameter

Primer Sand the table and chairs if necessary. Make sure they are clean. Use the 2-inch foam brush to coat them with primer. Let the primer dry.

Sky Use your 1½-inch paintbrush to paint the tabletop and the chair backs (including the spindles) light blue. Let dry.

Waves To protect the paint on the spindles, wrap each (where it meets the backrest) with low-tack masking tape. On each of two strips of Con-Tact paper (each at least 4 inches high and 2 inches wider than your chair back), trace a wave pattern using the bottom of the lid (see **A**). Cut each strip along the drawn lines. The top

piece is your stencil.

Adhere one length of the stencil over the top half of the front of the backrest, and use the other length for the back. Use your 1-inch brush to fill in the waves with dark blue paint (see **B**). Paint from the stencil downward. Remove the stencil promptly and let the paint dry.

Use the same method for the table waves, except create four lengths of stencil (each the length of a table side plus a few extra inches). Adhere all four stencils a few inches in from the table's edge and trim them where they overlap. Paint from the stencil toward the edge of the table. Remove Con-Tact paper promptly and let the paint dry.

Set the chairs and table upside down on a clean area. Coat all the legs, plus the table underside and outside edge, with the wave color. Let it dry.

Sun Center your plate on the tabletop (be sure you have space for the sun rays) and trace it in pencil.

Along the perimeter of the circle, make light pencil marks every 2½ to 3 inches. Using a ruler and these marks as guides, sketch triangular sun

rays. Tape along the lines. Use the 1-inch brush to apply orange paint inside the tape, brushing inward. Don't paint inside the center circle. Let it dry.

Use the 1-inch brush to paint the circle yellow. Let it dry, then pencil in a spiral and use the ½-inch detail brush to paint it orange.

Beach Ball Seats To protect the bottom of the chair spindles from the seat paint, apply tape to them.

Use a pencil and a ruler to lightly draw two lines across the seat in a cross shape. Then divide those four sections in half, like you're cutting a pizza to make eight sections. Lightly trace the 2½-inch plastic lid in the center of the seat.

Apply tape over your radiating lines (see **C**). Painting inward from the tape, do four alternating sections in the colors of your choice. Try not to paint inside the circle. Remove the tape and allow those sections to dry.

Place new tape on the edges of the painted sections. Paint the remaining four sections of the ball, remove the tape carefully, and let the paint dry. Use the detail brush to paint the circle dark blue. Let it dry. You're done!

Hand-painted Kitchenware

When kids make their own kitchenware, they'll feel right at home in the kitchen — plus, you'll have a lovely keepsake to treasure. We like those paint-your-own pottery studios, where we decorated these colorful mugs. Similarly painted, ceramic tiles make playful trivets or they can be installed behind the kitchen sink as a kid-friendly backsplash.

If your child paints one piece of kitchenware every year — whether it's a dinner plate, butter dish, cereal bowl, or color-coordinated mug (like the ones on the left) — you'll have a beautiful and useful record of the passing time. Look in your local yellow pages for a paint-your-own pottery studio, or invest in a handful of ceramic paints (available at art supply stores) to use at home.

FAMILYFUN SUCCESS STORY
Mixed Chairs

"When we moved into our house, we didn't have the money to spend on a new dinette set. One day my husband came home with a serviceable table that he'd found at a garage sale for $20. I knew that I'd never find five matching chairs in my price range, so I looked in thrift stores for sturdy wooden chairs that didn't match. Once I found five (they arranged from $5 to $9 each), I set to work stripping and sanding all the chairs and the table. When it was time to paint, I selected a base color and four accent colors that would look good in our kitchen. Then I handed each of my three kids a brush and let them go at it.

"My ten-year-old son, Christian, painted each rung of his chair a different color, and my 11-year-old daughter, Alexandra, put freehand designs on hers. Even Seth, our four-year-old, was able to decorate his chair — he used a round sponge brush that I found at a craft store to stamp on polka dots. My husband and I likewise painted chairs in individual styles. For the table, I applied the base coat, and the kids splatter-painted over it. The finished set looks great, cost little money, and has the most important quality of all: it will live in my kids' memories as a fun family project."

— Julia Konopasek
Everett, Washington

Pretend Kitchen

Kids love to keep you company in the kitchen, and a set of toy pots, dishes, and food will keep them busy pretend-cooking while you get to the real thing. But even kid-size playthings can leave a big mess, and a play kitchen for storing them can be pricey. Jean Williamson from San Marcos, California, came up with the perfect solution for her two wanna-be gourmets: an easily and inexpensively constructed play kitchen that houses all the paraphernalia of her budding chefs. The kitchen's base is stacking shelves intended for closet organization. Jean stacked a pair on each side; our local Lowe's had larger units (around $14 each) that we cut down with a jigsaw.

MATERIALS

Tools
- **Jigsaw**
- **Drill and screws**

Other supplies
- **A pair of stacking shelves**
- **Plywood**
- **Rimmed metal bowl**
- **Latex and acrylic paints**
- **Assorted hooks**
- **Junk mail CD-ROMs**
- **Wooden sink and stove knobs**
- **Café rod**
- **Fabric-scrap curtain**
- **Play kitchenware, such as dishes, pots and pans, cutting board, pot holder, and pretend food**

Set the shelves about a foot apart, then measure and cut a countertop and backsplash from plywood. Drill a starter hole, then use a jigsaw to cut a hole in the countertop just large enough to hold a rimmed metal bowl. Next, screw the backsplash to the counter and give the unit a coat of latex paint.

Fun details really seal the deal: painted flowers on the backsplash, a spout fashioned from the scrap wood from the sink hole, hooks to hang pot holders, junk mail CD-ROMs for the range burners, and wooden sink and stove knobs painted with acrylics (drill a pilot hole, then screw them in place). For the elegant finale, a café rod and clip-on hooks hold a fabric-scrap curtain. Now it is time to stock the kitchen with kitchen toys and tools — and don't forget the pretend food.

"It worked out great and gets many hours of use!" Jean gushes. "And when the kids outgrow it, I can reuse the shelves to organize my closets!"

Family Meals

Mom's Menu

With a little bit of planning and creativity, family meals can be the kind of soul-satisfying experience you crave.

For *FamilyFun* reader Krystyna McPhall of Stoughton, Massachusetts, this means creating an easy breakfast menu. Krystyna used to struggle to get her six-year-old twins to decide what they wanted for breakfast. One day, in frustration, she grabbed a piece of paper, folded it in half, scrawled "Menu" on the cover, and listed the usual choices inside. "To my surprise, Robert and Samantha instantly made their decisions," says Krystyna. She refined the list, typed it up, and made two copies. Mom's Restaurant is open for business daily,

and even the waitress is satisfied.

Prompted by similar desperation, Diana Treadway of St. Ann, Missouri, stuck a wipe board on the side of her refrigerator, where every day she lists the breakfast choices for Joshua, 13, and Alysha, nine. Her eatery offers pancakes (cooked in bulk, frozen, then popped in the microwave) and omelets (with add-ins, such as cheese, meats, and vegetables, precut, frozen in separate bags, and tossed in as desired).

QUICK TIPS
Reading to kids while they eat is a simple bickering buster several *FamilyFun* readers swear by.

Dad's Breakfast Buffet

Before leaving early for work, David Vining of Winston-Salem, North Carolina, sets the table for breakfast, puts a vitamin at each child's place, and leaves out a selection of cereal, muffins, and fruit. When his four daughters (ages two to nine) come down to eat, they serve themselves, using small pitchers of milk and juice filled and refrigerated the night before. "Even our two-year-old can fill her bowl with dry cereal," says mom Birdie Lynn.

Lunch Packing Station

When her son Jacob started first grade, *FamilyFun* reader Dee Martin of Cleveland had to pack three lunches — one for Jacob, one for her older son, Kyle, nine, and one for herself — so she established a new lunch system. She rounded up three plastic baskets and filled one with fruits, another with vegetables, and a third with snacks and desserts. Dee lets the boys choose one item from each basket for their lunch bags, then she adds a sandwich.

So far, the system is earning rave reviews. The kids like it because they're in charge. Even healthy foods such as carrots and apples have turned into treats. Dee isn't ready to let her kids choose all the food, though. "We'd have catsup sandwiches if I let that go on!" she says.

School Lunch Chart

Liz Ruff of West Chester, Pennsylvania, didn't want to get into the classic morning debate over who would take what for lunch. So she asked her four sons — Bobby, 11, Joey, nine, Matt, seven, and Timmy, four — to post a list of favorite foods on a chalkboard. The boys agreed to eat what their mom packs, as long as it's on the list.

The chart turned up some surprises, says mom Liz. "I had no idea Joey liked granola, but he said he always trades for it with his friend at school." The boys also make note of their changing tastes, which is part of the system's strength. "The boys know what they like to eat matters."

Sand-wiches	Fruits	Snacks	Desserts
Turkey	Apple	Granola	Brownie
Ham and cheese	Raisins	Pretzel rods	Chocolate Chip cookies
Salad in a pita	Grapes	Carrot Sticks	Applesauce
Jelly roll-ups	Pineapple Chunks	Popcorn	Pudding
Bologna	Melon	Yogurt	

Kid-friendly Kitchens & Baths

A Family Cookbook

Tastes and smells — whether Dad's famous pancakes or a savory Thanksgiving turkey — are powerful reminders of people, places, and good times. Making your own family cookbook will keep those meals and memories simmering for years to come. The basic idea is to create a culinary history of your tribe, but *FamilyFun* readers offered many different ways to do it.

◆ Mary Hess-Quinones of Kalamazoo, Michigan, placed her recipes in three-hole binders (easy for tab-dividing and updating) and personalized the covers for each of her kids.

◆ Terrie Shortsleeve of Shaw Air Force Base, South Carolina, opted for a 6- by 6-inch scrapbook to hold her handwritten recipe cards, photos, and recipe memories.

◆ Other readers wrote in about books that include snapshots of holiday meals, cooks' recipe ratings, and even an entire family tree! If your kids want to add to the soup, they might suggest recipes, interview cooks, or design a cover. As Terrie notes, "My seven-year-old daughter, Hannah, loves looking at 'The Family Cookbook.' It helps me pick out what to make for dinner and at the same time reinforces her ties to friends and family."

What's for Dinner?

Sometimes, the hardest part of putting dinner on the table is deciding what's on the menu. If you're in a pinch, try this simple dinner solution — an inside-the-cupboard list of dinner ideas everyone in the family will eat. Brainstorm favorite dinners with your children: spaghetti and sauce; rice and bean burritos with salsa; fish sticks, couscous, and peas; chili and cornbread; steak, baked potato, and salad; and so on. Before you do your weekly shopping, scan the list to be sure you stock up on all the ingredients for your pantry or refrigerator.

OUR FAVORITE DINNERS

BEAN BURRITOS
SPAGHETTI AND MEATBALLS
STEAK, BAKED POTATOES, AND PEAS
FISH AND COUSCOUS
CORN CHOWDER AND BISCUITS
LASAGNA, GARLIC BREAD, AND SALAD
HONEY MUSTARD DRUMSTICKS, RICE, AND BEANS
SPLIT PEA AND HAM SOUP AND ROLLS
PASTA AND PESTO
REUBENS AND FRIES
QUICHE AND SALAD
FAJITAS WITH LOTS OF TOPPINGS
CHICKEN STIRFRY AND RICE
TACOS
ROASTED CHICKEN AND MASHED POTATOES
TURKEY BURGERS
PEPPERONI PIZZA
CHILI AND CORNBREAD
LAMB CHOPS AND TABBOULEH
PANCAKES FOR DINNER!

FAMILY TRADITION
Make Mealtime Special

Why not treat your own family like extraspecial company? A few gracious details will transform any workday meal into a celebration.

◆ Set the table with elegant place mats (here, we show the Onion-print Place Mats on page 20).

◆ Eat your mac and cheese off the good china and pour the kids' milk into long-stemmed wineglasses (feel free to invest in a few plastic ones!).

◆ Dress for dinner in your fanciest duds, or snazz up the ambience with a little bistro-style jazz.

◆ The Watters of Seminole, Oklahoma, simply light candles. "For some strange reason, lighting candles and turning off the lights changes the whole atmosphere and mood of our household," mom Angi tells us. Kids Andrew, age 12, Chelsea, ten, Mason, six, and Zane, four, enjoy "the quiet" (and blowing out the candles, of course!), and dad Lewie loves "the romance" of the candlelit dinners. "I guess it goes to show you that romance is a state of mind!" Angi laughs.

Kitchen Crafts

Home-to-school Place Mats

If getting your family out the door has started to feel like a treasure hunt ("Mom, where's my math workbook?" "Has anyone seen my recorder?"), these breakfast place mats will go a long way toward restoring morning sanity.

MATERIALS

- **12- by 16-inch piece of poster board**
- **Markers**
- **Clear Con-Tact paper**
- **Stick-on Velcro**
- **Grease pencil**

For each place mat, start with one piece of poster board. Draw a home on the left side and a school on the right. On the home, make a morning to-do list (for prereaders, glue on magazine photos). On the school, make a checklist of items your child might need on any given day — lunch money, sneakers for P.E., and the like. In the middle, where the cereal bowl will go, draw your dashing kid (for added realism, affix a photo of her face).

Cover the mats with clear Con-Tact paper or have them laminated. Affix a small piece of stick-on Velcro to the mat and another to a grease pencil, which we found works well as an erasable marker (just rub it off the mat with a moist paper towel). At breakfast, check off what's needed for the dash out the door.

FamilyFun **Home**

Scented Coasters

Filled with a blend of spices, these no-sew cloth coasters emit a pleasant fragrance when you place a hot cup on them. Here's how to assemble a set of four.

MATERIALS

- 2 tablespoons ground cinnamon
- 2 teaspoons ground cloves
- 2 teaspoons ground nutmeg
- 1/4 yard printed fabric
- 9- by 12-inch piece of felt
- 1/4 yard tightly woven muslin
- Fabric scissors and tacky glue

First mix the spices together in a small bowl. Cut out eight 5-inch squares from the printed fabric, four 4-inch squares from the felt, and eight 4-inch squares from the muslin. Place four of the printed fabric squares right side down on the table. Top each one first with a felt square, then with a muslin one.

Sprinkle a spoonful of the spice mixture on the center of each muslin square, then apply glue along the edges of the muslin. Top with another muslin square, lightly pressing the edges together so they will hold. Next, apply glue to the edges of the printed fabric that extend beyond the muslin. Top with another printed fabric square, again lightly pressing the edges together. Let the glue dry, and the coasters are ready to use.

Wooden Spoon Bouquet

Round up a bouquet of these bright-hued wooden perennials to liven up a countertop or kitchen table in no time.

MATERIALS

- **Long-handled wooden spoons**
- **Acrylic or tempera paint**
- **Paintbrush**
- **Mug**
- **Assorted flat wooden craft shapes (sold by the bagful at most craft stores)**
- **Wood glue**
- **Wooden beads (colored or plain)**

Have your kids paint the wooden spoon handles green and stand them stem end up in a mug to dry. For petals, glue flat wooden craft shapes to the bowl of each spoon (this step works best if you lay the spoons on a flat surface). Once the glue is completely dry (see manufacturer's directions), your kids can paint the flowers (both front and back) and stand them in a mug to dry. Lastly, glue a cluster of wooden beads in the center of each flower.

Place Mat Template

Fashioned from shapes of colored paper that show the proper location of the plate and silverware, our place-setting place mat effortlessly teaches the fine art of setting the table. Kids will feel good about being able to help out, and they'll get practice in following a diagram.

MATERIALS

Colored paper
Glue stick
Clear Con-Tact paper

Cut a place mat and place setting out of colored paper. Tack the pieces in place with glue, then laminate both sides with Con-Tact paper.

Please Pass the Tasks

"To help smooth out our otherwise harried mealtimes, we implemented Task Place Cards for dinnertime. Each person, including Mom and Dad, gets a 4- by 6-inch index card decorated with stickers and labeled with a responsibility. Whoever has the card labeled "utensils," for example, takes care of setting the table ahead of time, while the person with the "refrigerator" card is in charge of retrieving anything needed from the fridge during the meal. Other responsibilities cover answering the telephone and the door. We keep one card blank as a freebie, and the cards are rotated each night so no one feels like he is always stuck with the same job."

— Margaret Tindol
Beeville, Texas

HOMEMADE DECORATION

Papier-mâché Veggies

This fun papier-mâché project celebrates one of the most important — and delicious! — food groups. Plus, it makes a beautiful centerpiece for your dinner table.

MATERIALS

Newspaper
Masking tape
String
Bamboo kitchen skewers
Colored tissue paper
Mod Podge (or similar clear sealant)
Paintbrush

Help your kids crumple up sheets of newspaper to resemble any vegetable shapes they like and use masking tape or string to secure the forms. (They don't need to be perfect, just close enough to identify.) Cover any dark printed areas with tape too. Then fashion stems (if applicable) from additional pieces of tape and tape the stems, in turn, to the appropriate vegetables.

Stick a bamboo skewer through the bottom of each newspaper veggie. Then cut several sheets of colored tissue paper into 3-inch squares. Holding each vegetable by its skewer, brush the entire vegetable first with Mod Podge and then add a single layer of tissue squares. Let the sealer dry. Repeat the process, adding more layers until you get the desired shade. Use the same method to cover the various stems with green or brown tissue paper.

When the vegetables are complete, remove the skewers and arrange the veggies in a bowl for a vibrant centerpiece.

Kid-friendly Kitchens & Baths

Magnetic Personalities

These mix-and-match refrigerator magnets provide hours of silliness, as kids create hilarious configurations of heads and bodies. Not only that, they'll encourage kids to keep the refrigerator door closed!

MATERIALS

- **Full-body photos of 2 or more people (the more the merrier)**
- **Flexible, self-adhesive magnetic sheets (available at craft stores) or recycled nonadhesive magnets (like those that come in the mail)**
- **Glue stick (if you use nonadhesive magnets)**

Cut the figures from the photos. They don't have to be perfect; slightly rounded outlines are okay.

For each figure, cut a piece of magnet slightly larger than the cutout, peel away the backing, and press the cutout firmly onto the magnet. If you're using recycled nonadhesive magnets, coat the backs of the cutouts, especially the edges, with glue. Then press the cutouts onto the printed side of the magnet. Allow the glue to dry (about 45 minutes).

Trim away the excess magnet around the shape of the person. Next, cut each figure into 3 sections (for instance: head, torso including arms, and legs). Now stick them on the fridge and let the fun begin.

Family Magnetism

The fridge door is a window into a family's soul. And what makes a door truly shine? Magnets, of course. Some of our favorites:

Fractiles-7. Magnetic shapes that teach geometry — and hold the week's school lunch menu (www.fractiles.com).

Alphabet letters. The classic, as simple as A-B-C.

Poetry magnets. Now in kid and adult sets, they let us all write like e. e. cummings (www.amazon.com).

Homemade fridge art. The most expressive of all. Glue magazine photos or snapshots to magnetic sheets and then cut them out. Voilà!

Frigits. Make a marble raceway from chutes, spinners, and buckets (www.fridgedoor.com).

Hand-colored Oven Mitts

Kitchen fun doesn't get much easier than this. All you need is fabric markers and a child's creativity to turn plain oven mitts and pot holders into handy kitchen art. We recommend using Marvy or FabricMate brand pens.

MATERIALS

Oven mitt or pot holder
Scrap paper
Colored fabric markers

Trace the oven mitt or pot holder onto a sheet of paper so that your child can experiment with different designs. Once he has settled on one, he can resketch it on the mitt and color it in with the fabric markers.

Kid-friendly Kitchens & Baths

CREATIVE SOLUTION

Toothbrush to Go

Sue Davis of Sycamore, Illinois, wrote to *FamilyFun* with a simple yet brilliant idea for easing bathroom gridlock: each person in the house gets a basket (Sue favors plastic-coated metal) for toiletries. In a two-bathroom house like the Davises', there's no more waiting to use the "good" bathroom — just grab your basket and head for the other one. Plus, cleaning is so much easier — you just lift up a few baskets, instead of maneuvering dozens of oozy bottles and tubes to scrub under them.

Sue credits her mother with the idea. "I grew up with three sisters, all of us in the same house — four girls, four girl teenagers, all of us in the bathroom at the same time. My mom had to think of something!"

TIPS AND TECHNIQUES

Family Bathroom Basics

- ◆ **Try scheduling bathroom times to prevent at-home traffic jams.**
- ◆ **Assign a color to each member of your family, then coordinate all the towels and washcloths so that everyone will know whose are whose.**
- ◆ **Designate a hook for each child, set at their level, so they know where to hang up their towels.**
- ◆ **Keep a nonskid stool handy for little ones.**
- ◆ **Invest in bathroom organizers, such as mesh bags for tub toys and a shower caddy for shampoos and soaps.**
- ◆ **Give each child a shelf in the bathroom where she can keep all her toiletries.**

Under-the-sea Bathrooms

The household bathroom is a fun place to decorate with an underwater theme. Paint your bathroom deep-sea blue, then pick out beach-themed accessories (shower curtains, towels, bath mats, toothbrush holders, or even bath panels). Here are some seaworthy designs.

◆ **Underwater World: Turn your bathroom into an underwater sea exhibit. Paint the lower half of the walls cobalt blue, then add self-adhesive fish, whales, and dolphins. Accessorize with blue towels and a fish bath mat.**

◆ **Sailor Kids: Make the bathroom look like the interior of a sailboat, and paint portholes on the wall to display underwater sea life. A fishnet hung in a corner is perfect for holding bath toys and plastic boats.**

◆ **Mermaid: Sketch and paint a fantasy mural on the walls with a turquoise sea, sea stars, pretty mermaids, and a pink sunset.**

PERSONALIZED CRAFT
Handprint Soap Dish

This sentimental dish offers more than soap: it's also a clean record of your child's handprint.

MATERIALS

1 pound of white air-hardening modeling clay (like DAS Pronto)
Rolling pin and waxed paper
Butter knife
2 toothpicks
Paintbrush
Acrylic waterproof sealer

Knead the clay to soften it up, then roll it out between two sheets of waxed paper so that you have a 1-inch-thick slab. Help your child firmly press his clean hand into the clay. Deepen or smooth the impression with a wet fingertip, if needed. Trim the edges of the clay with the butter knife, leaving a ½-inch border around the handprint.

From the excess clay, shape four 1-inch-wide balls to serve as the soap dish feet. Carefully invert the dish onto a clean section of waxed paper. Cut 2 toothpicks in half and use each half as a peg for attaching a ball under each corner of the dish. Wait 1 hour for the assembled dish to firm up before turning it back over, then let it dry completely as specified on the clay package.

Finally, apply a few coats of waterproof sealer according to the manufacturer's directions (a parent's job). Once the sealer dries completely, the dish is ready to use.

Bathtub Catamaran

This clever catamaran turns your bathtub into a regular port of call.

MATERIALS
- **2 1-liter plastic soda bottles**
- **Rubber bands**
- **Colored plastic tape**
- **Craft knife**

Remove the labels from the plastic bottles. Clamp the bottles together temporarily with the rubber bands, then wrap them with colored tape, as shown. Remove the rubber bands, then, with a craft knife (a parent's job), cut the oval seat openings. Sail away with a crew of fashion dolls, action figures, or waterproof plush toys.

Bath Paints Kit

The easy alchemy of turning plain soap and food coloring into vivid bath paints will delight children — and thrill parents when they see how quickly the kids get into the tub to play with them.

MATERIALS

Small, lidded, plastic containers
Creamy liquid body soap
Toothpick
Food coloring (or gel icing)
Paint-mixing bucket
Plastic palette
Foam brushes and sponge shapes

Fill the containers half full with the liquid body soap. Use the toothpick to stir a few drops of food coloring into each container. (Gel icing makes gloriously bright colors, but use only a drop or two or the colors might stain.) Arrange these paints in a paint-mixing bucket (about $4 at hardware stores), along with a plastic palette for color mixing, foam brushes, and some sponge shapes for printing. Have your child design a label: "Rub-a-dub-dub, make art in the tub" or simply "My Bath Paints."

TIPS AND TECHNIQUES
Tubtime Totables

Sure, you can buy toys for the tub. But why bother when everything you need for unsinkable fun is almost certainly stashed somewhere around the house? Some of our favorites:

* Plastic measuring cups and spoons
* Latex gloves (for filling, not wearing)
* Handheld mirror (for shampoo hairstyling)
* Turkey basters and ear syringes (for squirting)
* Empty shampoo and bubble bath bottles (we love using the mini ones from hotels)
* Spongy cleaning tools (unused)
* Swimming goggles or masks
* Empty clear plastic soda bottles (for, among other things, creating miniature whirlpools: fill a bottle with water, then swirl it gently as you let the water pour out)
* Plastic funnels and colanders

HOMEMADE TOY
Tic-tac-tub

Everyone knows how to play tic-tac-toe, but how do you do it in the bathtub? Easily, if you've got a pair of scissors and some sheets of colorful craft foam, which boasts a remarkable ability to stick to bathtub walls. To cut the craft foam into a tic-tac-toe grid, first use a ruler and pencil to divide a sheet into nine equal squares.

Cut out the grid so each line is roughly 3/4 inch wide. Next, cut out at least six sea stars and six minnows, making sure each fits within the squares of the grid. Wet the pieces of foam and stick them to the sides of the tub. The player with the pruniest fingers gets to go first.

Kid-friendly Kitchens & Baths

Towel Cape-r

Your squeaky-clean kids will love wrapping themselves up in one of these capes. The smaller towel forms a cozy hood, making it a warm and snuggly post-bath wrap.

MATERIALS
Hand towel (about 27 by 16 inches)
Bath towel
Needle and thread

To fashion one, have your child fold the hand towel in half lengthwise (A) and again widthwise, then help her to sew along one long side of the towel (the open edges) to form the hood (B).

Next, help your seamstress find the center point of the bath towel by folding it in half and marking the point on one of the long sides. Open the hood and lay it facedown on the larger towel, making sure the hood's seam is aligned with the center point of the larger towel (C). Sew the two towels together where the edges meet, turn the hood right side out, and let your little dry babies go.

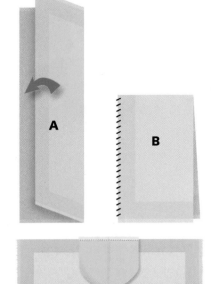

FAMILYFUN SUCCESS STORY
Sea Soap

"My son, Max, age five, wanted to do something special for his teachers to say thank-you at the end of the year. So we decided to make them some homemade hand-soap holders. I purchased clear liquid soap dispensers filled with blue hand soap and removed the front labels from each of them. We poured out a little of the soap to make room for a few clean pebbles, small plastic aquarium plants, and various small plastic sea animals, all of which we placed in the soap dispensers using a clean bamboo skewer. Lastly, we resealed the bottles, and Max used a permanent marker to personalize the back labels."

—Tamarah Henderson
Tampa, Florida

FamilyFun **Home**

First-aid Kit

Kids will be kids — and that means a few inevitable bumps and bruises along the way. Keeping a well-stocked first-aid kit at home allows you to treat these minor injuries without much ado, and creating the first-aid kit may even teach your youngsters a thing or two about basic medical intervention.

Begin by selecting a container — say a plastic box that your child has decorated with a red cross of tape. Consult with your pediatrician or with a reputable website (kidshealth.org offers a handy checklist) to obtain a list of first-aid essentials, which should include a basic first-aid book or chart and a list of emergency phone numbers. Now take your kids on a field trip to the local drugstore to stock the kit, and remind them what each item is for as you find it. Be sure to keep the finished kit out of reach of very young children.

MAKE-IT-YOURSELF
Boo-boo Bunny

Sometimes a clever trick, such as transforming an ordinary washcloth into a cuddly toy bunny, can work like a charm to brighten your child's spirit when she's feeling under the weather. Designed with a hole in its center, this little terry cloth critter slips onto a fingertip for an instant puppet show, or you can quickly pop it over an ice cube to help soothe an unexpected bump or scratch.

MATERIALS

- 1 baby washcloth
- Rubber band
- Tacky glue
- Googly eyes
- 1 small pom-pom
- 1 large pom-pom

To make a bunny, place the washcloth on a tabletop and evenly roll two diagonally opposite corners toward the middle. Fold the rolled washcloth in half, as shown. Then fold the cloth in half a second time and wrap the rubber band around the second fold to form the bunny's head. Gently pull apart the rolled ends that extend above the rubber band so that they resemble rabbit ears.

Next, glue the googly eyes onto the face and the small pom-pom in place for a nose. Glue the large pom-pom onto the back of the original fold to serve as a cottony tail, and the bunny is finished.

Kid-friendly Kitchens & Baths

Whale Water Scoop

The Old Washtub

As dismal as water seems to kids when it's streaking down the windows, it's a blast to pour, splash, and otherwise play with indoors. Your kids might like to sneak up on their rubber duckies with this great whale scoop (it also makes washing one's hair much more fun).

MATERIALS
**Clean plastic gallon milk jug
Permanent marker**

Begin by turning the gallon jug onto its side so that the handle is at the top. With the marker, draw a mouth shape on the base of the jug and extending partway up the sides, as shown. Cut along the lines with scissors, creating a wide-mouthed scoop (a parent's job). Using the marker, outline the edge of the mouth and add eyes and a blowhole.

"One night, our electricity went out just as my kids were going to take their baths. I found a candle and told Brian, age five, and Matthew, age eight, that in the old days, children had to bathe by candlelight. They were intrigued and excited to try it themselves. I set the candle in a safe place, and for once the kids didn't complain about having to take a bath. Now we sometimes have candlelight tubs on nights when the electricity is working just fine."
— Jeanie Ransom
O'Fallon, Missouri

Tiger Step Stool

We have to say it: this tiger step stool is simply the cat's meow. And your kids will be grateful for the sink-side boost it offers.

MATERIALS

Paints

1 quart water-based primer

(For paints below, we used semigloss interior latex paints by Crayola, except where noted)

1 quart Halloween orange

1 quart Burnt Sienna (red-brown)

1 quart Black

2-ounce bottle of pink acrylic enamel paint (available at craft stores)

Other supplies

Wooden step stool

2-inch-wide foam wedge brush

1½-inch-wide polyester paintbrush

Scissors

2 rectangular kitchen sponges

Disposable plates or trays

Pencil

½-inch-wide detail or artist's paintbrush

Sand your step stool if necessary. Make sure it's clean, then use the 2-inch foam brush to coat the stool with primer. Let it dry.

Turn the step stool upside down. Use your 1½-inch paintbrush to apply orange paint to the legs and outside edge of the seat. Smooth out any drips with your brush and let the paint dry.

Turn the step stool right side up, paint the top orange, and go over any spots you missed earlier. Let it dry.

A Use scissors to trim one sponge into a rectangle with rounded corners (ours was 3 by 3½ inches) and the other sponge into a triangle (2½-inch base, 3½-inch

sides) as shown in figure **A**. Save the parts you cut off.

Pour a small amount of red-brown paint into a disposable plate or tray. (Plan to do a test on paper before you start on the step stool.) Slide the sponge with rounded edges around in the paint, then drag it against the edge of the tray to take off excess paint. Blot the sponge on paper, then make your sponge print on the step stool. You want the print to be dark enough to make a pattern, but light enough

that the orange paint will show through (see **B**). Cover the step stool with overlapping sponge impressions. You can keep the stool right side up for the whole process. Allow the paint to dry.

Pour black paint into a plate or tray. You want bolder imprints this time, so wipe excess paint on the tray

edge, but do not blot. To make tiger stripes, press the triangle sponge firmly as you repeat the shape around the edge of the step stool top (see **C**). If you like, curve the sponge down around the edge of the seat, as shown below. To stripe the legs, curl the sponge around them as you press. Let the paint dry.

Pencil in your tiger's face. Use a ½-inch detail brush dipped in black to paint the eyes and mouth. Let them dry.

You can either use the detail brush to paint the ears and nose freehand (in pink) or do the following: cut one of your leftover pieces of sponge into a mini triangle. Pour a small amount of pink paint into a tray. Dip the sponge, wipe off the excess, and press it onto the step stool. *Grrr!*

CHAPTER THREE

The Family Room

Turn your family room into a place where kids —
and parents — feel right at home

The old-fashioned, velvet and lace parlor has gone the way of the cracker barrel, and it's a good thing. We have precious little time to spend with our family and friends — who wants to waste it on stuffiness? For many of us, even the less formal living room is a thing of the past, and we are turning more often to the family room as our entertainment and hangout headquarters.

Add children to this equation, and you have a lot for one room to juggle. The family room might be the game room, the library, or the den — or, more likely, all of these rolled into one. You expect it to be comfortable and practical, and you need it to house a range of entertainment equipment, from puzzles and board games to the more high-tech trappings of CDs, VCRs, and video games. That's a pretty tall order, right there. But you also want it to be a comfortable place for grown-ups.

Sound impossible? It's not. The trick, as you'll see in the pages that follow, is to organize the room around kid-friendly furniture, clever storage ideas that whisk toys out of sight, easy tips for organizing books and videos attractively, and hand-crafted decorations that show off both your family photos and your kids' art. From our clever Rain Gutter Bookshelves (page 60) to our space-saving Trunk Table (page 46) to our instantly festive Snapshot Racks (page 55), you'll find everything you need to put the family back in family room.

Self-portrait Pictures, page 51

Store toys out of sight. Forget about banning toys from the family room: if it's where your family relaxes, kids and toys are sure to follow. But make sure there are convenient and attractive places to put them — and put them quickly. We are especially partial to baskets, either by the door (these are easily transported to the kids' rooms) or lined up under the coffee table.

Keep the TV under cover. There will likely be a television in your family room, but you can store it in an armoire or drape it with pretty fabric to keep it from being the focus of the room. Its invisibility may, on occasion, encourage your kids to take up more creative pursuits.

Slip on a slipcover. Even if you're putting off buying nice furniture until the kids go to college, spiff up the stuff you already have with a machine-washable slipcover.

Use it or lose it. Because of its versatility, the family room is likely to gather a motley assortment of clutter. Evaluate it every couple of months: if you notice things that your family's not using (like a set of outdated encyclopedias or a stack of old magazines), get rid of it, move it to the garage, or find a more suitable home for it elsewhere in the house.

Family Room Essentials

Remember, the family room means a room for the family. Think of everyone's organizational needs. Ask yourself, "What collects in this room the most?" Then decide where to put it. These are some family-friendly clutter busters we swear by:

- Buy baskets or wooden boxes of varying sizes and shapes. **These can store (and hide!) games, newspapers, catalogs, toys, or even that cluster of remotes.**
- Invest in an armoire. **Use it as a computer station, TV cabinet, or entertainment center, or for holding board games and hobby paraphernalia.**
- Shelving is a must-have. **You can display framed vacation photographs, your kids' sculptures, potted plants, or knickknacks up and out of reach from small children, or, use it to hold your book collection.**
- Coffee tables with drawers, storage ottomans, or bench-seat toy boxes offer extra storage — as well as a spot for misplaced junk before company stops by.

A Project Table

The kitchen table is a great place for crafts, but not those that take more than a few hours to complete. For anything longer, crafts-in-progress must be cleared away for meals. To avoid this ebb and flow in creativity, set up a small table and chairs in the corner of your family room and dedicate it just to puzzles, models, and other long-term projects. Make this the one area where kids can work without having to clean up each day.

Put Toys on Wheels

If your kids are constantly bringing their toys into the family room to play, think about creating an attractive toy storage area right in the room. Some ideas: bookshelves (labeled so each child has his or her own), an old chest, or sets of labeled baskets. Still too cluttered? Pick up a small cart with wheels, like the one above, and haul it out when the children want to play, then have them load it back up and wheel it out of the way (or even out of sight in a closet) until they want it again.

Trunk Table

Since you're likely to have a coffee table anyway, why not make it do double storage duty? Consider swapping your standard-issue table for an attractive, flat-topped trunk. Wicker is nice, as is wood, and who says you have to buy it new? We like to rummage for flea-market gems that we spiff up with a coat or two of cheerful paint.

What to put inside? How about all those extra afghans that seem to multiply overnight on the couch? Or those stacks of board games and puzzles teetering on your end tables? Now to deal with all those old newspapers and empty glasses on *top* of the table...

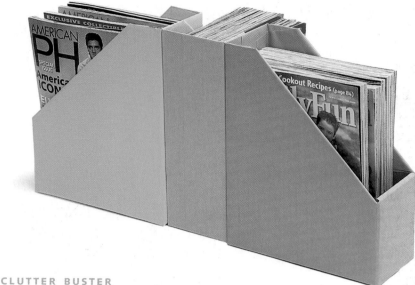

Family Room Music Box

If you want to foster impromptu jams and performances in your house, create a music box (or basket) and keep it handy. To fill it, start with some of the following instruments, and keep an eye out for used instruments at tag sales and flea markets: kazoo, triangle, shakers, finger cymbals, sticks, bells, drums, inexpensive guitar or ukulele, recorder, or harmonica.

Magazine Tamer

If you're overrun with magazines and catalogs, we have a line of defense. Store them attractively up on a shelf in decorated cardboard holders. You can buy these at an office supply store, or make your own by cutting one side panel out of a cereal box. We like to cover the holders with wallpaper or Con-Tact paper, or decoupage them with photos or cutouts. Now sort your magazines into the holders — after you drag the piles out from behind the couch, of course.

Couch Cushion Blocks

"While I was thrilled with the idea of trading in our old beat-up couch for a nice new one, my sons, Joel, eight, and Eric, six, were sad to see their longtime playmate go. They had enjoyed hours of fun jumping and playing on the cushions. So at the last minute, I decided to keep just the cushions and re-cover them in bright, soft fabric. They have become my sons' most-used toys of all time. The boys use them as giant building blocks for forts, obstacle courses, and hideouts. The cushions also make great padding for slumber parties and work wonderfully at drive-in movies. The best part is, my new couch has stayed new."

**— Ellen Thomas
Port Townsend, Washington**

Creative Decorations

Lighthouse in a Bottle

Here's a bright idea for the family room mantel: a toy lighthouse made from a sport water bottle lit with a flashlight.

MATERIALS
1.5-liter sport water bottle
Aluminum foil
Red acrylic paint
Black tape
Baseball-size ball of clay
Flashlight
11¹/₂- by 10-inch sheet of white craft foam

Use a craft knife (adults only) to cut the bottle in half. Glue aluminum foil inside the cone-shaped portion of the top half (this creates a reflective dome), then paint the outside of the foil-lined section. When the paint is dry, apply 3-inch vertical strips of black tape, spaced evenly, around the unpainted portion of the bottle top.

Pack the clay in the bottom half of the bottle. Stand the flashlight upright in the clay and press down to secure it in place. Cut a notch down from the bottle's edge (see photo, above) to allow access to the flashlight's switch.

Next, wrap the craft foam around the bottom half of the bottle (the foam will extend about 4 inches above the bottle) and note approximately where the flashlight switch opening is. Remove the foam and cut out a switch opening, as shown. Rewrap the foam around the bottle and secure the overlapping ends with clear packing tape.

Finally, fit the cut edge of the bottle top just inside the foam sleeve, and securely tape the foam to the bottle with colored tape.

DECORATE IT

Window Art

With these soapy (and easy to wash away) window paints, your kids can decorate the family room window or French doors with a seasonal painting.

MATERIALS
Clear dishwashing liquid
Tempera paints and paintbrushes

For each color of paint, mix about 1 tablespoon of dishwashing liquid with ½ tablespoon of paint (the mixture should have the creamy consistency of house paint). Foil-lined muffin tins or plastic containers work well to hold different colors. Using a different brush for each hue, paint onto the window (being careful to avoid sills and woodwork). To remove the painting, just wipe with a moist paper towel.

Colored-sand Vases

This is a cheerful way to fill a sunny windowsill: recycle assorted jars and bottles into a rainbow of colorful vases.

MATERIALS

Newspaper
Tacky glue
Plastic cup
Paintbrush
Clean glass bottle or jar
Spoon

Colored sand (sold at most craft supply stores)

Cover your workspace with newspaper (this will make it easier to clean up later). Pour ¼ cup or so of tacky glue into a plastic cup and dilute it slightly with a teaspoon of water. Now show your kids how to use a paintbrush to coat the outside of a clean bottle or jar with the glue solution and then sprinkle spoonfuls of colored sand over the glued surface, rotating the bottle to spread the sand evenly. Allow the glue to dry completely.

Once your kids get the hang of it, encourage them to experiment with multicolored designs. Or they might apply the glue in swirls or other shapes to create interesting patterns.

Displaying Kids' Art

CREATIVE SOLUTION

Hall of Frames

The entrance to your basement den is the perfect place to show off some of your children's masterpieces. Jocelyn Robinson of Troy, Michigan, discovered this when she was grappling with the problem of a crowded fridge — as covered with papers as it was full of food. "You know how it is," she says of the masses of artwork, certificates, and school photos piled up precariously under every magnet. "They're so important, but then they fall off and get lost behind the refrigerator, or they just get covered over with the next thing."

To create a more prominent gallery for her kids' achievements, she painted dozens of decorative faux frames right onto the wall, and now she hangs up whatever current awards or artwork her kids are most proud of, regularly rotating new papers onto this colorful wall of honor. To make the frames, Jocelyn marked off rectangles along the wall, using masking tape and variously sized school art papers as a guide. She painted the insides of the rectangles white, removed the masking tape, and then painted showy frames around them employing every creative technique she could think of, including sponge printing, splatter painting, and geometric prints. (Her daughters even embellished the frames with their own thumbprint hearts and flowers.) Jocelyn uses double-sided tape to hang up the kids' work. "It's been such a big hit with the kids," Jocelyn tells us.

Self-portrait Pictures

DO-IT-YOURSELF
Showcase Kids' Art

With inexpensive picture frames and the help of your local copy shop, you can decorate your walls and make your artists-in-residence proud. Look for frames at yard sales (just remove the original pictures and swap in your children's). Or pick them up at discount stores; paint them, if you wish, for a consistent look. Have matting cut at a frame shop. Finally, for a slick look, use a copy shop's color photocopier to make a color copy just the right size to fit the mat. When the next masterpiece comes along, reduce or enlarge the new work with the photocopier and swap in the artwork.

To record what your family's life is like today, you can create self-portraits, either by taking photographs, by painting, or as we show below, by drawing with markers — a technique that works well for families with small kids. This project starts children thinking about the things that are meaningful to them and encourages them to consider how their everyday lives are actually history in the making.

MATERIALS

> **Acid-free heavy-stock paper (at least 5 sheets per family member)**
> **Acid-free markers**

Each person should think about how she would like to be remembered years from now. What objects would she hold to best reflect her personality? What should the setting be like? Should she place anything in the portrait that reflects her ethnic heritage? What emotion would she like to express? Encourage everyone to assemble any items they would like to use as references while they are drawing.

Set up your work area for drawing and give everyone enough paper to try several versions of their self-portraits. (Set a good example for your kids by favoring fun over perfectionism!) When everyone is done, set aside each person's favorite self-portrait.

Mark on the back of each portrait the date, the artist, and the place it was drawn.

Frame your self-portraits, then hang them together in a prominent place in your home so the kids can show off their family gallery to guests.

FAMILYFUN SUCCESS STORY
The Art Wall

"My husband and I have three children, Jennifer, ten, Christopher, seven, and Samantha, three. The older kids are always bringing home art projects, so I came up with a new and easy way to display their work.

"I hung five or so clear plastic box frames on our wall and designated it the Art Wall. The kids and I slip their favorite paintings and drawings into the frames. They love walking by and admiring their art and are especially proud when friends and relatives visit.

"As new work comes in, I take down the old pictures, put clear Con-Tact paper on each side, punch holes down one side, and put each child's work in individual binders. Now as they get older, they will always have their Artists' Portfolios to look back on."

— Linda Ludwig
Woodstock, Illinois

The Family Room

Family Photos

FAMILY KEEPSAKE
Wall of Fame

If there's one project that's just perfect for the family room, it's a visual representation of your clan's roots. A traditional family tree will do the trick, but for a fun, kid-friendly twist on the usual jumble of names and dates, try hanging up framed baby pictures from various time periods, as shown at left. Seeing a newborn cousin's resemblance to Great-Grandpa as a baby can be a sentimental way to make the connections between family members, regardless of the years or miles that separate them.

To create your own wall of fame, solicit copies of baby and early childhood photographs from relatives. Place any unframed shots in era-appropriate frames, then assemble your tree on a wall in your family room or playroom. You can arrange your photos with elder relatives either at the bottom (like the trunk of your family tree) or toward the top of your tree (so descendants, well, descend, along family lines). You might also add labels or captions. Your decorative gallery will no doubt prompt discussions about family history: "What did Grandpa do at school?" "Where did Uncle Brian get that horse?" "Why do the baby boys wear white dresses?" Kids might even interview relatives about their childhoods and compile a book of "When I was young" stories to go with the tree.

ORGANIZE IT
Themed Photo Albums

Ginger Barr Heafey, *FamilyFun* **senior art director, was fed up with her big, disorganized photo albums. "It was a chore to arrange all the photos on a page," she says, "and after all that work, the books still didn't always make sense." Her solution? Mini 4- by 6-inch albums that hold a few dozen photos in each. The best photos can be gathered quickly and easily into themed books — "Summer in Maine" or "Danyelle's Graduation" —**

and Ginger always knows just where to find them. Flip through her ongoing "Christmas Morning" album (she adds a few new pictures every year), and the kids seem to grow up right before your eyes. Why not keep a few on the coffee table, to entertain guests or to prompt fits of nostalgic conversation with your own family?

How to Organize Your Photos

Organizing expert Julie Morgenstern's photo strategy offers, as she puts it, "dramatic relief at every stage."

Stage One: Gather all of your photographs and negatives. Hunt them down from every drawer and closet and put them on a table. "Already something's done!" she notes. "The photos are all together."

Stage Two: Sort the photos into categories that make sense to you, either chronologically or by topic, depending on how you're most likely to look for them. Get a number of storage boxes (we covered regular shoe boxes with pretty wrapping paper, below), label the fronts of the boxes, and file in your piles. (Following archivists' advice, we transferred our negatives and photographs from their photo-shop envelopes to PVC-free plastic negative sleeves and files made from folded acid-free paper.) "Now you've gotten complete command over your photos," Julie says, "even if you never do another thing!"

Stage Three: With the bulk of the sorting behind you, relax, pick one box at a time, and put the photographs into albums. Give yourself a generous deadline and make one night a month Photo Album Night.

Stage Four: Maintain your storage system. Even as you're still filing old ones, new photos are incoming. We pick our favorite five pictures from every roll and put them into albums immediately, then file the rest into boxes. Donate bad shots to the craft basket; store duplicates with stationery — handy for sending to doting grandparents.

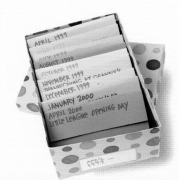

The Family Room

Picture Garden

This family photo stand makes a lovely end table decoration — and an easy beginning woodworking project for your child to try her hand at (with assistance from you).

MATERIALS

11½-inch-long 1- by 8-inch pine board
Pencil and ruler
Saw and drill
Sanding block
2½ feet of ³/₈-inch dowel
Wood glue
7 pinch-style clothespins

Help your child measure and mark the board, as shown. Using a ³/₈-inch bit, drill holes a half inch deep into the wood where marked. Use the sanding block to remove any pencil lines and smooth all the edges.

From the dowel, cut two 2-inch lengths for the front row, three 4-inch lengths for the middle row, and two 6-inch lengths for the back row. Sand the upper front of each dowel to create a flat spot, then use wood glue to attach a pinch-style clothespin (you can clamp the pieces together with another clothespin until the glue dries). Finally, fit the dowels into the appropriate holes and attach your photos.

3"		3"
1" 4½"		4½" 1"
3"		3"

Snapshot Racks

This clever snapshot holder is easily assembled from inexpensive hardware store supplies, and just as easily mounted. Plus, because photos slide in and out so readily, it encourages regular updating — even kids can change the display. The whole project can be made for under $10.

MATERIALS

Saw
Decorative wood frame molding
Latex wall paint
Finish nails and hammer

Cut the molding into 2-foot lengths and paint it. Nail the sections to the wall, spacing them so they just grip a snapshot. Or, use lengths of the double-channeled plastic known as paneling division bar ($2 for 8 feet). It can be cut with scissors and affixed to the wall with white thumbtacks.

The photos slide between the molding rails or into the plastic channels. Because the photos aren't protected and will curl over time, be sure to update the racks regularly or use duplicate prints.

PAINTING PROJECT

Skyscraper CD Tower

The family room inevitably doubles as a dance club, and the cool downtown look of our skyscraper CD tower will make any kid want to groove.

MATERIALS

Paints

1 quart water-based primer

We used semigloss interior latex paints by Crayola, except where noted)

1 quart Purple Mountain's Majesty

1 quart Sky Blue

1 quart Parrot Green

2-ounce bottles of acrylic enamel paint for people in windows (available in craft stores)

Other supplies

Unfinished CD tower

Sandpaper

2-inch-wide foam wedge brush

1-inch-wide polyester paintbrush

Ruler

Marker

Craft knife and scissors

About 1 square foot of corrugated cardboard

1 piece of felt (any color)

½-inch-wide detail or artist's paintbrush

Disposable plates or trays

Low-tack painter's masking tape

1. Sand your CD tower. Make sure it's clean, then use the 2-inch foam brush to coat it with primer. Let it dry.

2. Use the 1-inch paintbrush to paint the tower purple, inside and out, except for the roof and base. Let it dry.

3. Next, make the stamps (see **A**). Using a

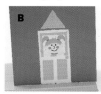

A

ruler, marker, and craft knife, cut two shapes from corrugated cardboard: a rectangle for windows and doors (ours was 2 by 2½ inches), and a triangle for details (ours was a 1½-inch equilateral). You may want to vary yours, depending on the size of your tower. Trace each cut shape two times on cardboard and once on felt. Cut these out (using scissors for the felt). Stack the identical shapes with the felt on top and use the ½-inch detail brush to apply a light coat of paint between each layer (in this situation, paint holds the layers together better than glue). Press the stamps down on a flat surface to bond, then let them dry.

4. Pour blue paint into a tray, then press the rectangular stamp into it, felt side down. The felt should be thoroughly coated: test the stamp on paper. Apply the door by making one stamp on top of another, overlapping slightly depending on how tall you want the door (see **B**). Wait for steps 6 and 8 to add details.

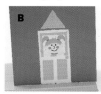

B

5. Before you stamp on your windows, create a guide with low-tack masking tape so they'll be even (see blue tape, **C**). Stamp on the windows, working up from the door. Tape and stamp windows on the other side of the tower. Remove the tape when done.

6. Use the triangle stamp, coated in green paint, to add detail work along the top of the tower and over the door. Let it dry.

7. Use the 1-inch brush to coat the roof and the base with green paint. When dry, use the window stamp to

shingle your roof with an alternating pattern of stamps in blue paint (see **D**).

D

8. Use the ½-inch detail brush and enamel paint to add people and other details in the windows. Consider curtains, cats, plants, aliens . . . the sky's the limit.

Handy Holder

This no-sew caddy tucks under the cushion of a couch or favorite chair and keeps the television remote control and viewing guide within easy reach.

MATERIALS

11¹/₂- by 44-inch piece of fabric
Yardstick and chalk
Washable fabric glue (we used Aleene's OK To Wash-IT)
Iron
Iron-on patches or rickrack (optional)

1. First, place the fabric facedown and use the yardstick and chalk to measure and mark a ¾-inch hem at one narrow end. Iron the hem flat (parents only), then glue it in place against the back of the fabric. Turn over the material and repeat at the other end, this time pressing and gluing a ¾-inch hem against the front of the material (**A**). Allow the glue to dry.

2. With the material right side up, mark a horizontal line across it, 6 inches from the hem you just made. Then mark a vertical line 4¼ inches in from one side of the material, as shown (**B**).

4¼"
6"
Glue

3. Apply 3 vertical lines of fabric glue as shown, then fold up the bottom of the material along the 6-inch line (**C**). Allow the glue to dry.

4. Turn the material facedown. Press flat a ¾-inch hem along each long side of the holder (**D**). Secure the hems in place with the fabric glue and allow to dry. If your child likes, he can decorate his holder with fabric patches or lengths of rickrack, as we did.

Trade Tokens for TV

Like many *FamilyFun* readers, the Bakers have found it a challenge to limit their kids' TV time. So they began giving each of their girls five tokens a week. Each token is worth 30 minutes of TV time. The kids — Carly, age 12, Sydni, nine, and Regan, six — write their TV choices on the calendar and pay for their viewing time just before a show starts. The kids can also choose to save their tokens; any left at the end of the week are cashed in for 25 cents apiece. The payoff? The kids are choosier about TV and are reading more. Even better, though, says Traci, is that the family spends more real time together instead of just plunking down in front of the tube.

The Family Room

Foldaway Puppet Theater

The family room is the perfect venue for this foldaway puppet theater: the audience can make itself comfortable on the couches to take in an evening's performance. And after the final bows have been taken, your kids might want to use it as a grocery store, a drive-through restaurant, or a lemonade stand.

MATERIALS

- 4- by 8-foot sheet of $^1/_2$-inch plywood, finished on both sides
- Cardboard (for template)
- Paints, rollers, and brushes
- 4 feet of 1- by 6-inch pine (for stage shelf)
- 3 feet of 1- by 2-inch pine (for stage shelf brace)
- Carpenter's wood glue
- Nails, 2-inch finish
- 2 feet of $^3/_8$- by $^3/_4$-inch pine (for window stops)
- 4 2- by 2-inch hinges
- 2 1-foot lengths of light-gauge chain
- 4 medium screw eyes
- 4 1- by 2-inch hinges
- 4 small pull knobs
- 1$^1/_3$ yards velvet for curtains (or old curtains)
- Thread
- Curtain rod, cloth loops, and thumbtacks

Tools

- Circular saw
- Straightedge and clamps (optional)
- Sandpaper
- Drill with bits
- Jigsaw
- Hammer
- Screwdriver
- Measuring tape
- Sewing machine (optional)

1. Using a circular saw (with a straightedge and clamps, for extra stability), cut the sheet of plywood into the theater's front and two sides, as shown. Sand all edges until smooth. An easier option: for a nominal fee, have your lumberyard cut the stock when you purchase it.

2. Create a cardboard template for the rounded windows and trace the pattern on each side piece. Drill a

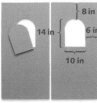

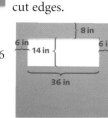

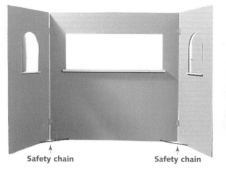

¼-inch hole just inside the line, insert the jigsaw, and cut out the window. Sand all cut edges.

3. Draw the rectangular stage opening (14 by 36 inches), drill a pilot hole, and cut out, using a straightedge if necessary. Sand the edges.

4. Paint the theater. We chose a three-color scheme. For a fancier look, consider painting the front with chalkboard paint or hanging a bulletin board or dry-erase marker board there for notices of upcoming shows.

5. The removable stage shelf consists of a notched 1 by 6 board glued to a brace of 1 by 3 (see photos). First cut a 39-inch length of 1 by 6 pine, then round and notch the ends (see inset). Cut a 36-inch strip of 1 by 2 for the brace, then

glue and nail it in position along the underside of the 1 by 6. When in place, it should rest against the theater's front. Countersink the nails and let dry.

6. For the window stops, cut two 11- by ¾- by ⅜-inch strips of pine, quarter rounding the ends, if desired. When the paint on the theater is dry, glue the strips so a ¼-inch lip sticks up above the windowsill, preventing the window door from swinging in.

7. Attach the sides to the front with the 2-inch hinges, screwing the hinge plates to the inside walls. Install two safety chains at floor level, suspending them between screw eyes. The chain should prevent the hinged sides from opening more than 120 degrees. Hinge the window doors in position, hardware on the outside, using 1-inch hinges. Glue

the pull knobs on both sides of each door. Insert the notched stage in position.

8. Use an old curtain or make a new velvet one, as follows. Cut the velvet into two 24- by 36-inch rectangles. With each, turn under and stitch a ⅝-inch hem on the two shorter sides and the bottom. Turn under 2½ inches from the top, then stitch ⅝ inch down from the top and 1⅞ inches down from the top to create a pocket for the curtain rod. Slip in the rod.

9. Hang the curtain rod using thumbtacks and cloth loops. (Other hardware may prevent the sides from folding in completely.) Dim the lights, open the curtain, and its showtime!

Family Library

Rain Gutter Bookshelves

Books are a natural in the family room, but they can truly monopolize the space. When the Meliezers of Douglasville, Georgia, were awash in kids' books, it was this humble rain gutter that bailed them out.

MATERIALS

10-foot piece of standard vinyl rain gutter
Brackets

To make bookshelves, the Meliezers started with a 10-foot piece of standard vinyl rain gutter. (They had it cut in half at their local home center, but you can also do it yourself with a hacksaw.) Dad Hans then used brackets (sold separately) to install two 5-foot lengths in the room — one at the right height for each child. "We are avid readers," mom Catherine tells us, "but our house got so full of books, we could never see them. These

shelves really display the books, and the covers look so nice." We're not recommending that you judge a book by its cover, but it sure is nice to be able to see it.

Tip: The hanging brackets for vinyl rain gutters come in a number of styles in addition to what we show here. Those looking for a more ornate look might also consider affixing vinyl end caps, available from gutter suppliers, to the ends of the gutter.

Story Tent

"Getting my kids excited about doing their reading assignments was not an easy task! But when I realized how much they love camping, I decided to combine the two. We set up a small tent in our family room and furnished it with beanbag chairs, oversize pillows, quilts, and flashlights, as well as a bowl of popcorn or some other favorite snack. The only rule of The Reading Tent is that once you enter, no talking is allowed. The tent has been a success: the kids' reading charts for school are now full."

— Linda Hardy
American Fork, Utah

HOME STRATEGY

At-home Library

Books motivate, enlighten, and paint pictures in our kids' minds. We cherish our book collections and tend to enlarge them happily, but let's face it: books are a major clutter culprit. Here are some tips to help all you bookish types organize and enjoy your family's home library.

- Set up a reading nook next to a window or fireplace, with a cozy chair and a blanket.
- Remember who will be reading what. It is nice for your younger readers to be able to pick and choose their books at a comfortable level. The bottom shelf should be devoted to them.

- For extensive book collections, it may be helpful to alphabetize your books or categorize them by subject matter. For large families, you could also organize them by reading level (for example, preschool, early and late elementary, junior high, and high school).
- Keep a book basket in each room. When it fills up, carry it back to the main library and reshelve the books.
- For books that come with audio tapes, store them together in gallon-size freezer zip bags, attached to the wall or the side of the bookcase with universal clips.
- As an incentive to read stories that jump-start the imagination, start up a family book club. You and your kids can all read and enjoy the same book, and then get together weekly to share thoughts. For younger readers, you can read aloud while they listen and draw along to the story.
- Create a pretend library. Leave a date stamp and ink pad on a table near your bookshelf and have kids "check out" their books. Their deadline might encourage them to get through their books faster.
- Finally, consider weeding out some books that you no longer read. You can donate them to your local library.

LEARNING AT HOME

Decorate Globally

Pump up your kids' enthusiasm for geography by keeping a globe, or hanging a colorful world map, in the family room. Besides gaining familiarity with the world's countries and cities, they'll always be ready to pinpoint where something comes from. Next time you get mail from a distant locale, have them find the letter's origin. Or as you're putting away groceries, have them locate the home country of the olive oil or sardines.

CHAPTER FOUR

Kids' Bedrooms

Turn your child's kingdom of chaos into coolness with these clever decorating and organizational projects

For a child, his room is the most valuable real estate in the house — a place to play, daydream, listen to music, or just hang out with friends. Plus, it's where he keeps and showcases all his favorite things. For a parent, however, a child's bedroom can feel like a clutter zone — a place where laundry, toys, schoolwork, hobbies, and sleep mix too chaotically. Where a child sees treasures, we are more inclined to see a mess. It's no mystery why "Clean up your room!" may be the most-uttered phrase in the history of the English language.

**Sticker Tickers,
page 71**

The trick is to keep the jumble under control without dampening your child's pride in his very own room. More than in any other part of the home, he should be able to play a leading role in deciding how to decorate it. He can spiff up the furniture, show off his collections, and even help paint the walls. Let him try some of the fun ideas in the following pages, from an artwork-covered lampshade (pages 67 and 70) to a Glow-in-the-dark Mural (page 80), all adaptable to individual tastes.

Not only will these decorating ideas foster your child's creative expression, but they may even help organize his room in the process. And if he needs a little extra help in that department, you can sneak in some of our inventive clutter busters, like a laundry hoop (page 72) or the Kids' Room Bookshelf (page 83). Just keep these tips in mind before you start.

Get your child involved. Kids are not short on ideas, and when it comes to their own space, it's nice to let them have a say. Give your child a piece of paper and colorful markers and have him design his dream room. In his sketch, he can suggest where to put his bed, desk, collection shelf, and more. He can even draw a mural or painting idea for his walls. Even if the resulting design isn't feasible or affordable, it may inspire your efforts: how about helping him create a stencil for painting his wall (see pages 76 and 77)?

Create a secret hideout. Kids love to crawl into a cozy place made especially for them. Even if you don't have the resources to build the full-fledged loft bed on page 85, small spaces may present themselves. Scope out the closet: is there room for a pillow and a wall lamp? Or divide the room with a bookshelf, curtain, or mosquito netting to create a private nook.

Bear in mind that childhood passions are fleeting. Remember Smurfs? Instead of decking out your child's room in the theme of the moment, choose accessories and paints that are changeable — and furnishings that will last for many years.

Kids' Room Essentials

When it comes to a child's room, we believe in having reasonable goals to keep clutter at bay. Here are some steps you can take.

* **Make sure there is a place for everything.** Dresser drawers (that aren't stuffed to bursting!) for clothing, plenty of clearly labeled storage containers for special treasures, and bins and baskets for toys. When it is time to clean up, kids will at least know where to put things.
* **Use space wisely.** Try setting up a closet organizer to keep shoes, dress clothes, and bulky sweaters neatly stored. Hang hooks on the backs of doors for jackets and bathrobes, and use shoe holders creatively (see page 74).
* **Thin the ranks.** With each season, change and sort clothing. Evaluate toys with a critical eye, and donate (or store) any that aren't getting regular play time.
* **Remember the basics.** Buy a desk with drawers for organizing supplies and homework; consider a bookshelf headboard for displaying stuffed animals; and keep a laundry basket and a wastebasket handy.

Playful Decorations

CLUTTER BUSTER
Bedroom Door Bag

This handy bag does double duty: hanging on a bedroom door, it proudly announces the name of the child who lives there. Plus, it makes a clever place to tuck away all the bits and pieces that belong in that child's bedroom (you know what we mean: all those Barbie shoes and Matchbox cars and pop-it beads that end up strewn around the family room or, worse, your own bedroom).

It couldn't be easier to make one. Start with a small, solid-colored canvas tote bag (these are available inexpensively at craft stores). Have your child use fabric pens, fabric paints, or glitter glue to write his or her name on it, and then decorate it further. Let it dry, hang it up, and your child will have the perfect, personalized knob accessory.

MAKE-IT-YOURSELF
Pocket Curtains

Here's a quick way to jazz up a window and provide your child with a convenient place to stash away action figures or other lightweight toys. There is a little sewing involved, but it's all straight seams.

MATERIALS

- **Solid-color cotton curtains**
- **12 bandannas and cloth napkins**
- **Straight pins**
- **Sewing machine**
- **Fringe trim (optional)**

First, transform each bandanna into a pocket by folding it in half diagonally so that it resembles a triangle with one corner facing directly down. Then fold under both sides and press all the edges. With the cloth napkins, create rectangular pockets by folding them in half once, then again, and pressing all the edges.

Now lay the curtains flat on a smooth working surface and pin on the bandannas and napkins, arranging them in staggered vertical rows, as shown. Machine-stitch the sides and bottoms of each pocket to the curtain, removing the pins as you go. Finally, stitch fringe trim to the pocket bottoms, if desired.

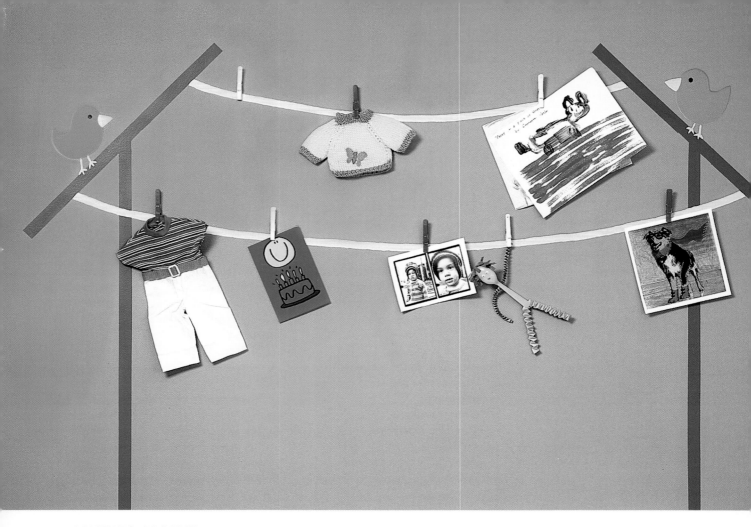

Artistic Hang-up

Here's an idea that makes displaying kids' art a breeze: clip the creations with real wooden clothespins nailed to a trompe l'oeil line. Angela Judd of St. George, Utah, got the idea when her fridge front was spilling over with the artwork of Haley, five, a prolific painter.

Like daughter, like mother, Angela grabbed a pencil and drew a picture — right on Haley's wall. She filled in the decorative clothesline scene with a brush and some acrylic paints before securing the clothespins with finishing nails. (**Tip:** Drill pilot holes for the nails to avoid splitting the clothespins.) Now Haley can pin up all her own pictures, special letters, and cards, and she doesn't even have to wait for a sunny day.

FAMILYFUN SUCCESS STORY
Lending a Hand

"When my husband and I purchased our home, I was pregnant with my second child, a girl. I wanted something special for her nursery, but money was tight and I knew my daughter would quickly outgrow the baby motifs that were in the stores. Instead, we went to the paint store and bought white paint, brushes, and rollers. We painted the entire room white, then invited our closest family and friends over for an evening to help decorate. We had each person pick a place on the wall for his or her handprint. Then, armed with a bottle of hot-pink tempera paint, we each made our prints on the walls, signed, and dated them. It made for a lovely room!

"Lia is now three years old, and we have continued this tradition with friends who come visit — her wall currently sports more than 100 hand-prints. Some of the printers have passed away, and although Lia never will remember them, we talk about them and look at photos to help her understand. We did reserve one place just for her handprints; she now puts her own prints on the wall each year on her birthday. We have fun comparing them to see how much she has grown."

— Cheryl LaVecchia
Olmsted Falls, Ohio

Home

Colored Lamp

This project sheds a whole new light on displaying your kids' art or handiwork.

MATERIALS

- **Your child's crayon artwork**
- **White or beige lamp shade**
- **White glue or a commercial brand of decoupage matte (sold at craft stores)**
- **Paintbrush**
- **Craft wire**
- **Small toy**

Have your child pick out his favorite coloring creations: monsters, people, a landscape, you name it. Cut out the shapes and glue them to the outside of the shade. If the shapes are too large, you can take them to a local copy shop to have them resized on a color photocopier.

With a solution of 3 parts glue to 1 part water (or you can use a decoupage matte), paint over each of the cutouts on the shade, taking care to coat all the edges. Apply two or three coats, allowing the glue to dry between applications. Use the craft wire to attach the small toy to the end of the pull chain.

Kids' Bedrooms

Height Chart

For those who like keeping records, there's nothing like pencil marks moving up a wall to document a kid's weedlike sprouting. The Rodriguezes of Round Rock, Texas, have taken the growth chart even further by posting dated photographs of their daughter, Analisa, next to her twice-yearly measurements. Now they can remember exactly what she looked like at each height, and Analisa herself is sure to get a big kick out of the pictures as she grows up.

Mom Amy made the chart out of scrap lumber (you'll need a board 4 to 5 feet long), which she sanded and painted before adding a strip of molding that she'd marked off into inches and feet. Amy then decorated the chart with acrylic paints before screwing it to the wall 2 feet above the floor. Analisa's only two now, but those first measurements still inspire waves of nostalgia in her mom. "It's so sweet to look back at her little round baby face," Amy sighs. "Now she's such a big girl!"

Toy Mobile

Kids just seem to love hanging lots of things from the ceiling, but making lots of holes in the wallboard is a prospect no parent relishes. This homemade mobile offers the perfect compromise. Suspended from a single hook, it features nine dangling objects attached with pinch clips that make it a cinch to exchange items whenever the mood strikes.

MATERIALS

- **1 5-inch-wide wooden embroidery hoop**
- **1 10-inch-wide wooden embroidery hoop**
- **Acrylic paint and paintbrush (optional)**
- **Fishing line**
- **9 plastic-coated pinch clips**
- **Assorted small toys**

To make the mobile, separate the inner and outer circles of the two embroidery hoops and paint them, if desired. Once the paint dries, tie three 18-inch lengths of fishing line to the inner circle of the smaller hoop, spacing them equally apart. Tie a pinch clip to the bottom of each length, then reattach the outer circle of the hoop. Similarly, attach six 2-foot lengths of fishing line and pinch clips to the larger hoop.

Next, tie the ends of two equal-length pieces of line to the smaller hoop so that the ends are evenly spaced apart. Gather the midpoints of both lines and hang the hoop from the ceiling. With 10-inch lengths, hang the larger hoop from the smaller one so that the two are about 6 inches apart, and the clips hanging from the top one fall through the center of the bottom one. Now help your child clip on toys in a way that balances the weight.

Collectibles Corner

Let's face it. No dresser top could ever be big enough to display all the stuff our kids collect. You can capitalize on an area of the room that's rarely used by installing a row of corner shelves, like the Shelf Master ones pictured here. Sold in pairs or sets of four on-line at www.telebrands.com, each shelf can be positioned wherever you want it. Slide a lever on the bottom to lock it into the corner.

Picture Pals

6. Draw and cut out hair and clothing from craft foam (**G**). We also had fun making clothes out of Mylar (buy it or recycle a balloon).

7. To make shoes, form the polymer clay into four balls, each 1½ inches in diameter, and flatten the bottoms. Press the tips of each leg into the shoes until they nearly reach the bottom (**H**). Slip out the legs and bake the shoes according to package instructions.

8. Prepare the base by sanding, if necessary, then apply a coat of acrylic or tempera paint to the top and sides. Let it dry. We don't recommend painting cardboard bases since the paint warps the cardboard.

9. Glue the photo face to the head (**I**). Glue on hair and clothes. (If you like, back pieces of hair and clothes can be glued to matching front pieces.) Again, hot glue (a parent's job) is our preference since it's easier and dries faster, but tacky glue works too.

10. Form arms into loops for hands (**J**). Slide the legs into the shoes and position the shoes on the base. Using a pencil, mark the shoe positions and remove the figures. Glue only the shoes to the board; let them dry, then insert figures. If needed, apply a dot of glue in each shoe hole.

This best friends' photo frame is easy to make and cool to look at on a dresser. Plus, kids will love moving the figures of themselves into different poses.

MATERIALS

- **6 pipe cleaners**
- **Close-up photographs of each pal's face (approximately the same size)**
- **Colored craft foam sheets and (optional) Mylar**
- **Polymer clay such as Sculpey (you'll need about 3 ounces)**
- **Strip of either basswood (available at craft and hardware stores), balsa wood, or cardboard, measuring 3½ to 4 inches wide by ¼ inch thick and 9 inches long**
- **Sandpaper**
- **Acrylic or tempera paint and paintbrushes**
- **Hot glue gun (best option) or white tacky glue**

1. For each body, place three pipe cleaners as shown (**A**), then fold down legs (**B**).

2. Wind the legs two or three times below the head and arm pieces (**C**) to secure them.

3. Lift the head pieces upward and twist them tightly three to five times to create a neck (**D**).

4. Keeping the face sizes of your photos in mind, create a head (**E**). Fold down the pipe cleaner ends.

5. Place the head on the photo, adjusting the pipe cleaners if necessary, and trace around the outside (**F**). Cut out the face.

draw a straight line connecting the beginning (A) and ending points (B) of the traced line. Cut out the template and mark several points about 3 inches up from the rounded edge. Draw a curvy line connecting the points to create the dips and the peaks of the dirt hills, then cut along the line. Wrap the strip of paper around the bottom of the shade, curvy side up, and use your pencil to trace lightly along the top edge of the strip on the shade. Finally, cut this strip into 6-inch-long pieces and use them as templates to cut identical pieces from the tissue paper for hills. Set aside the hills.

Next, your child can cut basic animal and vegetable shapes from the colored paper. Use permanent markers to add details, such as eyes, whiskers,

or stripes. Once you have all the shapes ready, brush a layer of clear sealer onto the shade and press on the paper shapes, using the pencil line as a guide for placement. For instance, a carrot root should be below it, whereas a bird would be placed above it. Gently smooth out the shapes with your finger to remove any air bubbles trapped underneath. Apply another layer of sealer over the shapes and allow the shade to dry completely (1 hour).

Attach the dirt hills by applying an even coat of sealer along the bottom half of the shade and carefully pressing each tissue paper panel in place over the shapes, lining them up with the pencil line and flattening them with your fingertips as you go. Allow the dirt panel ends to overlap slightly and trim where needed. Dab sealer along the seams where the tissue papers

meet but do not brush a layer of sealer over the brown tissue, as the color may run.

Garden Lamp-scapes

Your kids will dig transforming a plain lampshade into a garden scene like this one. The best part is turning on the light to reveal the veggies growing "underground." Although the following directions are for a medium-size lampshade, you can use this decoupage technique to decorate one that's any size or shape.

MATERIALS

Large sheet of plain paper, 36 by 25 inches

Tape

Plain white lampshade, 7 inches tall and 10½ inches wide at the bottom

Brown tissue paper

Lightweight colored paper

Permanent markers

All-surface sealer glue and finish (we used Plaid brand Mod Podge) and paintbrush

Make templates for the tissue paper dirt hills by first taping the large sheet of paper to your work surface. Set the shade, seam up, on top of the paper and roll it one full revolution, tracing along the lower edge as you go. Then

Hairstyling Station

Both functional and whimsical, this window-style mirror features a colorful plastic window box just right for storing brushes, detangler, and any other accessories your child needs to style her hair. There are even hooks for hanging her necklaces and bracelets.

MATERIALS

2 decorative bent-wire hooks with screws to attach them to the mirror frame
Window-style mirror (sold at many department stores)
$1/2$-inch screws
Plastic shower caddy (the type with suction cups on back)
Hot glue gun
Assorted silk flowers
Feather butterflies and silk dragonflies

First, attach the hooks to the upper corners of the mirror frame by drilling starter holes in the wood and then screwing the hooks in place.

Next, transform the shower caddy into a window box by removing the suction cups from the back. Then predrill a couple of screw holes in the lower portion of the mirror frame that will match up with two of the holes in the back of the caddy. Turn the screws into the holes until the heads stick out of the wood a quarter of an inch. Next, hang the caddy from the screw heads.

For a finishing touch, hot-glue the silk flowers, feather butterflies, and silk dragonflies to the mirror frame. Finally, hang the mirror on a wall at a height that suits your child and fill the window box with her supplies.

Sticker Tickers

When Cindy Bruch of Davis, California, redecorated her two-year-old daughter Angela's room, she wanted a clock to match both the jungle theme and her budget. Lickety-split, stickers came to the rescue, transforming an inexpensive wall clock into a kid-friendly eye-catcher. Cindy used a flathead screwdriver to pop off the clock's plastic cover, enlisted her kids' help in decorating its face with stickers, and then replaced the cover. In no time at all, Cindy had customized a clock for every room, including one with tank engines for four-year-old Ryan, a passionate Thomas fan. Her kids don't tell time yet, but with such watchable clocks, we bet it won't be long.

Kids' Clothing

Slam-dunk Success

We all know the gross anatomy of a peeled-off outfit — that bedside heap of dirty-kneed jeans (underwear still inside) topped by an inside-out T-shirt/sweatshirt combo. Becky Sprague, a mother of four from Richmond, Indiana, knew it all too well. Backed by the if-you-can't-lick-'em-join-'em philosophy, she installed a basketball hoop hung with a laundry-bag net. "I never have to pick up laundry anymore," she says.

The hoop was a yard sale find, repainted, then screwed to her sons' bedroom wall. The net was a mesh laundry bag with a zipper closing. She cut open the bottom and hooked the bag to the rim, zipper end down. When laundry day comes, she places her laundry basket beneath the full mesh bag and opens the zipper. Swish!

Very Special Pillows

"My son, Jason, age ten and a half, has a number of T-shirts from sports teams he's played on, camps he's gone to, and places we've visited. Jason's aunt, Linda, came up with a creative way to preserve those memories after he has outgrown the shirts. She cuts a section from the front and back of each shirt, sews them together, and lightly stuffs them to make mini pillows. She then sews the pillows together to make a soft and comfortable quilt. It's a great keepsake, and as Jason gets older and taller, the quilt just grows with him."

— **Debbie Emery**
Northboro, Massachusetts

Personal Shoppers

"It used to be quite a chore to get my daughters, Katrina, seven, and Valerie, three, to try on hand-me-downs and the prior year's clothing whenever a new season rolled around. That was until I created The Clothes Store Game. For each girl, I spread out a categorized selection of clothes: pants, pajamas, dresses, and the like. The girls come "shopping" and select items to try on in the dressing room (my closet). When they've tried on enough for that day, they bring their purchases to the cashier (me) to be tallied. My daughters each pay with real money, given to them just for this purpose, and get to take the clothes back to their rooms in a shopping bag. Depending on how many outfits there are to be tried on, we play the game one or two more times and always have fun."

— Theresa Medoff
Wilmington, Delaware

Ready-to-wear

Choosing an outfit is one of those seemingly simple tasks that inevitably takes up a lot of precious time on a school-day morning. With one of these handy stands, your child can set out her apparel the night before. Here's how to build one.

MATERIALS

Supplies
- **Two 10-foot-long 1- by 3-inch clear pine boards**
- **Three dozen 1¼-inch wood screws**
- **Pitch and Toss disk or Frisbee**

Tools
- **Handsaw**
- **Drill (for making the holes for the screws)**
- **Screwdriver**

Cut the following pieces. From one of the 10-foot boards, cut two 35-inch lengths (A and B), two 22-inch lengths (C and F), and a 5-inch length (D). From the second board, cut a 10-inch length (E), an 18-inch length (G), and four 12-inch lengths (H, I, J, and K). Mark and cut H, I, J, and K as shown to shape the pieces of the base (see figure **1**).

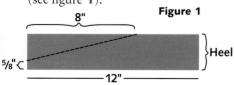

Figure 1

8"

5/8" Heel

12"

Assemble the post. The post is formed by sandwiching the crosspieces (F and G), spacers (C and D), and neck (E) between the face (A) and back (B). Start with piece A facedown on a flat surface (see figure **2**). Set C on top of A so that the bottoms and sides are flush, drill screw holes, and screw it in place. Now center and attach G horizontally to A so that its lower edge is centered against the top of C. Attach D vertically and F horizontally, as shown. Then screw the lower portion of E to A so that E's bottom edge rests against the top of F and its upper portion extends beyond the top of A. Finally, set B on top of all the attached pieces so that all of its edges are flush with A's and screw it in place.

Figure 2

Attach the base. Attach H to the bottom of the post so that H's heel and bottom are flush with the right side and bottom of A. Attach I, J, and K in like fashion, rotating the post one turn counterclockwise each time (see figure **3**).

Top it off. Lastly, strap the Pitch and Toss disk (or screw the Frisbee) to the upper part of E, and the rack is ready to "dress."

A

K

H

J

I

Figure 3

The Pocket Shoe Holder

Whoever designed the first pocket shoe holder most probably imagined a solid, honorable life of shoe holding for her invention. *FamilyFun* readers beg to differ. According to the mass of letters we've received, this pocketed wonder combines storing and sorting like no other product, and it inhabits space you are guaranteed not to miss — the front or back of a closet door. Besides, when your kids grow out of all their tiny, sortable passions, you can always return it to its humble shoe-holding origins.

Closet in a Bag

The shoe holder can have no greater fan than Liz Gasper of Bellevue, Washington. "I have them in almost every room in my house," she cheers. The shoe bag that started it all? A coat-closet organizer for hats, scarves, gloves and mittens, compact umbrellas, and the bane of every soccer parent, those shin pads that always seem to be underfoot. "It worked!" Liz boasts. "My closet is no longer a clutter collector."

Beanie There, Done That

More than one reader has written in about the need to control packs, flocks, and herds of stuffed animals. Annette Entin of North Caldwell, New Jersey, employed a see-through pocketed shower curtain, which she nailed to her daughter's wall (Mom covered the nailheads with Sculpey clay — a nice touch). Vicki Watson of Columbus, Ohio, had similar luck with the trusty shoe organizer, and now all of her daughter Madeline's "favorite bears and bunnies" have room of their own while remaining visible to — and reachable by — their doting keeper.

Blue-ribbon Idea

Tammy Lindsay of Carrollton, Virginia, uses a clear pocketed organizer to keep her daughter Chelsea's hair accessories in order. They sorted all the barrettes, bows, ribbons, and scrunchies by color and grouped like items in each pocket. The organizer hangs in the closet near all of Chelsea's school outfits, which makes for easy color matching. "What a difference this has made in the mornings before school," Tammy writes.

Other uses for a pocket shoe holder:

◆ Art supplies and craft odds and ends (see page 119)
◆ Sewing and knitting supplies
◆ Tiny trinkets, toys, and prizes
◆ Toiletries
◆ Keys, sunglasses, wallets, a flashlight (hang one by your front door)
◆ Car junk (hang one over the front seat)

Where to find them:

Try a discount department store like Target or Wal-Mart (a 24-pocket model costs about $15). Bed Bath & Beyond sells a 24-pocket canvas shoe holder for $20 (go to www.bedbathandbeyond.com).

FamilyFun Home

Morning Routine Picture List

Kids who are just starting school — as well as those who know the drill — sometimes need extra help getting through the morning routine to make it to school on time. Many *FamilyFun* readers say they have luck using a picture list like this one.

MATERIALS

Construction paper
Magazine, catalogs, and photos
Glue
Markers

Have your kids select and cut out images, such as brushing teeth, eating breakfast, and combing hair, from magazines or photos. Arrange the pictures on paper, glue in place, and describe each step in writing.

CLUTTER BUSTER

Hand-me-downs Down Under

Alix Kennedy, editorial director of *FamilyFun,* and mother of two young sons, devised this terrific hand-me-down system to keep track of her kids' outgrown and to-be-grown-into clothing. Besides keeping dresser drawers unstuffed, the system prevents the frustration of forgotten hand-me-downs.

1. Begin by investing in a set of plastic bins (we like the under-the-bed ones with wheels). Label each bin with a size and sex (5–6, boy), and as your children outgrow clothing — or as you receive hand-me-downs from other families — add it to the bins. When a bin is full, either store it under the bed of a younger child or give it away.

2. Create a special clothing keepsake box for the sentimental items that you can't part with, such as hand-knit sweaters and baby booties.

FAMILYFUN SUCCESS STORY
Clothes Kid

To make choosing clothes more fun, **Hannah and Mackenzy Derrick** of **Rock Springs, Wyoming,** made a pact with their mom, **Kandi:** each night the girls would lay out the next day's clothes on the floor in the shape of a person (including everything from socks to hair accessories). Whatever their "Clothes Kid" wore to sleep, they wore to school the next day.

The result? A big reduction in the number of fits thrown, says a very satisfied Kandi.

Kids' Bedrooms

Painting

The Climbing Tree

We think that you shall never see a stencil as lovely as a tree. Using just a few branch and leaf patterns, you and your kids can create a single stately elm or transform an entire wall into a lush forest of laurel. You might even add a few hooks to hold plush tree dwellers, like owls or squirrels.

MATERIALS

- Manila folders
- Paper towels
- Vegetable oil
- Craft knife
- Chalk
- Acrylic craft paint (two shades of green, brick red, and dark brown)
- Masking tape
- Paper plates
- Stencil brush

Cut a manila folder in half, then use paper towels to rub each piece with a light coat of vegetable oil (it makes the paper more durable and flexible). Let the oil absorb for an hour or so.

On one folder half, draw a few basic leaf shapes and clusters. For a more traditional stencil look, draw the two sides of the leaf, leaving a vein down the center.

On the other folder half, draw various branch sections. Use a craft knife (adults only) to cut out your leaves and branches.

Lightly outline a large tree shape on the wall with chalk. Pour each color of paint onto its own paper plate. We used two shades of green for the leaves (letting them mix on the brush), a brick red for the trunk, and a darker brown for the branches.

Using masking tape to secure stencils to the wall, begin painting clusters of leaves and connecting branches, alternating between the two and moving from spot to spot to allow the paint to dry (see tips at right). Wipe any paint from the underside of the stencil before you reposition it.

When the design is complete and the paint is completely dry, wipe off the chalk outline.

TIPS AND TECHNIQUES
Stenciling 101

◆ **Keep it cheap.** Plastic report covers, manila folders, and masking tape work as well as more expensive specialty materials, as do acrylic craft paints or latex wall paints.

◆ **Keep it simple.** Start with a stencil shape that's no more intricate than a cookie cutter. Remember, straight lines are easier to cut than curves.

◆ **Keep it dry.** Pour some paint on a paper plate, coat your stencil brush (available at craft stores), then blot it on a dry area of the plate. Use a "pouncing" motion to dab paint on the wall (brushing could cause seepage). Work from the outside of the stencil in.

Fabric Pattern Stencil

When redecorating her then two-year-old son Kip's bedroom, Tracey Herburger of Tulsa, Oklahoma, used an ingenious stenciling technique. Struck by the bold, cheerful designs of the room's curtains, Tracey decided to repeat their images around the room. First, she photocopied the fabric to enlarge the designs. Then she traced the designs onto a see-through report cover, from which she cut her stencils: a train, sun, boat, and star. Painted in matching colors, the shapes echoed the festivity of the curtains, much to Kip's delight. We adapted Tracey's idea here, beginning with a set of Garnet Hill sheets and ending with a room full of friendly snails.

Trace one or more of the fabric's designs on a plastic report cover. If you want to enlarge or shrink the designs, use a photocopier, then trace the copy. Make separate stencils for each area of color, as we've done with the snail's shell and body. Cut the designs from the plastic.

Use masking tape or stencil adhesive spray (follow the label directions) to position the stencil. Pour some paint onto a paper plate. Dab the brush in the paint, then on a dry part of the plate, then fill in the stencil, from the edges to the center.

Move the stencil and repeat to make as many images as you like.

Sticker Stencils

Calling all stargazers! We turned a plain lampshade into a celestial beacon, illuminated by a galaxy of shining stars. And the technique couldn't be easier:

1. Draw stars (or other simple shapes) on low-tack shelf liner paper, cut them out carefully with a craft knife (parents only), then stick them all around the lampshade. These become a kind of reverse stencil.

2. Smear an oil-paint stick (we used Shiva brand Artist's Paintstik) on a paper plate. Wipe a cosmetic sponge into the smear, then rub the paint over the edges of the stencils — always working from the centers of the stickers out — and onto the lamp.

3. Continue to apply the paint until the lampshade is colored to your liking. Carefully remove the stars and allow the lampshade to fully dry.

4. If you've cut out the stars carefully, you now should have several traditional stencils — ready for use on a nearby wall or ceiling, as shown above. Affix them in place and apply latex wall paint with a pouncing motion, as described in Stenciling 101 on page 76.

Stencil Ideas Basic shapes make the best stencils. Some themes we like:

Dinosaurs (such as this diplodocus)

Insects: dragonflies, butterflies, ladybugs, inchworms

The beach: fish, shells, sun, clouds

Cars and trucks and things that go

Wall-to-wall Fun

This is a room design where kids will feel right at home: the very street where they live. Here, they can check the mail, take the dog for a walk (or draw him a pal on the chalkboard), hang up doll clothes on the line, play with magnetic fish in the pond, or open the door to see who's in the house.

Best for kids ages four and up, this design is fairly complex, incorporating many materials and a large wall (note: for information on any of the materials, turn to page 215). But you can simplify it to suit your family's needs or personalize it with elements that reflect your own home — a felt board garden or magnetic street signs, say — or invent a new scene altogether, such as a barnyard or rain forest.

Once you and your child decide which elements she'd like, lay out your design with masking tape. Paint on the big blocks of color first, then add in the details. As your child grows and her interests change, you can always paint over your original design or include new features. Consider adding a mini basketball hoop, a doorbell, a Lego building base on a doorstep, or any of the other ideas you're bound to come up with as you go.

Pond

Apply a circle of magnetic paint. To  cover the gray color, we added a top coat of light blue glitter paint.

Mailbox

Cut the top off a cardboard milk container, then wrap the outside with electrical tape.

Tape on a cardboard door flap. Cut out a flag and attach with a brass fastener. Mount on a cardboard tube.

Door

Paint a 2- by 4-foot chalkboard paint door. To add a screen door, cut matching openings in two 2- by 4-foot cardboard pieces and sandwich screening between them. Hang with small hinges.

Window

With electrical tape, we outlined panes on a 13- by 19-inch mirror. The shutters are cut from corrugated cardboard and hung with hinges. Kids can peek in the mirror.

Fence

To make a picket fence, cut the shape out of corrugated cardboard. Paint, and then glue on a few cardboard flowers, if desired.

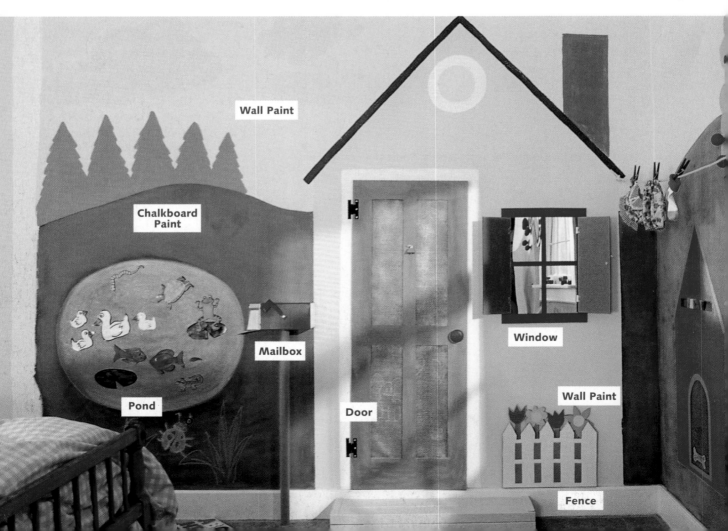

Wall Paint

Chalkboard Paint

Pond

Mailbox

Door

Window

Wall Paint

Fence

along the cork tree (see below) so that kids can track their growth with a pen mark or, for older kids, a thumbtack.

Apple Tree

Cut a tree trunk out of cork, then glue or tape it to the wall. Paint the leaves on with wall paint. For a crop of pickable apples, we added Velcro dots and Ping-Pong balls, painted red, with Velcro attached. When kids are old enough to use tacks, they can hang messages and pictures on the tree.

Owl

Glue or tape on a felt oval. We added a felt owl (with a changeable felt face), but a squirrel or bird might be equally at home here.

Doghouse

Using wall paint, we painted a 3-foot-high dog-house on the wall. A metal ruler nailed to the top holds movable magnetic letters for spelling out the dog's name.

Dog

The dog's body is also painted on with wall paint. His head is cut out of felt, as are the pieces that make up his changeable face. We put a screw eye into the wall (where a stud is) on his collar, then clipped on a dog leash.

Clothesline

Attach two screw eyes to the wall (into wooden studs), then string a clothesline between the two. Kids can use clothespins to hang up artwork, small toys, or doll clothes.

Tape Measure

Using double-sided tape, vertically attach a cloth tape measure to the wall, starting at the floor. We put ours

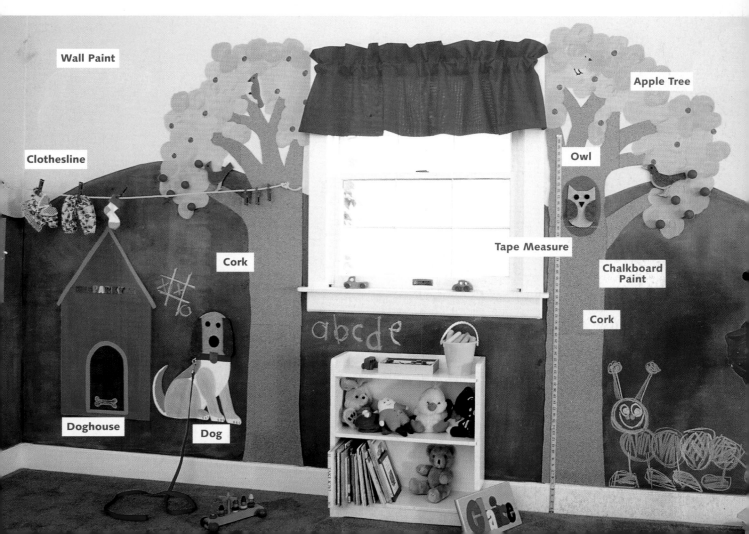

Glow-in-the-dark Mural

By day, this cityscape mural makes an imaginative backdrop for playing with toy cars and trucks. When the sun goes down, all it takes is a night-light to illuminate the buildings and night sky.

MATERIALS

**Interior acrylic white wall paint
2 or 3 sponges of assorted sizes
Paintbrush (optional)
Interior acrylic glow-in-the-dark paint (generally available in several colors and sold at most hardware or craft stores)
Night-light (the moon-shaped one shown here, manufactured by Lightning Bug Ltd., is battery-operated)
1 or 2 dozen glow-in-the-dark stars**

First, make sure the wall you plan to decorate is clean and dry. Then pour a shallow layer of white wall paint into a flat-bottomed container (you need an opaque white undercoat to make the buildings clearly visible during daylight). Dip one of the sponges into the paint to coat its surface evenly, then holding it upright, evenly press the sponge against the wall just above the baseboard to create a "building" imprint. You may want to practice on newspaper until you are able to achieve an effect you like.

Continue in this way, using all the sponges to stamp a row of buildings. You can even trim a sponge into a triangular roof or steeple shape or use a paintbrush to add finer details. Once the paint is dry, use the same method to apply a topcoat of glow-in-the-dark paint to all the buildings. Let the final coat dry thoroughly. Then attach the night-light and glow-in-the-dark stars to the wall.

DECORATE IT
Switch Plate Art

When your kids dress up light-switch plates and hang them on their walls, rooms become galleries for their artwork.

Collage

Offer your child a supply of magazines, candy wrappers, comics, old photos, and even postage stamps, and let her cut out images to cover a switch plate. Help her arrange the pieces until they are just right, reminding her to leave the openings for the screws and switch clear. Set the collage aside and stir up a mixture of 3 parts white glue and 1 part warm water. With a soft paintbrush, coat the back of each cutout before mounting it on the plate. Apply a final layer of the sticky stuff when the collage is complete. For pieces that extend over the edge, fold them under the plate to prevent them from curling up. If curling persists when the glue is dry, apply a second coat or fold strips of clear tape along the edges of the plate.

Painted Light Switches

Select shades of acrylic paint that complement the color scheme of the room. To achieve the splashed-on Jackson Pollock look, cover your area in newsprint, then dip the brush deeply in paint and, holding the tip of the handle, wave the brush down and sideways above the switch. Because the target is small, the motion of the brush should be quick and compact. While you have the paints out, cover another switch plate with a repeated pattern, such as polka dots, stripes, stick figures, or spirals. Or paint a smiley person with freckles and attach a pair of googly eyes with glue. Then, flick his nose to turn off the light.

Wallpaper

Place a switch plate facedown on a piece of wallpaper. Trace the openings with a pencil and draw a ¾-inch square from each corner. Open the rectangular switch slot by cutting an X from corner to corner with scissors or a craft knife. The two screw openings can be poked with a sharp pencil. Attach the paper to the front of the plate with an even coat of tacky glue. Fold the borders and the corner and switch slot flaps around to the underside of the plate.

Kids' Bedrooms

Fun Furniture

HOMEMADE DECORATION
Custom Drawer Knobs

Not only will these handmade knobs spruce up your child's dresser — there's also a chance (okay, a long shot) that, because the knobs are fun to use, your child may actually close his drawers once he's grabbed the clothes he needs.

MATERIALS

- **Polymer clay, such as Sculpey III or Fimo**
- **Round wooden screw-on dresser knobs**
- **Small, heat-resistant trinkets or beads, permanent colored markers, or acrylic paint**

Knead the clay until it is malleable, then flatten pieces of it into ⅝-inch-thick "pancakes." Wrap the pancakes around the knobs, as shown, firmly pressing the clay to the wood to make it stick. Now you can embed decorative items into the clay on the front of the knob. Or, to make a baseball like the one shown here, use the end of a toothpick to create two curving rows of indents for "stitches." Bake the decorated knobs according to the clay manufacturer's directions. Once they're cool, the knobs are ready to attach to

your child's dresser. (To finish the baseball, simply fill in the indents with permanent red marker or acrylic paint.)

DO-IT-YOURSELF
Changeable Chair Upholstery

Goldilocks never would have wasted time trying out other chairs if this cushy, customized seat had been among the three bears' furnishings. The furry cover is attached with Velcro, so you can easily launder it — or even swap a different patterned fabric when your child is ready for a change.

MATERIALS

- **Painted wooden chair**
- **Thin foam cushion**
- **½ yard no-fray faux fur**
- **Velcro strips**
- **Hot glue gun**

Trim the foam cushion to fit the chair seat, then cut out a piece of faux fur that's an inch or so larger than the cushion all around. Cut the Velcro strips into lengths that match the fabric edges, then hot-glue the top portions of the Velcro to the underside of the fabric and the bottom portions to the surface edges of the seat. Lastly, set the cushion in place and cover it with the fake fur, using the Velcro to secure it.

Kids' Room Bookshelf

This bookshelf offers a solution to a problem most parents are faced with every day after school: that pile of backpacks, papers, shoes, coats, and sporting equipment that floods the foyer when the kids get home. It will take a little extra effort to put this shelf together, but it will ultimately save you time — and stress.

Use the ideas below as a starting point. Families with more than one child may want to divide one bookshelf (for two kids, for instance, paint each side a different color) or customize multiple clutter busters.

1. Check out stores or garage sales for an inexpensive wooden bookshelf or pull an old one down from your attic.

2. Recycle a yogurt or frosting container (or a dressing cup from a deli, as pictured) for lunch money.

3. Attach plastic hooks with short screws. On the shelf's front edge, add a plastic 3M hook with Command adhesive.

4. Display favorite objects, such as a trophy or something made in art class.

5. Create an in-box-style organizer by cutting the front off an empty cereal box and laying it on its back. Excellent for library books that are due or for prized haiku.

6. A plastic milk crate and a clean pail can hold umbrellas, sporting equipment, and any other large objects.

7. For papers that need a parent's signature, affix one or more sturdy plastic file holders (available at office supply stores) with short screws or mounting tape.

8. Attach a dry-erase board (a corkboard would also work) to the front of the shelf with Velcro tape.

Sleeping Car

"I wanted to make something home-made for my younger son, Drew Christian. Since he was about to grow out of his crib, I decided to build him a race car bed. I put the frame together using 2 by 4's and plywood and made the car-shaped sides also from plywood, high enough so he wouldn't fall out. I designed the headboard to look like a rear spoiler, and it doubles as a bookshelf. As a finishing touch, I attached real reflectors and painted a '96' on the side for the year he was born. The total cost was $75 (compared to $300 for a store-bought plastic version). When Drew gets too old for it, we can disassemble it and save it for his own kids."

— **Chevelle Kelly
New Bedford, Massachusetts**

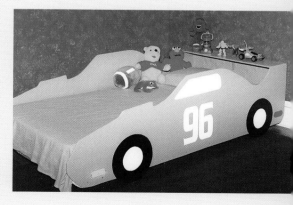

Kids' Bedrooms

Polka-dot Nightstand

This bold dresser is bound to add zing to any kid's morning, and you won't go dotty applying the spots, thanks to our Con-Tact paper stencil. Tricksters will appreciate the camouflaged drawer pulls.

MATERIALS
Paints
1 quart water-based primer
(For paints below, we used semigloss interior latex paints by Crayola, except where noted)
1 quart Parrot Green
1 quart Red
1 quart School Bus Yellow
2-ounce bottle of light-blue acrylic enamel paint (available in craft stores)

Other supplies
Unpainted dresser
2-inch-wide foam wedge brush
1 square foot corrugated cardboard
1½-inch-wide polyester paintbrush
Low-tack painter's masking tape
1 small roll of repositionable, medium-adhesive Con-Tact paper (available at hardware stores)
½-inch-wide detail or artist's paintbrush

1. Sand your nightstand if necessary. Make sure it's clean, remove the drawers and the drawer pulls, and then use the 2-inch foam brush to prime everything (including the fronts of the drawers and the pulls). Let the nightstand dry. Store the pulls in a safe place.

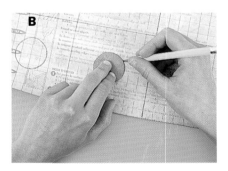

2. With the drawers still out of the nightstand, place small pieces of cardboard under each leg to prevent them from sticking to your surface if any paint drips. Use the 1½-inch paintbrush to cover the body of the nightstand — everything but the top and the bottom front — with green paint. Let the paint dry completely.

3. Set the drawers faceup. Use the 1½-inch brush to paint the front of each drawer red.

4. Using low-tack masking tape, tape the edges of the body wherever the green and yellow paint will meet (see blue tape in figure **A**). Your tape should be on the green paint and will serve as a guard so that if your brush slips, you'll get yellow paint on the tape rather than on the green surfaces. Use the 1½-inch brush to apply yellow paint to the top and bottom front of the nightstand. Remove the tape carefully and allow the paint to dry.

5. Trace a drawer pull, upside down, on the corrugated cardboard. Cut out the circle. Now trace the card-

A

board circle repeatedly on the reverse side of the Con-Tact paper, leaving a couple of inches between each copy of the circle (see figure **B**). Cut the Con-Tact paper into a series of squares, each with a circle in its approximate center. Last, cut out the circles (fold

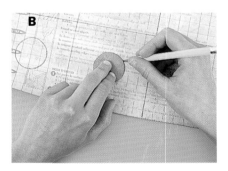

B

the squares in half to do so). These squares with cutout centers are your polka-dot stencils.

6. Slide the dry drawers into the dry nightstand. One at a time, remove the backing from the stencil squares, fold back a corner for an easy removal tab, and scatter the squares randomly over the nightstand. Remember that the drawer pulls will be polka dots too, so don't apply any dots too close to where the pulls will be.

7. Use the ½-inch detail brush to apply light blue, yellow, and green dots through the stencils (see **C**). Paint

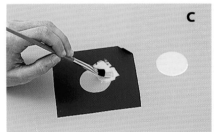

C

toward the center of the circle to avoid getting paint under the stencil. Remove the Con-Tact paper promptly.

8. Randomly paint the drawer pulls with the dot colors for a camouflage effect. Let all of the paint dry, then reattach the pulls.

Decorate With Decoupage

Give your flea-market finds, such as step stools, wooden boxes, or even collection shelves, a new look with this lively decorating project.

MATERIALS

Step stool, box, or shelf
Magazines, catalogs, or maps
Decoupage medium (we recommend Golden Soft Gel Matte, available at craft stores)
Clear varnish (optional)

Once you have chosen something to decorate, have your kids select and cut out a variety of favorite images from catalogs, magazines, maps, and other sources. For a collection shelf of miniature race cars, for example, one child might want a backdrop of pictures of real NASCAR drivers. A box for keeping special pen-pal letters could be covered with cool stamps. Or an old step stool might take on a new life when covered with a hodgepodge of another child's favorite things: Shetland ponies, daisies, baseballs, and parrots. If the artwork is very thick — or conversely so thin the words from the other side show through — try color-copying it first.

To apply the images, first clean your surface, then paint on a thin film of decoupage medium. Apply the art and let it dry for 5 minutes. Paint a thin film of gel over the artwork. **Tip:** For surfaces that will see lots of traffic (say, a step stool), add a layer of clear varnish for a durable finish.

CLUTTER BUSTER
Lofty Bed

When *FamilyFun* writer Charlotte Meryman decided to bring some order and fun to her daughter's bedroom, she settled on building this amazing loft bed. The unit, which was designed by contractor and parent Kent Hicks, has a twin bed, a ladder, bookshelves, and even room for a puppet stage. For step-by-step plans for your very own loft bed, go to familyfun.com and do a search for "loft bed."

CHAPTER FIVE

Playspaces

Tame the mountain of toys in your home so your kids can have hours of independent play

Child's play is serious business: kids never look more industrious — or joyful — than when they are hunched over a scattering of toy cars or immersed in a sea of Barbie belongings. For us grown-ups, however, business as usual looks more like cleanup and tidying than a two-day game of Risk. And when it comes to spirited child's play and our homes, this is the real tension: we want our kids to enjoy their toys, but we also want a home that isn't carpeted in Legos.

Establishing a play area will solve part of your problem: your kids get a space of their own, and you get a place to stash their toys. But what if you don't have the space? Let the kids play where they may, but make it easy for them to do so independently and tidily. Helping us in that goal are the dozens of toy storage solutions and play stations on the following pages. Each one will engage your child in imaginative play and then cleverly store her playthings when the fun is done. Play's the thing. Just follow our tips to keep it neat.

Storing Stuffed Animals, page 91

Keep your kids in mind. Design a toy storage system that accommodates the particular needs of your children. Consider factors like a child's height, her interests, the toys she uses most frequently, and the most likely place she will go to look for things. Some general principles seem to work well for most toys — such as storing similar toys together and putting them in labeled, transparent bins (see our Picture-perfect Toy Boxes, page 97).

Put it on a shelf. Shelves can be an attractive and useful tool for displaying dolls, games, and toys, but not all shelving is designed with kids in mind. Look for low, sturdy units that won't topple, shallow shelves that allow kids to reach all the way to the back, and a surface material that easily wipes clean. Shelves also make a great base for play stations, such as the Doll Condo (page 91).

Rethink your toy box. A toy box is a lovely piece of furniture — and it offers convenient storage space. But, thanks to its cavernous holding tank, it can become an abyss of toys, and your kids may forever be rummaging through it or, worse, dumping its contents to look for that missing Lego piece. The best way to enjoy it? Assign it a specific function holding larger items like balls or board games.

Rotate your toys. When it comes to kids and toys, familiarity breeds disinterest. Keep some of your child's toys in a stored bin, then rotate them in and give others a time-out. Their absence will clear space in the play areas, and their reappearance will be cause for celebration.

Get creative with cleanup. Put on a song and ask your kids to spend its duration tidying. Stage silly contests, with prizes awarded for the speed of your children's cleanup efforts. If all else fails, throw stray toys in the Toy Jail (page 94).

Playspace Essentials

Need more ideas for creative play? Try setting up fun stations in your home:

- A reading nook with a beanbag chair, a good light, and a stack of books
- A portable art studio with an easel, a pad of paper, and a bucket of coloring supplies
- A bin of toy cars and a raceway with a rug or floorcloth decorated to look like a road
- A puzzle or board game platform — a piece of Fome-Cor or cardboard that lets you move everything intact
- A tent with a flashlight and cozy blankets, for portable privacy or hideaway adventures
- A music bin with a child's cassette player (ideally one with a microphone) plus a handful of blank and prerecorded tapes and a couple of songbooks
- A dress-up box with clothes and hats, jewelry, and dress shoes (page 93)
- A play kitchen (page 23) with pretend food, empty cereal boxes, and plastic utensils
- A cleaning station with a small dustpan and broom, a sponge, and a spray bottle of water

Stuffed Animals & Dolls

Vertical Menagerie

"My husband and I found a fun and practical way to display our son's ever-growing collection of stuffed animals. We mounted a 7-foot piece of furring strip to the wall in a corner of our playroom, then added mug hooks every 6 inches. Nicholas, age three, then selected his favorite animals for display, which we hung up by their ribbons or arms, creating both a practical storage solution and an eye-catching decoration."

— Karen Langford
Erie, Pennsylvania

STORAGE SOLUTION

Bedroom Beanie Lift

f small stuffed animals are threatening to take over your child's room, our hoistable Beanie tram is a fun way to get them out from underfoot.

MATERIALS

Plastic tubs (ours once held berries)
Ribbon
S-hooks
Clothesline pulley
Ceiling hook
Braided plastic rope
Wall cleat

For each tramcar, punch a hole in the bottom center of a plastic tub. Weave two lengths of ribbon through the slits on either side of the tub as shown, above. Gather the four ends, tie them in a knot, and insert an S-hook into the knot. Hang a clothesline pulley from a ceiling hook. Thread a length of braided plastic rope through the pulley to the floor and secure the other end to a wall cleat. Thread the rope through the bottom of each tram and insert the S-hook into the strands of the rope. Release the rope from the wall cleat to lower the trams, fill with Beanies, and hoist away.

A Doll's Suitcase

"Years ago at a garage sale, I bought a train case (a small, deep suitcase with a mirror and side pockets) for holding my daughter's doll clothes. It's perfect for little shoes, hats, hair ribbons, clothes, and other accessories. My daughter, who is now 23, had fancy clothes for her doll (such as a Queen Elizabeth ball gown and crown) that she would fold neatly into the case like a miniature wardrobe. I still have it, so when she has her kids, it will be right there."

— **Sandy Russell**
Malibu, California

STORAGE SOLUTION

Baby Doll Bassinet

As your children will remind you, dolls are not just toys — they are babies. So what better place to store them, along with their myriad clothing and accessories, than in your former baby's old bassinet? It's pretty, it's portable, and it fits better with the baby theme than a plain old plastic bin would. Show your child photos of her own tenure there (you could even frame one nearby), then encourage her to organize her dollies and their belongings inside. No bassinet? A baby bathtub, a cradle, or even a changing table can also provide fitting storage for the growing family.

HOMEMADE TOY

Baby-sitter Kit

Store those all-important doll accessories — baby bottles, brushes, and so on — in your child's old diaper bag. Toss in a few fun extras, such as a board book, stickers, newborn diapers, and onesies and call it a Baby-sitter Kit. At playtime, your child gets to be in charge — and make sure Baby gets changed, brushes her teeth, doesn't watch too much TV, and is read to before bedtime.

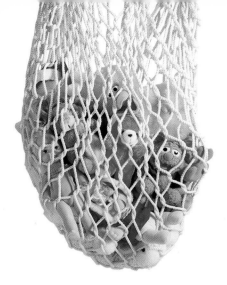

Storing Stuffed Animals

Bright, colorful, and ever cheerful, stuffed animals are cute, yet too often they're hidden away, left to wrestle on the floor, or get tangled in a pile on your child's bed. Why not let your cuddlers add charm and character to your child's room? The following storage ideas give them the visibility they deserve.

Hammock: Give your child's furry favorites a place to hang out by stringing a hammock in the corner of her room, low enough to reach.
Shoe bag: For maximum display impact (and ease of grabbing), fill each pocket of a clear shoe bag with a stuffed animal (see page 74).
Bookshelf headboard: Give the cuddlers a shelf of their own — within reach of your sleepy child at bedtime.

ORGANIZE IT
Barbie's Own Dresser

Did your husband really think he could hang onto that adorable set of tiny plastic drawers? You know, the one he bought at the hardware store to sort all his nuts and bolts? Forget it. Barbie's been shopping again, and she's got big plans for organizing her small belongings: shoes in this drawer, purses in that one, hairbrushes, bathing suits. Never again will she (or any of her human playmates) have to turn the house upside down to look for that lost feathered mule.

FAMILYFUN SUCCESS STORY
Doll Condo

"I made this home for my daughter Sydney's Barbie dolls using inexpensive stackable plastic shelves. To create the facade of the house, I decorated one side of a piece of cardboard (the same size as the shelves) with windows, doors, and flowers. Then I covered the other side with scrapbook, wrapping, and Con-Tact papers to resemble wallpaper and glued the cardboard to the shelving. Now Barbie and friends have a fabulous, affordable new home."
— **Carol Forsyth**
Eagan, Minnesota

Dress-up Clothes

Instant Dressing Room

We tweaked the idea of Superman's phone booth to create a kid-size transformation station — a place for kids to keep and play with their costumes, dress-up attire, and play jewelry. Its many virtues include ease (you can make one in about a half hour) and portability (it's featherlight, so you can move it from one room to another).

MATERIALS

36- by 48-inch cardboard display board (available at office or craft supply stores for about $5)
Mirror
Foam mounting squares
Colored tape and stickers
Pair of battery-operated touch lights
Self-adhesive hooks
Berry baskets
Paper fasteners

First, affix the mirror to the center panel of the cardboard display board with foam mounting squares. Use colored tape and stickers to create a trompe l'oeil vanity, then add a pair of battery-operated touch lights and a handful of sticker-adorned self-adhesive hooks for clothes and accessories. Berry baskets, attached with paper fasteners, hold brushes, ribbons, and other things of beauty.

DISPLAY IT
Chain of Hats

If you've got a clothesline and a handful of clothespins hanging around (maybe in a bin in the basement?), then put them to good use. Strung near a mirror, or in any other popular dress-up spot, the clothesline is the perfect way to display your child's collection of hats, which can be clipped right to the line. Alternately, you could use it for that growing collection of baseball hats. Because up, up, and away always means less clutter at ground level.

PLAY STATION
Costume Case

To encourage hours of magic, masquerade, and make-believe, pack old suitcases with dress-up items and disguises and store them under your child's bed. We recommend scouring your closets, attic, and local thrift stores for the following:

- Fancy vintage dresses, scarves, and purses
- Hats — top, straw, witch, and cowboy hats; fedoras; Easter bonnets; baseball caps; chef's toques
- A feather boa
- A piece of sheer, velvet, or heavy fabric with a dress clip — an instant cape!
- Shoes of all kinds — cowboy boots, feathered mules, Chinese slippers, high heels
- A bathrobe or kimono
- Wigs and fake fur for beards and sideburns
- A bandanna
- Costume jewelry, including bangle bracelets and clip-on earrings
- Eyeware — think nonprescription glasses, shades, and swim goggles
- Lipstick
- A black eye pencil (and cold cream) for whiskers and mustaches
- Plastic fangs
- Wands
- A tiara
- Angel wings
- A tutu
- Masks
- Old neckties
- Silk flowers

FAMILYFUN SUCCESS STORY
Clothes Quarters

"My daughters, Chandler and Kelsey, just love to play dress-up. The sight of their clothes all wrinkled up in a box drove me crazy, so we made each of the girls a portable closet from cardboard boxes. We cut openings for the clothes and shoes, added bars for hanging, and covered the boxes with Con-Tact paper. Now the girls each have a wardrobe fit for a princess."

—Robin Giese,
Trappe, Pennsylvania

Cars & Trains

Toy Car Parking Lot

Does your playroom (or garage or basement) have a traffic jam of ride-on push cars and trikes? Designate a section of the room as a parking garage and gas station for your child's larger toy cars. Simply lay out colored tape so the kids know where to park after their road trip. While you have the tape out, you could also mark a roadway around the perimeter of the playroom.

FAMILYFUN SUCCESS STORY
Toy Jail

Even if there's a place for everything, someone has to put it there. To give her children a strong incentive to do this themselves, reader Therese M. Stenzel of Broken Arrow, Oklahoma, instituted a toy jail. "When it is time to start tidying up, I set a small kitchen timer (one that ticks loudly) for five to ten minutes," she says. When it goes off, any toy not put back where it belongs goes into the "toy jail," a box on the top shelf of the closet, where it stays until Saturday.

FAMILYFUN SUCCESS STORY
Train Table

"My kids, Bradley, four, and Whitney, two, love trains, race cars, and farm animals. Many of our friends have store-bought train tables, but we wanted to make our own. We primed, painted, and sealed a hollow door from Lowes (ours was 36 by 80 inches). We placed the door on top of plastic stack shelves and secured them in place with Velcro. Underneath, we put color-coded bins for storing horses, cars, trains, and dinosaurs. We decorated the top with rubber 'road' tape (from a hobby store) and painted on ponds. It was the best gift, and we made it ourselves!"

— Laura and Jimmy Dyke
Crozier, Virginia

Tube Cubbies

These inexpensive display racks can be made from whatever size cardboard tube best suits your child's toy car and truck collection. We used builders' tubes (sold at lumberyards and home supply stores) for the large version shown above and mailing tubes (available at office and postal supply stores) for the Matchbox car holder at right. Using a craft knife or hacksaw (parents only), cut the tubes just longer than the items to be stored, neatening the cuts with scissors, if necessary. (**Tip:** Draw a line around the tube to ensure a straight cut.) Paint the tubes if you like and let them dry.

We assembled the smaller cubby by first marking each line of contact, then gluing with a bead of low-temperature hot glue. The larger model is fastened with black metal binder clips, whose road hazard motif was created with strips of yellow craft tape.

Playspaces

Collections

Collection Containers

Recycled and low-cost containers bring order to any childhood collection:

Glass jars: For balls, buttons, and other durable items

Film canisters: Store beach sand, dead bugs, and other "samples"

Plastic cases: Great for marbles and other items that get carted around

Clementine boxes: Ideal for bulky things such as rocks and pinecones

Egg cartons: Still the cheapest solution for beads, shells, and acorns

STORAGE SOLUTIONS

Bits & Pieces

Legos breed faster than rabbits: turn your back for a minute, and three become 30 — burrowing under the couch cushions, hiding under dressers, biting your bare feet. Like K'nex and Tinker Toys, and sets such as Hot Wheels and Brio, these multipiece toys demand places of their own. Here are some suggestions:

Set up a workstation. Some heavily used toy sets are best "stored" at a workstation, where they can be left out and returned to as the needs of a project demand. For a Lego station, glue a large base plate to the top of a kid-size table, then paint the surface around it to resemble an aerial view of a farm scene. The Lego blocks can be stored in containers nearby or spread across the farmyard.

Buy a bucket. Looking to buy a toy container? Keep in mind that the ideal design may not be marketed as such. A jumbo nuts-and-bolts drawer box from the hardware store, for example, might be just the thing for sorting and separating Lego pieces. You might also try a tackle box (bigger blocks fit in the bottom half, and the lift-up tray stores Lego accessories such as heads, wheels, and trees). Lunch boxes, plastic dishwashing basins, and pretzel or popcorn cans might also suit your needs.

Preserve those plans. Use plastic sheaths and a three-ring binder to protect those essential assembly instructions. Keep the binder on hand so your builders have a ready supply of plans if their imaginations run dry.

Picture-perfect Toy Boxes

The culprits? A gang of Barbies loitering on the floor after playtime with a motley crew of tiny accessories, plastic food, and dress-up clothes. The solution? Mug shots of the offending suspects, which are posted on storage boxes so your kids can see where all their loot belongs.

Julie Filbeck of Auburn, Washington, thought up this idea when her daughters, Janelle and Jenna, were still too young to read. She guessed,

correctly, that photographs would encourage the girls to unjumble their stuff and restash it neatly. The picture-box system especially helped when other kids came to play. "They'd look at the pictures, and then they'd get the necklaces back into the necklace box, the Barbies in the Barbie box, the horses in the horse box," Julie explains, before describing a post-play floor of unearthly tidiness. "And the kids can find what they're looking for without

digging through a gigantic pile."

Julie covered a bunch of cardboard boxes with decorative Con-Tact paper, grouped like toys inside each one, and then took a close-up photograph of a few representatives from each box. These she glued onto white paper, labeled with bold markers, laminated (you could also cover them with clear Con-Tact paper, or leave them as is), and attached to the boxes with clear packing tape.

Playspaces

Cardboard Townhouse

Are your kids itching for a change of scenery? With a quick trip to your local appliance and hardware stores, you can offer them the keys to a sparkling new playhouse. Fashioned from a refrigerator box, this elegant townhouse looks like a million bucks but costs just pennies to make.

Here, we've laid out a foundation of building tips from creating the blueprint to applying the faux brick finish to hanging real curtains for the cutout windows. After your young architects pitch in on the design and decor, this life-size backdrop will inspire hours of creative play. Our favorite feature? When the kids are

done visiting friends, ringing the doorbell, and delivering the mail, the whole neighborhood can easily be folded up and tucked away.

MATERIALS
Cardboard refrigerator box
Utility knife
Chalk
Tempera or acrylic paints
Paper plates
Sponge(s), about 2³⁄₄ inches wide by 5 inches long
Paintbrushes (regular and foam)
Two ¹⁄₄-inch dowels, each approximately 21 inches long
Four ¹⁄₂-yard pieces of fabric
Tacky glue or Stitch Witchery tape

Cut Apart the Box

Using a utility knife (parents only), cut lengthwise down one corner of the box, separating two main panels along a fold. If the top or bottom flaps are still secured together, unfasten them and spread the box flat. Remove the top flaps. Trim the bottom flaps to 6 inches, but don't remove them; they will help to stabilize the final standing structure.

Make a Blueprint

Have your kids dream up a townhouse design. They should plan it out on scrap paper first, then outline their blueprint on the cardboard with chalk. (**Tip:** Have the kids test their design ideas on a piece of paper folded in four panels just like the box.) Alternate between spreading the box flat (so the kids can reach any part of

the box) and standing the box up (so they can step back and check their progress). In addition to doors, windows, window boxes, and front steps, they can also include other fun details like flowers or vines, a mail slot, a cat door, or an entry light.

Paint!

To paint your townhouse, work on a section at a time either on a table (fold the other panels under), spread out on the floor with a tarp underneath it, or outside. To make the brick walls, squeeze some red, brown, and tan paint onto a paper plate. Dampen a sponge, then blot it in the different colors for a mottled effect and stamp it onto the box. (To make smaller bricks, simply trim a sponge to the right dimensions.) To paint the trim, doors, steps, and flowers, pour paints

onto paper plates, then apply them with either a foam brush or a regular paint-brush. Use

different brushes for each color, or rinse one brush thoroughly between colors. For delicate trim, a small foam brush is handy, and it's the right size for kids to use easily.

Cut Out the Windows and Doors

Next, cut out the windows and doors using the utility knife (a parent's job). Before you start, draw a half circle 3 inches in diameter on

the inside of each side of the window frames. These will become supports for the curtain rods and should be at

the top of the window frame. When you cut out the window panels, cut around the curtain holders and any window box flowers that extend over the sill, as shown. When you cut the doors, remember to leave one long side uncut for a hinge.

Make and Hang Curtains

To make the curtains, fold over 1 inch on the sides and bottom of each piece of fabric and secure in place with tacky glue or Stitch Witchery tape (follow package directions). For the curtain rod casing, fold down 2 inches of fabric from the top and glue or tape it in place, leaving enough room for the curtain rod and being careful not to close the ends. Cut a ¼-inch dowel approximately 3 inches longer than the width of each window. In the center of each cardboard half circle (on the window frame), cut a hole ¼ inch in

diameter. Fold the half circles to the back, thread a pair of curtains on each dowel, and insert the dowel ends into the holes.

Decorate!

Our townhouse design includes a brass bell, a mailbox slot, a flowerpot, and rope doorknobs (a piece of heavy rope threaded through a small X cut in the door and knotted at both ends). Your architects, however, can brainstorm any number of add-ons. Try stringing indoor holiday lights around the windows or roof or set a floor-lamp lamppost outside. Clip a small notepad to the door for neighborly messages and use houseplants for landscaped greenery. If they're gung ho decorators, they can even design and paint an indoor scene on the flip side.

Store It

When your kids are done being homeowners for the day, the townhouse is a breeze to close up: just fold it, tie it with a length of clothesline, and store it in a closet or under a bed for another day.

CHAPTER SIX

Workspaces

Keep your family organized with our creative and practical systems for home offices, craft areas, and laundry rooms

Children are busy people. You are probably too familiar with the sight of a small scholar hunched over a computer monitor to finish her homework, or a sweaty young athlete tossing his soccer uniform into the hamper, or a budding artist in the messy throes of passionate creativity. What do these images have in common? They're all about kids engaged in the everyday work of being kids — studying, creating laundry, making art. And this is, of course, work that intersects with the kind of work we need to get done as adults: like doing our taxes on the computer, or coordinating washing efforts so we don't feel like we're running a 24-hour Laundromat. As you'll see in the ideas that follow, when it comes to shared workspaces, the trick is to develop a system that works for you.

Mouse Pad, page 108

Get the message across. With our ever-busier schedules, the family information center is becoming a crucial component of family sanity and order. More important than *how* it works is *that* it works: set aside time for a regular family meeting (page 104), pick a system for organizing your schedules, and treat your family like a team. With a little practice, you'll all be communications experts.

Take a byte out of computer chaos. Our home offices are doing double, even triple, duty these days — as adult work areas and homework stations, game arcades and music booths. There is bound to be bickering over turns and time on the computer, a proliferation of paraphernalia, and not enough desk space. Sift through the ideas on pages 108–110, and decide which might help you share the space more easily, considering issues like time management, keeping track of belongings, and general clutter.

Craft a craft area. Kids and crafts are inseparable. We've found no better way to encourage their creative work — and keep their projects from taking over the entire house — than designating a specific space just for crafts. As you'll see, this can be as simple as a rolling cart full of supplies or a converted bookcase (page 116) that organizes everything for ongoing or spur-of-the-moment artistic endeavors. The trick is keeping everything in one place so that creativity doesn't become an occasion for clutter.

Get rid of wash-day blues . . . and whites. It's a basic fact of family life, and it's no dirty secret: laundry piles up daily. Our best advice for taming towers of grubby clothes? Get your kids involved — on the front end, sorting and loading, or on the back end, folding and stashing. We offer you dozens of tips and tricks (pages 120–123) to help your kids learn to help, and to keep it fun while you get it clean.

Workspace Essentials

Workspaces should be functional, efficient, and neat. Keep in mind the following:

◆ Location, location, location. **Whether it's a computer, a laundry bin, or a craft table, consider who will be using it and how. Everything should be easily accessible — or, in the case of things like glue and important files — not accessible. Should it be placed on a high shelf? Tucked away in a drawer or cabinet? Down low for easy reach?**

◆ Lighten up. **Most work requires good lighting. Invest in a good desk light for your home office. A craft center or an ironing station may require a bright floor lamp or overhead track lighting.**

◆ Run a tight ship. **Designating specific days or times for work like laundry, bill paying, and computer use will keep your house running smoothly and will let your kids know what to expect.**

◆ Music sets the mood. **Wherever a task beckons — be it folding towels, mailing out utility bills, or finishing a project — keep a CD player or radio for cheering tunes. A job set to music will often fly by pleasantly.**

Family Communication

Custom Corkboard

Today's busy families can have schedules more hectic than a rock band's. To keep track of who's doing what, you need an organizing system that's a bit more sophisticated than the refrigerator door and a bunch of magnets. Here's one idea: hang a bulletin board to post all your important messages. Corkboard (inset at left) can be bought at lumberyards and office supply stores, then customized with fabric and ribbon to match your decor. We tacked our fabric to the back with thumbtacks (see photo, below), then created a grid with ribbon for holding important tickets and invitations, securing each crossing point with upholsterer's tacks. Screw the board to the wall with Sheetrock screws, hiding the screw head behind the ribbon if possible. Place it beside a monthly calendar (for recording all family events) and a small chalkboard or dry-erase board (for day-to-day notes and reminders).

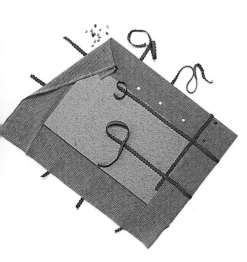

Clip Key Papers

Keep a firm grip on important papers such as soccer schedules, school lunch menus, and permission slips with these personalized clips. Each bulldog clip is screwed to a strip of painted wood and customized with a circular name tag (held on by an upholsterer's tack). More frenetic households may need to give each member an in-box (a wicker basket, decorated shoe box, or an actual in/out box as described on page 129) for holding mail, phone messages, and schedule reminders.

Family Meetings

Several readers of *FamilyFun* **set aside time to go over the week's activities, plan holidays and vacations, and even divvy up household chores. Here are their creative tips:**

Sunday after-supper meeting. For the Osleys of Bolton, Connecticut, the process of getting ready for their busy week ahead begins each Sunday after supper. With mom Melanie traveling frequently for her job, dad Robert working a physician's hours, and assorted activities to arrange for Michael, nine, and Nicholas, four, it's a real juggling act. The Sunday powwow allows them to get everything out in the open so there are fewer surprises during the week, like forgotten sports equipment or sudden science projects.

Let's make a deal. Ronnie Rom of Northampton, Massachusetts, came up with a regular family meeting time (midday Sunday), a rotating schedule of leaders, and the following agenda:
1. Sharing (a family version of show and tell)
2. Problem-solving
3. Family plans/announcements
The real success of the forums, says Ronnie, is that they now ward off grumbles with the refrain, "Bring it up at the family meeting!"

Plan for the weekend. Every Friday after dinner, the Zobels of Dublin, Ohio, have a family night that doubles as a weekend planning session. They make popcorn and sit down at the kitchen table with a list of ideas — berry picking, swimming, a local festival, or a picnic — for orchestrating the weekend. Everybody gets to put their two cents in, and the family settles on a plan before the conversation evolves into a check-in about the previous week. Mom Lori says, "Friday nights have become 'our night.'"

ORGANIZE IT
Message Center

This cardboard message board makes keeping track of phone calls and important dates — such as sports meets, field trips, and get-togethers with friends — a snap. Instead of writing directly on the board, your kids can just tuck their messages under one of its rubber band holders and then remove them when they're outdated.

MATERIALS
4 9-inch squares of corrugated cardboard

Glue
12 or so broad rubber bands
10-inch-long piece of string
Masking tape

First, glue together the cardboard pieces one on top of the other to create a four-ply square. Then, stretch the rubber bands around the board, randomly crisscrossing them, as shown. Lastly, fashion a hanger for the board, by knotting the ends of the string and taping them to the backside of the cardboard.

Suggestion Box

Kids are often bursting with good ideas that have no place to go. By crafting a suggestion box and then making a big deal of the ideas you find inside, you let your kids know how much you value creative thinking. And everyone gets practice in brainstorming and writing persuasively.

With paper and pencil handy, our suggestion box is ready for action. It lets your family focus its brainpower on what to have for dinner, where to go on vacation, or any other pressing family problem (post a request for ideas nearby).

We made our version from an oval paper box from a craft store, decorated with stencils and ribbon. The notepad is glued on, but the paper lightbulb is removable and reversible (the other side is shown at left) so idea writers can let others know a new suggestion is inside.

Secret Journal

Amy Laidlaw noticed that her fourth grader, Morgan, was struggling with writing and spelling in school. How could she encourage her daughter to practice writing without making it feel like more homework?

Acting on a hunch, the Sterling Heights, Michigan, mom addressed a journal entry to Morgan in a new notebook and snuck it under her pillow. That night, Morgan responded, then tucked the journal under Amy's pillow. The secret swap has been going strong ever since.

"We write about things she likes," says Amy, "and the things that happen at school, my memories of her as a baby, and even things she'd rather not talk about face-to-face, like guns, drugs, boys, or times when she's mad at me." As Morgan faithfully keeps up the journal, she's developing confidence in her writing and an ever-deepening relationship with her mom.

Phone a Friend

"To make it easier for my daughter, Hannah, now age six, to make phone calls to friends and relatives by herself, we made her a phone book of her very own. I listed a name and phone number on each page and put the pages in a three-ring binder. We then looked through our stacks of pictures and found photos to add to each one. Finally, we slipped a picture of Hannah inside the plastic cover of the binder, which we titled 'Hannah's Phone Book.' Hannah loves using her book to find the photo and number of the person she wants to call."

—Anne Robinson
Cuyahoga Falls, Ohio

SEPTEMBER

HOME SOLUTION
Mark Your Calendar

If you're tired of trying to decipher the scribbles on your family calendar, here's a fun way to make sure that important school dates, like sports meets and field trips, really stand out. With a fine-point marker, print the events on round, color-coding self-adhesive labels (available at most office supply or department stores). Your kids can even embellish them with mini sketches. Then press the stickers onto your calendar. Keep extras handy for highlighting significant dates throughout the year.

CLUTTER BUSTER
Paper Triage

A pile of paper tends to spell procrastination, and so it is with those school memos — whether they mount up on your desk, in the kitchen, or by the front hall, the stacks suggest that you have things you should be remembering (bake sales? soccer games?). But why keep the pile of papers, when all you really need are the important dates? FamilyFun.com visitor Lynn Schumaker offers this easy plan for purging: "When my son gets off the bus, I go through his book bag immediately and enter new stuff in my 'Week-at-a-glance' day planner — and throw out that paper immediately. That way everything is in one place. By doing it right away, I drastically reduce 'that pile.'"

The Three-ring Binder

Even in an age of megabyte hard drives, it's hard to beat the simple utility of this organizational old-timer. It's cheap, sturdy, comes with handy tabbed inserts, and it brings method to the madness of a mess of loose papers.

Keep Tabs on Your Kids

Tanya Beeler of Hillsboro, Oregon, keeps a binder for each of her three kids, its dividers labeled with headings like Activities, School, and Sports. "Any papers that I get for each child have their own place to go," Tanya writes, "and if I need to find out what time the next game is, I know where to look." Suzi Campbell of West Valley, Utah, keeps one binder divided into sections for each of her four kids. Suzi writes, "My kitchen has gone from notes and papers stuck on every empty surface to just one easy-to-locate notebook."

Family Notebook

Beth Kelley of Potomac, Maryland, keeps one master binder for her entire family. Its tabbed sections include Carry-out Menus, Current Phone Lists (class lists of all three kids, her own book-club list, and volunteer lists), Emergency (especially good for baby-sitters), Institutional Info (the school calendar and the county library directory), and Team Schedules. "Everyone old enough to use the phone knows where 'The Notebook' is," Beth writes. That would be right by the phone.

Fun-finder Binder

We don't like to boast (okay, maybe just a little), but it turns out that *FamilyFun* magazine occupies quite a few three-ring binders out there:

- Sue Davis of Sycamore, Illinois, has pages from the magazine organized into Crafts, Games, Outside (this is further divided by the seasons), Parties, Recipes, Travel, and specific holidays. Many of her sections are subdivided into age-appropriate categories, making it a snap to match up the right activity with the right kid.
- Janet Brewer of Salt Lake City has three binders, one each for Crafts, Recipes, and Holidays, and hers are also further divided into specific categories. **Tip:** Photocopy any pages that need to be in two places at once.

Tips of the Trade

- Keep a three-hole punch in a central location so that to-be-filed papers don't pile up.
- To distinguish among binders, decorate the spines with photos or stickers, or label with gold markers.
- Let your kids decorate their own binders distinctively, and you'll always know whose is whose.

Consider keeping binders of:

- Frequently used recipes photocopied from cookbooks.
- Copies of your kids' best art, organized by year (see page 51).
- Photocopies of color photographs. These are good first photo albums for small hands.

Workspaces

Home Office

Mouse Pad

Help your kids craft this cute mouse pad — a study buddy who'll be as quiet as, well, a mouse.

MATERIALS
- **9- by 12-inch piece of gray craft foam**
- **Nonslip liner (sold at most department stores)**
- **Purple craft foam**
- **Black, gray, and purple felt**
- **Purple ribbon and string or yarn**
- **Tacky glue**

Round the corners of one short side of the gray craft foam and trim the other short side to a point. Trace this shape onto the nonslip liner and cut it out. Create a face by tracing the pointed side of the gray foam onto a sheet of purple craft foam. Add a curved line as shown below, then cut it out.

Glue yarn to the foam for the mouse's tail, then cover with the nonslip liner. For ears, glue two purple felt circles to the centers of two slightly larger gray felt circles, then glue in place. Glue ribbon whiskers to the end of the snout and cover with a black felt nose. Glue on black felt eyes. Finally, glue the purple face in place on the gray body. Cover the mouse with waxed paper, set a large heavy book on top, and allow the glue to dry completely.

Sharing a Computer

Nowadays, computers have a range of applications that make them indispensable — or, more to the point, irresistible — to everybody, especially kids. Between writing reports, finding homework help, playing games, and instant-messaging friends, your children could easily occupy every waking hour with the computer. Short of acting as traffic cops, how do you as parents ensure they're not overdoing it? And how can you get your kids to leave the computer ready for the next person (especially Mom or Dad)? Let's take it step-by-step.

1. Enlist your kids' help. One of the best strategies for managing computer use is to require that your kids record each session in a logbook the minute they sit down. Then add a prominent clock or a kitchen timer (see the Ticky Tock Mom shown at right) so they know how long they've been sitting.

2. Play it safe and use backups. Kids, as well as adults, can inadvertently delete important files, so it doesn't hurt to back them up regularly.

3. Organize your computer station. Sharing is easier if you keep the space both accessible and uncluttered — not to mention ready to use by the next person. Organizing the software your kids like to use is a good start. Assign each child a separate bin where favorite programs can be stored and then easily returned after each use. For prereaders, color-code software jewel cases with stickers. (For more ideas, see the custom CD holders at right.) Also, dedicate a shelf for instruction manuals and reference cards, which tend to get scattered or lost.

These strategies aren't going to eliminate all of your problems, of course; only a 24-hour baby-sitter could do that. But at least they can make your computer a part of the solution.

Custom CD Racks

Ever-proliferating CD-ROMs can wash across your computer desk like so much technological flotsam and jetsam. Here are a few ways to rein them in:

Pan-o-rama: For kids who can't yet read, most disc racks just don't work: the thin spines on CDs offer no visual cues beyond words, and kids tend to scatter discs as they search. The Keefe family of El Dorado Hills, California, discovered that their youngest daughter, Allie, could never find the games she was looking for. Their solution? A cat litter pan (brand-new, of course!). It keeps disks tidy but allows kids to flip through them easily to scan their covers. Our 18- by 15- by 5-inch box is adorned with sticker dots, and we think it's just the cat's meow.

CD storage rack: A colorful label will motivate kids to put their CDs away. We like the appropriateness of labeling discs with a disc, and it gives us a way to recycle some of those junk-mail CDs. Use a marker and ruler to draw a line down the middle of a CD, then cut it in half with scissors. Hot-glue the halves to make a right angle. Add a name or a category (like "Games") and decorations with puffy paints. Then glue the signs onto a store-bought CD rack.

MAKE-IT-YOURSELF

Ticky Tock Mom

Kids, confronted with limitations on their computer use, can bear a disconcerting resemblance to lawyers — contesting all claims about time spent and time allotted and offering eloquent discourses on the letter of the law versus its spirit. But while they may be budding legal geniuses, why waste time in court while the computer sits idle?

That's why we turn to the Ticky Tock Mom, a kitchen timer decked out in pipe cleaners and googly eyes to look like your kids' favorite computer ref. They set it for the agreed-upon period of time, and when the bell rings, the computer goes off. No more Mrs. Nice Guy. We used hot glue to affix the pipe cleaners and googly eyes.

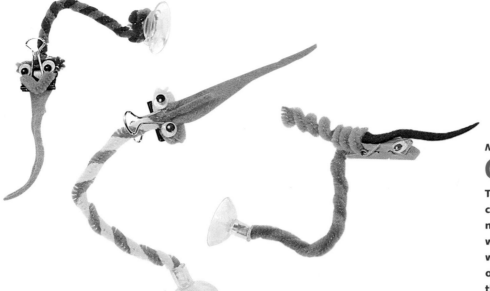

CD Marquees

This cute billboard announces your child's game of the moment, and more importantly, it saves hunting (or worse, not hunting) for the case when play is done. We made the sign out of craft foam and puffy paint, then used low-temperature hot glue to attach a thick craft foam support to the back. We then glued the whole thing to a coated-wire plate holder.

KID-FRIENDLY CRAFT
Hands-free Paper Holder

Stuck to a computer monitor, these bendy clip critters put some teeth into the task of holding papers while you work. Start with a small-diameter suction cup (available with hooks for bathroom use or clips for holding fish tank hose). Twist together a pair of 6-inch pipe cleaners and attach one end to the suction cup. On the other, glue a small clothespin or binder clip decorated with googly eyes, craft foam, and whatever else you'd like.

FAMILYFUN SUCCESS STORY
Computer Communiqués

"My eight-year-old son has a tough time staying out of my office at home. It seems the minute I begin working he is drawn to my computer like a magnet. To divvy up our computer time, we have devised this system: as soon as Gregory comes home from school, he races up to my office to tell me about his day — via the computer.

We set a limit of 20 minutes for him to transcribe his daily events, while I keep him company as I perform other office duties. When the time is up, he prints his news for later use, leaving me free to get back to work. I also prepare a quick record of my own tidings.

"At dinner, we read our dispatches aloud. It's a wonderful way to share our experiences, and we usually end up in a fit of giggles over some silly sentence or incident. Gregory's writing and computer skills have improved enormously, and he saves his narratives in a binder to create a diary of his activities."

— Janine S. Pouliot
Green Bay, Wisconsin

Study Solutions

How do you encourage your kids to have good study habits? Try these creative ideas for organizing homework:

Accordion folder: To organize her fourth grader's exploding collection of school papers, Kim Donahue of Absecon, New Jersey, purchased a plastic accordion folder in a hip neon green and helped him carefully label each file. "The first day home from school with his new folder was the first day of peace, and it hasn't stopped since," says Kim. "Half the class has them now. I only wish I'd started this in third grade."

In/out boxes: With five kids ages 18 months to 20 years, the Finnegans of Richmond, Virginia, were drowning in paperwork. Their solution? A set of office-style in/out boxes. Terri Finnegan labeled boxes for each family member and put them in a central location. Any papers the kids need their parents to check or sign — such as homework, report cards, and permission slips — must be put in an in-box. Says Terri, "The children have really assumed responsibility. We no longer turn the house upside down looking for papers, and we've even stopped misplacing them ourselves."

Book report notebook: For Kevin Pazdziorny, a fifth grader from Middleton, Massachusetts, book reports were a huge and intimidating chore until his mom, Debbie, gave him a blank "Book Report Notebook" and had him write notes on his reading sessions. He didn't like it at first, but when book report time rolled around, to Kevin's surprise, he was all set. "Now it's automatic," says his mom, who is in turn surprised at how much her son writes. "One of his book reports last year actually required a reading journal," she says. "He had no trouble with that one."

FAMILYFUN SUCCESS STORY
Mom-Morandum

When Corwin Carson of Federal Way, Washington, started preschool, his mom, Debbe, had every intention of staying in touch with his teacher — but she soon realized there was no easy way to do that outside of parent-teacher meetings. The teacher wasn't in the room at drop-off time, pickup time was a madhouse, and catching her during a free period was almost impossible. So Debbe and Corwin invented a simple solution: the Mom-Morandum.

"It was just a few sentences on what had been happening at home, the skills we were working on with Corwin, any motivational secrets I'd discovered, and some of his accomplishments and triumphs," says Debbe. Corwin got a kick out of delivering the Mom-Morandum, and teachers told Debbe how helpful it was to have news from home. "It really helped us work as a team," she says.

Hot Chocolate Organizer

Cheryl Robinson is no stranger to crafts. About a year ago, in fact, she began holding monthly three-hour craft classes for kids, including her daughter, Maiah, age eight. This idea was born in a Walgreen's drugstore, where Cheryl saw ceramic mugs on sale. Like any true crafter, she had to do something clever with them. With a mid-February craft class approaching, she decided to fashion them into steaming mugs of cocoa that could hold pencils, pens, and scissors. "As a kid," Cheryl says, "I always liked drawing and coloring pictures of food. All my projects seem to be food-related. The kids all loved these. The parents loved them too — they can take them to work!"

MATERIALS

Ceramic mug
1-inch-thick Styrofoam block
Serrated knife
Brown acrylic paint
Modeling paste (such as Golden)
Rainbow-colored glitter
Cotton
Plastic spoon

Turn the mug upside down on the Styrofoam block and trace the rim. Cut out the circle of Styrofoam with the knife (parents only); the resulting disk should nest snugly in the mug, near the brim. Make a semicircular cut in the disk as an opening for the items you'll be storing.

Paint the top and the cut edge of the disk with the brown paint. With the paint still wet, place the disk in the mug's top and spread modeling paste over the Styrofoam until any gaps between it and the mug are filled and the paste mixes with the brown paint to reach the color and consistency of hot chocolate.

Sprinkle the paste with glitter and press in wisps of cotton for steam. Use a plastic spoon to add a dollop of modeling paste for whipped cream. Let dry and serve!

Computer Closet

How can you set up a family computer area so it's right in the thick of family activity when you need it but out of sight the rest of the time? Quite a riddle, but Gale Goeman of Waukesha, Wisconsin, wrote to us with one outside-the-box solution: "We updated a large closet in our dining area into a computer center. We inserted a small counter-top for the computer and a pull-out drawer for the keyboard. Above, four large shelves filled with baskets house all the essentials that four kids and two parents need. Since the computer is where the action is, everybody loves it. The best part? I can close the folding doors when no one's using it."

Hungry Alligator

Whereas a real alligator's meal of choice ranges from snails to snakes, this toothy reptile will be more than happy to munch on whatever pens and pencils your child has to offer.

MATERIALS

- **2 new green scrub pads**
- **Red felt**
- **White felt**
- **Tacky glue**
- **2 googly eyes**
- **2 green pom-poms**
- **Green rickrack ridges**
- **2 black pom-poms**

To make one alligator, start by trimming the scrub pads into elongated pocket shapes. Then cut two similar shapes from red felt. From white felt, cut triangular teeth and use tacky glue to stick several to the rounded edge of each scrub pad. Glue a red felt piece atop each scrub pad, covering the bases of the felt teeth.

Next, stack the scrub pads with the red felt pieces face-to-face. Glue all along the straight edges but leave the rounded, toothy edges unglued to create the alligator's open mouth.

To make the gator's face, glue the googly eyes onto the green pom-poms, then glue the pom-poms to the top of the head. Finally, affix green rickrack ridges and black pom-pom nostrils atop his snout, and your reptile is ready for the first course of writing utensils.

Pencil Pots

Looking for a way to put a lid on desktop clutter? Turn an empty coffee can, oatmeal box, or any other canister-style container that comes with a reusable plastic lid into a handy holder for school supplies.

MATERIALS

- **Construction paper**
- **Empty canister with plastic lid**
- **Glue or tape**
- **Markers or magazine cutouts**
- **Magnet**

First, wrap a piece of construction paper (trimmed to fit) around the container and tape or glue together the overlapping edges. Then your kids can draw personalized designs or glue magazine cutouts on the paper.

Next, use a craft knife (adults only) to cut a series of X-shaped openings in the plastic lid for inserting pencils, paintbrushes, scissors, or a ruler. Finally, glue a magnet to the side of the can for holding paper clips (keep the magnet away from your computer).

Workspaces

Writing Basket

Some kids enjoy writing letters
and others don't. But everyone is
more likely to pick up a pen when
it's right there in an enticing holder,
along with other supplies that make
the process easier and more fun.

First, help your kids pick out a cool
assortment of postcards, notecards,
stickers, stamps, an address book
(noting important birthdays), self-
address labels, pencils, and pens. Then
put all the write stuff in a tidy orga-

nizer and keep it within arm's reach of
a family gathering spot. You might
even set aside a special time each week
and call it "Write a Note Night."

Popsicle Paperweight

Though it may look like a melting mess, this ice pop paperweight is just the thing to keep papers neat and tidy on a kids' desk.

MATERIALS

- **Lightweight cardboard, such as a cereal box**
- **Masking tape**
- **Dried beans or rice**
- **Cotton balls or packing peanuts**
- **Craft stick**
- **Paintbrush**
- **Craft glue**
- **Green tissue paper**
- **Glitter**

Cut two matching 3- by 4½-inch ice pop shapes and two ½-inch-wide strips (one 3 inches long and one 10½ inches long) from the lightweight

cardboard. Use masking tape to attach the long cardboard strip between the two pop shapes, as shown, leaving the bottom of the pop open. (**Tip:** Cut the strip into smaller sections, if necessary.)

Bend the pop shape slightly and fill the top of it with dry beans or rice for weight. Fill the remaining space with cotton balls or packing peanuts. Slide one end of a craft stick into the bottom of the pop and secure it in place with craft glue. Tape the remaining cardboard strip across the bottom of the pop, making a small cut to accommodate the craft stick.

Next, trim a small piece of cardboard into a puddle shape and tape it to the bottom of the pop. With a paintbrush, apply a thin layer of glue to the pop and the puddle, then press on pieces of colored tissue paper to completely cover them. For a frosty look, brush on more glue, then sprinkle on some glitter. Allow the glue to dry.

Memo Blocks

With rubber stamps and precut memo sheets, your child can make these personalized notepads for your home office.

MATERIALS

- **Colored duct tape**
- **Memo cube pad, memo filler sheets, or scrap paper cut into small squares**
- **Ink stamps and ink pad**

Cut a strip of duct tape that measures 2 inches longer than the height of the stack of paper you plan to use (it should be 1½ inches or more). Lay the tape sticky side up on a table. Grasp the stack and tap the sides against a flat surface as you would to straighten a deck of cards, then hold it on end and press one edge down onto the center of the tape. Wrap the tape ends over the top and bottom of the stack, pressing down firmly to bind the paper. Use more tape to cover the edge, if needed. Now, lift the top sheet of paper and cut the tape just above the second sheet so that the binding is flush with the top of the pad.

Now your child can use the ink stamp and ink pad to print a design on the three untaped sides of the block.

Craft Area

part of a larger bookcase, or a rolling cart instead (see page 45).

2. The clear plastic bin is our storage unit of choice. One large bin holds bulky felt and fabric scraps; another holds coloring supplies — crayons, colored pencils, markers, and chalk — further divided into labeled ziplock bags.

3. Smaller bins hold themed supply sets, all further divided into labeled bags: clay (modeling clay, cookie cutters, rolling pin); string (embroidery floss, plastic lanyard, yarn, twine); paint (watercolor sets, small tubes and bottles of acrylics, powdered tempera paints), and so on.

4. Tall, clear plastic jars are best for collections of uniform materials such as pom-poms or pipe cleaners.

5. A shower caddy makes for a durable paint bottle holder. Hang smocks on washcloth hooks.

6. In/out boxes let you store paper, card stock, and sheets of craft foam in individual slots.

7. Fill the bottles of a spice rack with glitter, googly eyes, buttons, beads, shells, confetti, and other tiny materials.

8. Put a lazy Susan to work holding glue, tape, and other oft-used items.

9. Attach a paper towel holder where your kids can reach it with messy hands.

10. A cutlery tray provides open-air storage for still-damp paintbrushes.

11. A large basket holds miscellaneous recyclables, like egg cartons, empty bottles, and packing materials — the kind of bulky stuff that has "craft project" written all over it, but no particular assignment.

WORKSTATION

The Craft Center

This model organizer keeps art supplies where kids can find (and return) them. We suspect that tidy supplies will inspire even greater creativity in your kids, since they will always be able to find exactly what they're looking for, in addition to some other things (hey, glitter glue!) they didn't even know they had. With this inviting and user-friendly system, your craft projects won't begin with a frustrating preliminary scavenger hunt. And that, we hope, means you'll have more time for art, for art's sake.

1. For the base of our craft operations, we used a basic 3- by 4-foot bookcase. You could use a cabinet,

Craft Organizers

Magnetic knife strip. Keep scissors and hole punchers from straying.

Tackle boxes. The clear ones offer mini compartments just right for beads and jewelry findings.

Recyclables. Diaper wipe boxes and margarine tubs are unbeatable for medium-size craft supplies, such as markers, rubber stamp supplies, and stickers. Egg cartons, baby food jars, and small bottles can be used to store tiny beads, shells, and buttons. Gallon-size ziplock bags work well for holding half-finished projects and modeling kits.

Old briefcase. This can be stocked with materials and transformed into a portable art center, ready to take to restaurants or Grandma's house.

Skirt hanger. Use one to easily store a dozen of your child's works in progress.

Artwork Portfolio

Kids' artwork presents a notoriously sticky storage issue: on the one hand, we doting types want to preserve every shred of our children's creative output; on the other hand, the sheer fact of its volume makes this impossible. Here's our solution:

1. First, we start with a super-big, super-flat portfolio that we craft from two large pieces of poster board that we attach on three sides with duct tape (as shown). Write on your child's name and the year (she can decorate it more if she likes), find an out-of-the-way storage spot, and add each new piece of artwork to the portfolio until it is full.

2. Now, sort through the portfolio and pick your battles carefully. Save some artwork and toss some — if a piece is stunning, save it; if it doesn't knock your socks off, take a deep breath and throw it out. (We're talking about at least a seven-to-one ratio of chuck to save in the early years.) But beauty isn't the only reason to save a

piece of art. Consider saving anything that shows a developmental jump: the first scribbles, then shapes, the first sun, the first people and objects, and any self-portraits.

3. You can use the artwork you don't plan to save as gift wrap and greeting cards.

Keeping the Crafting Clean

- Try to contain crafting to one location, such as a project table in the family room or a movable easel.
- For large, messy projects, break out an old tablecloth, sheet, or plastic shower curtain to use as a drop cloth beneath the table.
- To ease the cleanup of tempera paint from washable surfaces, add 1 teaspoon of dish detergent to every ½ cup of paint.
- Rather than spread wet paintings on the floor to dry, clothespin them to a length of string hung on a wall, where they can remain on display. Alternatively, try the skirt hanger on page 117.
- To encourage kids to put away arts and craft supplies after a project, set up an easy-to-maintain storage system, such as The Craft Center on page 116 or the Craft Supply Shoe Bag at right. That way, similar supplies are kept together so kids can hunt logically for needed items, and they are labeled so kids can see where materials belong.
- Clean out your craft area on a regular basis, discarding any unusable supplies or materials. Relabel bins as their contents change.

MAKE-IT-YOURSELF
The Towel Apron

Nothing smothers the creative fire like having to clean a big glob of paint off your favorite shirt. This comfortable two-pocket apron — fashioned from an old hand towel that's folded and secured with a few stitches (or dabs of fabric glue) — neatly solves that problem. After your kid's creativity emerges, just toss the apron in the washing machine.

MATERIALS

Terry cloth hand towel
Needle and thread or fabric glue
2 yards of heavy cord or string
2 1-inch wooden beads

1. Lay out the towel (as shown) and fold up the bottom 5 inches to form a front pocket. Sew or glue the pocket's side seams, then sew or glue a center dividing seam to create two smaller pockets.

2. Fold back the top two corners as shown and sew or glue them in place, leaving a 1-inch-wide casing for the cord.

3. Starting at one side, thread the cord up through the casing and then down the other side, as shown. **Tip:** Attach a safety pin to the end of the cord to help work it through the casing.

4. To keep the cord ends from slipping back through the casing, thread beads onto the ends and secure with knots.

Craft Supply Shoe Bag

If you don't have room for the complete Craft Center on page 116, try stocking supplies in a shoe holder (see page 74 for buying information). In our space-frugal organizer, we stored a craft item in each pocket so crafters can find what they're looking for — whether it's buttons, bottle caps, or beads. A sample item is affixed to the pocket for easy identification.

MATERIALS

Hanging canvas shoe organizer (we used a 20-pocket model)
Needle and embroidery floss
Small craft materials, such as bottle caps, corks, buttons, craft sticks, googly eyes, pipe cleaners, beads, film canisters, assorted caps and lids, lanyards, pom-poms, modeling clay, old keys, clothespins, assorted small plastic toys, rubber bands, and packing peanuts

1. Determine what small craft supply items you'd like to store in your organizer and find a representative sample to sew onto each pouch. **Tip:** To make them easier to tie on, consider gluing together several similar items (as we did with the craft sticks).

2. With a loop of embroidery floss and a needle, sew through from the inside of the pocket (leaving a tail inside), wrap the thread around or through the object once or twice, then sew back through to the inside.

3. Tie together the two ends of the thread. Repeat for each item.

4. Stock with supplies and hang over the back of a door.

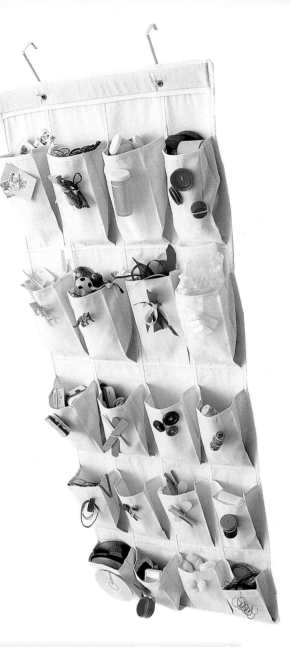

Wrapping Paper Station

Beth Moberg-Wolff, a mother of three from Augusta, Georgia, hit upon one resourceful idea to solve two perennial problems. First, she

wanted to do something with her old changing table. Second, she wanted to organize all her gift-wrapping supplies in a single easy-to-use, easy-to-maintain location. Recycling, it turns out, is the mother of invention: the changing table made the ideal wrapping station.

"We discovered that wrapping paper rolls fit perfectly on it!" says Beth. "The top shelf was a great height for wrapping books and other smaller gifts, and the organizer that held lotion and creams could also hold tape, tags, scissors, and ribbon. My third grader is into recycling, so she loved the idea!"

So do we. We couldn't find a lotion holder like the one that Beth's

sister had sewn, but we found that a mesh shower caddy or small shoe bag hung from the table's side with shower curtain hooks works just as well for holding odds and ends like tape and tags, and a basket full of bows tied to the other side puts those final touches right within reach.

Workspaces

Laundry Solutions

HELPING HANDS
Dishpan Ally

With **seven children** in the house, Krista Gafkjen's mother had to resort to innovation to keep laundry lugging from becoming a full-time job. So she bought eight plastic dishpans, assigned each to a family member, and lined up the dishpans in the laundry room. When it came time to unload the dryer, she simply folded the clothes, sorted them into the appropriate dishpans, and called in the kids to haul their own laundry to their rooms (you could even skip the folding if your kids can fold their own).

Now Krista lives in Panora, Iowa, with three kids of her own, and her mom's idea still makes sense: even two-year-old KC can take her brightly labeled dishpan up to her room and put away her own socks, although getting Dad to unload his basket, quips Krista, "still takes some encouraging."

FAMILYFUN SUCCESS STORY
Sock Sorting

"We used to have two baskets that were entirely full of unmatched socks," recalls Angela Mathis, a mother of five from Spartanburg, South Carolina, whose family produces almost a hundred socks a week. "If you wanted a pair, you had to go digging through them." Inspired to take action, Angela bought mesh lingerie bags, a different color for each person, and now the socks are sorted before the wash cycle even starts — everyone puts their dirty socks in their own bag and then matches their own clean socks after the bag emerges from the dryer.

Easy-sort Laundry Baskets

Sorting comes naturally to kids — you've seen them bent over seashells or jelly beans — so encouraging them to help with the laundry should be a snap. Happily, our handy dress-up doll tags help them identify which things go in which baskets, and keep you from folding up clean piles of gray (or, worse, pink) clothing.

We selected and cut out a bunch of clothes from old catalogs and magazines and then glued them onto kid-shaped pieces of card stock: one kid should be dressed in all lights and whites, one in all darks or colors. We covered the tags in clear Con-Tact paper, punched a hole in each one, and tied them onto our laundry baskets. (Note: This also works great for any laundry-challenged adults you might happen to know!)

Baby-pockets Chore Chart

Two unrelated conundrums produced Joi Giacopuzzi-Steven's creative solution. "All those cardboard chore charts taped to the walls and on the fridge never worked for us," she says. In addition, "I'm a keeper. I keep all the kids' baby clothes." Inspiration struck in the form of a doll-clothes decoration that Joi saw at a home in her neighborhood. Why not turn the cast-off clothing into a playful way to assign chores to her three kids?

Almost a year later, the system is still going strong. "Not only has our chore chart been fun and effective for the kids' daily tasks," Joi says, "but it is also a precious reminder of just how quickly our babies are growing up."

MATERIALS

- Pair of baby pants (for 2 kids' chores)
- 4 pockets cut from other baby clothes
- Hot-glue gun
- Various colors of fabric paint
- 1 larger pocket cut from big-kid pants (keep the back of the pocket attached so it can serve as a pouch)
- Large craft sticks
- Rope or twine
- 2 nails
- Clothespins

Hot-glue two of the small pockets down the front of each leg of the pants (parents only). Leave the tops open! Next, use the fabric paints to write a child's name on each of the pants' own front pockets. Write "Done" on each of the middle pockets, and "Special Treat" on each of the bottom pockets. Write "Chores" on the separate pocket cut from big-kid pants. For each chore, make a chore stick by using craft paint to write the chore on a large craft stick. Use the fabric paints to further decorate the jeans to your liking.

String the rope or twine on the wall between two nails or other fasteners. Use the clothespins to hang the finished jeans and chore pocket from the rope. Glue the clothespins to the pants if necessary to make the attachment more secure. Each day or each week, take the appropriate chore sticks from the Chores pocket and place them in each child's top pocket. When a chore is done, the child moves the stick to the Done pocket. After all the sticks have migrated to the middle pocket, the child gets the reward that's been written on a slip of paper in the Special Treat pocket.

wash car
pick up toys
sort dirty clothes
clean bedroom
read to Amber + Parker

Dazzling Dusters

Put a pair of work gloves to the task with these fun-to-use dust busters. The long-handled one is great for reaching cobwebs overhead. The other is just right for furniture — or you can tuck it into your car's glove compartment where it's ever ready for tidying your dashboard.

MATERIALS

- **Pair of work gloves**
- **Felt**
- **Fabric glue**
- **Plastic beads**
- **Wooden dowel**
- **Batting or newspaper**
- **Ribbon**

To make the pair, set each work glove on a piece of paper and trace around the four fingers and palm but not the thumb. Cut out the thumbless hand shapes. Then trace around the thumbs and cut out those shapes. Use the paper patterns to cut like shapes out of felt and attach them to the gloves with fabric glue.

Now your child can embellish the tops of the gloves by gluing on felt "fingernails" and plastic beads (tacky glue works best with plastic items). Once the glue is dry, slide the end of a wooden dowel into one of the gloves until it reaches the tip of the index finger. Then stuff that glove with batting or newspaper. Tightly tie ribbon around the wrist to secure the glove to the dowel, and you're ready to start dusting.

FAMILYFUN SUCCESS STORY
A Clean Swipe

"I found an easy and fun way for my three oldest children (Jessica, seven, Amanda, five, and Alex, four) to help with the dusting. I bought the kids bath mitts, letting them pick out designs they liked. On cleanup day, they put on mitts, squirt on some furniture spray, and are off to their respective room assignments to get tables, bureaus, and shelves (whatever they can reach) squeaky-clean. They are always happy to help — so far, anyway."

— Colleen Biondo
Beverly Hills, Michigan

CHAPTER SEVEN

Storage Spaces

Storage solutions that are easy and convenient for your entryway, basement, attic, or garage

A good storage space is like a good perm: if everything goes well, you won't even notice it. But this happy invisibility can take some creativity on the front end. Consider such workhorse spaces as the entryway, the garage, the attic, the basement — no other areas of the house get so much use and so little respect. For busy families, they become convenient dumping grounds, the place where the odds and ends of our lives collect — the sports equipment, seasonal paraphernalia, outgrown snowsuits, shoe boxes of family photos, and muddy boots that multiply so exponentially that they seem to need a home of their own.

That, in fact, is the solution we recommend. No, we don't mean a second mortgage. We're talking about giving everything a specific place, bin, hook, or basket so that your storage spaces don't turn into wastelands of unclaimed things.

What you'll find in the pages that follow are storage ideas that make more out of less — less space, less effort, and even

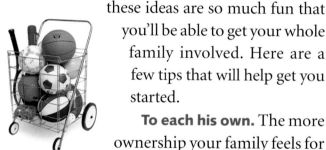

Ball Bin, page 139

less money (in case you're California dreamin' about one of those expensive made-to-order closet systems . . .). And, with regard to clutter, they'll surely make less out of more. From an easy-to-make memo board (page 132) to a whimsical duck-footed umbrella stand (page 131), these ideas are so much fun that you'll be able to get your whole family involved. Here are a few tips that will help get you started.

To each his own. The more ownership your family feels for their personal storage spaces, the more likely they are to use them — and to take responsibility for keeping them tidy. That's why so many of our ideas entail individualized solutions: a separate key hook for each family member; an assigned stair to keep things that need to return upstairs; a drawer for each child's mittens. Keep this principle in mind as you solve the specific storage issues of your own family.

Be courageous. Sometimes things have to get worse before they can get better. It may be worth your time to completely overhaul some of your storage spaces — this is especially true for garages, attics, and basements — before proceeding with new strategies. Devote a weekend to pulling out all your bags, bins, and boxes, examining their contents, relabeling them, and setting aside whatever you will no longer need to hold on to. Clearing the decks will dramatically decrease the amount of time you'll need to spend on day-to-day storage maintenance.

Hold a garage sale. This is a guaranteed win-win situation: you get rid of unwanted things; lucky buyers take home great finds; you end up with a big enough wad of ones in your pocket to take to the bank — or at least to take your family to lunch! For more tips on throwing a successful sale, see page 138.

Storage Space Essentials

If you have too many boxes of who-knows-what in your basement, attic, or garage, consider these storage tips:

◆ Before you lug books, baby clothes, and furniture down to the basement, ask yourself, "Do we really need to keep this?" If not, toss, donate, or sell it.

◆ Be sure your storage spaces are cool, dry, and clean. In the basement, use a dehumidifier to remove moisture from the air and open windows to promote ventilation. Your attic should be properly insulated and ventilated.

◆ Don't store things in huge boxes, or your back will never forgive you. Instead, use medium-size stackable bins. Label each one for easy access.

◆ Put like with like. Sort and store items in categories, such as clothing, toys, or sporting equipment. If you have the space, give each family member his or her own storage shelf or bin for favorite outgrown toys and memorabilia.

◆ Utilize wire shelving on wheels to hold storage bins and boxes (see page 136). These are essential if your basement floods.

◆ If you plan on storing dress clothes in the attic, invest in portable wardrobe closet bags or a cedar chest (and mothballs!).

Entryway

Family Cubbies

In many households, clutter walks right in the front door. As soon as the kids come home, an otherwise orderly house is transformed into a wasteland of boots, book bags, coats, and sports equipment.

The Lieberman family of Northampton, Massachusetts, found a way to rein in the chaos in their side entryway: they built in this useful cubby and peg system. The pegs keep high-use items like dog leashes and swim bags and cross country skis at their fingertips. The cubbies — a few for each person in the family — are packed with sweaters, bike helmets, and backpacks.

A Handy Hang-up

Take one cold winter and two outdoorsy kids, and you're bound to end up with a mess of mittens. That was the problem facing *FamilyFun* readers Lisa and Ken Schmidt of New Milford, Pennsylvania. Their inspired solution was the basis for our space-saving glove-and-mitten rack, designed to be hung on the back of a closet door.

The crosspieces and side slats are ¾- by 1½-inch lengths of painted poplar, cut to fit the door width and assembled with screws. The mitten grabbers are ⅝-inch micro-mini spring clamps (available at Woodworker's Warehouse, www.wood workerswarehouse.com) screwed into the rungs about 4 inches apart. For added neatness, we labeled each row

of clamps using rubber stamps and a permanent-ink pad (such as Archival Ink, available at craft stores).

Family Key Keeper

The key to a great entryway decoration is to hang something personalized and practical that your kids can have a hand in making, like this rack that everyone can use to keep track of car and house keys. You can even add an extra hook for hanging up the family dog's leash.

MATERIALS

- **2 picture hangers**
- **2¹/₂- by 12-inch pine board**
- **Small flat wooden spoons or wooden paint stirrers cut into 3¹/₂-inch lengths**
- **Colored markers**
- **Twine or yarn**
- **Glue**
- **Small brass cup hooks**

First, attach the picture hangers to the back of the pine board according to the package directions. Meanwhile, have your kids decorate the wooden spoons with colored markers to resemble each person and pet in your family. When they're done coloring, help them fashion hairdos by gluing on pieces of twine or yarn.

Next, glue the handle of each spoon to the back of the pine board, as shown, so that the characters are spaced equally apart. Once the glue dries, screw a brass hook into the board below each character, and the key rack is ready to hang near the front door.

Kids' In/Out Box

It starts in preschool and grows exponentially with each passing year: that barrage of permission slips, report cards, and other paperwork that somehow has to find its way from your child's backpack to you and back to school again. One solution is a family in/out box system that serves as a visual reminder to kids when they're loading or unloading their backpacks.

The key is to use a transparent office-paper sorter (about $9 at office supply stores) and to mount it at eye level, just above your child's backpack hook. Label one slot for each child and another for parents.

Each day after school, when your kids hang up their backpacks, they can remove important papers and place them in your slot. You read them, sign them if necessary, and place them back into your kids' slot. Your kids then return them to their backpacks the next morning.

Secrets of Successful Entryways

For an entryway that works for the whole family, these small details add up to big improvements:

- **Coat and other hooks hung low enough for kids to reach them (see page 130).**
- **Individual shelf, cubby, or other storage area for each person's glasses, wallet, and assorted gear (see page 127).**
- **A message board to leave notes for family members (see page 132).**
- **Seating, so boots can be slipped on and off, with boot mat or rack nearby.**
- **A convenient caddy for video rentals and library books (see page 130).**
- **A place for each child's backpack and school papers.**
- **A small basket on the back of the door, a dedicated shelf, or the Family Key Keeper to store house keys in one place (above).**

Catchy Hooks

These easy-to-make hooks just might lure your child to hang up his stuff.

Butterfly: Plastic hook body, self-adhesive fun foam wings

Elephant: Chrome hook trunk, card stock and marker body, googly eyes

Crown: Brass hook, stamped card stock

Octopus: Double chrome hook head, felt arms, googly eyes

KID-FRIENDLY TIP

A Peg Apiece

Take a lesson from your kids' classroom: kids do best when they have their own coat hook, cubby, and boot space. Give each kid her own hook for hanging her backpack and coat, and a shelf for shoes and boots. Place the hooks out in the open and at a kid's height to improve your chances that she'll actually use them.

HOME SOLUTION

Vertical Clothesline

Cold or rainy weather, and the assorted wet clothing that comes with it, only adds to the strain on entryways. One space-efficient way to deal with the influx of dripping hats, coats, sweaters, and foul-weather gear is to suspend a vertical clothesline from the ceiling (anchored with an eyebolt). Even little kids can reach the lower section and attach their wet items with clothespins.

FAMILYFUN SUCCESS STORY

Library Book Bag

"My five-year-old son, Eric, would routinely put away his library books with his own books, and they were impossible to find when it came time to return them. To fix this problem, we got Eric a small tote bag and labeled it 'Eric's Library Books.' We punched a hole through the corner of his library card, looped a piece of string through it, and tied it to his bag to keep him from losing it. When we visit the library, Eric can check out only as many books as he can fit in his bag, and when we get home, he makes sure the library books stay in the bag when they are not being read to keep from misplacing them."

— Marquesa Fedastion
Colorado Springs, Colorado

Fowl-weather Umbrella Basket

A rainy day conundrum: How do you prevent the umbrella that kept you dry outdoors from getting everything indoors soaking wet? Let it drip-dry into a special basket that you can empty out later.

MATERIALS

- **2 small identical white plastic wastebaskets that fit inside one another**
- **12- by 18-inch sheet of orange craft foam**
- **Ruler**
- **Duct tape**
- **Pushpin**
- **Hammer and nail**
- **3 1¼-inch-long metal paper fasteners**
- **2 12-ounce bags of floral marbles (or stones)**

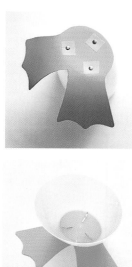

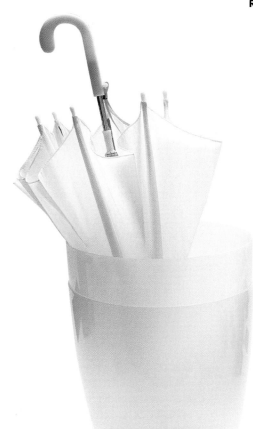

Place one of the baskets on the foam sheet at least ½ inch from one of the 18-inch sides. Trace around the bottom of the basket about ½ inch out from the base, then draw duck feet extended from the front of the circle. Cut out the shape in one piece.

To attach the feet to the basket, stick 3½-inch squares of duct tape to the foam as shown, spacing them evenly apart. Use a pushpin to make a hole through the center of each tape square and the foam. Center the feet, taped side up, atop the overturned basket. Press a pencil through the pinholes to make corresponding marks on the bottom of the basket. Then remove the foam and use a hammer and nail to make holes through the plastic at the marks. Realign the feet and insert a metal paper fastener through each pair of lined-up holes, spreading open the prongs against the inside bottom of the basket.

Finally, place some marbles or stone weights in the basket, then slide the second, water-collecting basket into the first, and the holder's ready to use.

FAMILYFUN SUCCESS STORY

A Drawer for Everyone

With three children, Rebecca Herschkopf, knew she needed something to organize hats, mittens, and scarves in her front hall. Not knowing exactly what would work, she took everything she wanted to store and stacked it up. "I realized what I needed was something with four drawers," she says, and then went shopping. "It was a lot easier buying some- thing when I knew what I needed, rather than hoping that it would hold everything I had." Now, when her children arrive home, they each have their own drawer — with the fourth for their parents.

Birdhouse Memo Board

This homemade chalkboard key track will help you remind your kids, or vice versa, of what's up next: sports practice, graduation parties, and so on.

MATERIALS

1¾- by ¼-inch strip of pine lattice (cut into one 10-inch length and one 12-inch length)
Pine board, 20 by 11 by ¾ inches
Handsaw or table saw
Green chalkboard paint (we used the spray type)
Chalk
4 #16 carpet tacks
Hammer
Permanent markers (black and other colors)
Drill with ¹¹/₆₄- and ⅜-inch bits
Golf tees
Craft glue (optional)

Hold the two pieces of lattice in place on top of the pine board to form the birdhouse roof, as shown, and trace along the upper edge. Remove the lattice and saw the board along the traced lines. Paint, dry, and season the board with chalk according to the chalkboard paint manufacturer's directions. Now nail the roof pieces in place with tacks.

With a black permanent marker, color a 2-inch-wide hole in the center of the board. Use the ¹¹/₆₄-inch bit to drill a row of four evenly spaced holes (for the key ring pegs) about 1 inch up from the bottom of the board. Next, use the ⅜-inch bit to drill a hole (it should angle slightly upward) centered just under the black hole for a chalk perch. Finally, color the white golf tees with permanent markers and, when dry, push them into the peg holes, securing them with glue if needed.

Dressed-up Doorstops

One of these fanciful customized doorstops makes a cheerful entryway decoration. You'll need to make a stop at your local garden store for a brick (the kind with holes in it), as well as at the craft store, which, these days, has tiny versions of just about everything!

MATERIALS

Newspaper
Brick with holes in it
Felt
Tacky glue
Modeling clay
Miniature decorations (see below)
Craft wire
Toothpicks

Cover your work surface with newspaper to keep the brick from scratching it. Cut out a piece of felt to fit the bottom of the brick and glue it on.

Fill the holes of the brick with balls of clay. Then arrange your decorations any way you like, sticking the bottom of each item to the clay. If necessary, you can use craft wire to attach a toothpick to certain items and then insert the toothpick into the clay.

VEGETABLE GARDEN

Mini white picket fence
Bamboo skewers (for tomato stakes)
Tiny decorative garden vegetables

CHICKEN ROOST

Small sticks and straw (fastened with wire stuck into the clay)
Ornamental chicken and rooster
Mini plastic eggs

FLOWER GARDEN

Silk butterfly and flowers
Mini wooden birdhouse
Wire

Hand-painted Welcome Mat

Canvas floorcloths have been around for centuries. Traditionally used to protect and decorate floors, the thick canvas rugs are attractive yet sturdy enough to hold up to lots of wear and tear (they clean up with a wet mop). And, as Cyndi Dabney of Gallatin Gateway, Montana, discovered, hand-painting a floorcloth makes a great family craft project as well as an artful entryway display. The blank cloth can be a canvas for just about anything a family imagines — from a welcome mat like the one pictured here to an activity rug for toy cars to a splat mat for under a baby's high chair.

MATERIALS

Untreated canvas, weight #10 or #11 (available at canvas stores or stores that sell awnings, tents, tepees, or boating supplies)
Yardstick
Duct tape
Light-colored latex paint (or gesso) for preparing the canvas or dark-colored latex, if you plan on using the color as your background
Hot glue gun
Acrylic craft paints and paintbrushes
Paint markers (available at craft stores)
Clear water-based polyurethane varnish

1. First, determine the size of your floorcloth, then cut the canvas a few inches larger on each side to leave room for a hem. If you are making a large rug (over 2 or 3 feet), duct-tape the canvas to a cement floor. This helps stretch the canvas and keep it flat as it dries. As you tape, start at the center of each side and then move to the opposite side, stretching the material tight as you go. Secure all four sides in the center, then continue to alternate sides.

2. Put on a base by painting the canvas with two coats of latex paint  or one coat of gesso and one coat of paint. Let the surface dry thoroughly, then inspect it in a bright light to make sure you haven't left any raw canvas.

3. Next, finish the edges. To do this, first measure and mark a hem on the cloth's unpainted side.

4. Cut off the tip of each corner as shown. This will ensure that, when folded, the hem corners will neatly butt up against each other, but not overlap and cause a bump.

5. With the yardstick as a guide, fold over the hem, then use a hot glue gun to seal the edges in place.

6. Next, rough out your design with a pencil, whether it is an ocean motif, handprints, an interactive design (a maze, town, or hopscotch board), or a simple welcome mat.

7. Then begin painting. One tip for keeping painted edges sharp (difficult to do with a brush) is to first outline the shapes with a paint marker in a color close to the one you'll be using, then fill in the outlined shape. Paint markers are particularly helpful if you'll be writing any words on the canvas. They can also help fix mistakes of splashed paint or wild brush strokes if you get one the same color as your base paint.

8. To finish your floorcloth and help it hold up to lots of dirty feet (as well as repeated moppings with soap and water), you'll need to coat it with five to six coats of clear polyurethane varnish. The water-based kind is easiest to clean up and work with, and very low-odor. Once you've varnished the cloth to a point where the surface is hard and the cloth feels thick, you are done for now, though you will want to add another coat every few years. To make the cloth stay in place  on a slippery floor, use a rug mat under it, or paint the back with liquid non-skid backing.

Storage Spaces

Basement

Special Occasion Storage

Holiday paraphernalia and special occasion cooking supplies can take up a lot of room in your house and make everyday living more cluttered than it needs to be. After all, Easter only comes once a year: you shouldn't have to move the lamb-cake mold every time you want to get at the muffin tins. FamilyFun.com visitor Lynn Schumaker offers this convenient, inexpensive solution for storing special occasion items: "I bought the cardboard legal boxes that are supposed to hold documents. Instead I turned them into storage boxes for holiday stuff, extra cooking or craft supplies, etc." Clearly label each box with a permanent marker, then stack them neatly in a utility room, basement, or attic where they will be easily accessible when holidays roll around.

CLUTTER BUSTER

The Out-of-sight, Out-of-mind Box

FamilyFun.com visitor Tish Keating-Skaronea offers this clever variation on the "Use it or lose it" theory of clutter control — though it's not for the faint of heart! "Box up all the clutter in your house and put it in the garage or somewhere out of the way. Leave it boxed for a month. If you don't miss it, don't open the boxes again — take them out and donate them."

Step Up

At the Parks household in Austin, Texas, everyone in the family is assigned a step at the bottom of the stairs. As belongings accumulate downstairs, they are sorted and piled on each person's step, to be returned to his or her room on the next trip upstairs. Laminated name tags hanging on the wall just above each step facilitate sorting and hamper anonymity should anyone's step become glutted. For Beth Parks, a mother of four, this system is certainly a step in the right direction, saving her countless trips up the stairs with armfuls of unclaimed stuff. "I can't tell you how much clutter four kids can generate," Beth laughs. "As it is, I'm glad that our stairs are hidden by the fireplace!"

FAMILYFUN SUCCESS STORY

Moving On

"We recently moved from Kentucky to Florida with our four-year-old son, Taylor. He was concerned how all his things would make the move. To ease his mind, I bought cardboard boxes that were covered with pictures of Power Rangers. We packed all his toys in these boxes, which the moving company didn't mind at all. When everything in the house was in brown moving boxes, he kept pointing out the Power Rangers boxes as his. And when the truck unloaded in Florida, we all knew which boxes went to Taylor's room."

— **Lynn Clemens**
Palm Harbor, Florida

The Multilevel Organizer

The family of multilevel organizers is large indeed, including open shelves, stackable bins, and rolling trolleys, each of which might be made from wire, plastic mesh, metal, or solid plastic. But whatever the form, *FamilyFun* readers agree that these budget-friendly space savers are organizing giants.

Holds Everything

For Kelly Malone of Cordova, Tennessee, the stackable bin is an organizational cure-all. "I have them all over the house," she says with a laugh. But she's not kidding: she's got them in the closet for toys and clothes, in the garage for stacking dirty shoes, in the house for artwork, papers, and school memos (one bin for each boy and one for their collective Boy Scout info). "If it would fit," she quips, "I'd keep a set in my car."

Saved From Doll-irium

If there's one member of the household who needs more closet space, it's usually Barbie. Solid plastic bins on wheels solve that problem. "My daughter can wheel it where she wants to play and push it back into her closet when playtime is over," writes Eva Hensbergen of Macomb, Michigan. Penny Huffman of Mobile, Alabama, is also a fan. "You can pull out each drawer and place it on the floor for easy access, and since the drawers are clear, we can see where everything is."

Highly Classified Objects

Air Force Major (and mother of four) Deborah Rieflin of Mount Pleasant, South Carolina, has flexed some serious organizational muscle to keep her house up to code. She enlists a four-drawer organizer, one drawer per kid, to sort and store (or is that rank and file?) all of the odds and ends that accumulate around the house — the assortment of "yo-yos, LEGOS, Scout handbooks, Hot Wheels cars, and diapers" that perpetually find their way underfoot. When the drawers fill up, the Rieflin kids sort through their stuff "and they usually find that lost wristwatch or favorite key chain I tossed in after finding it astray!"

Other uses for multilevel organizers:

- Art papers, craft supplies, and finished artwork
- LEGOs, blocks, toy cars, or action figures
- Sports equipment like cleats, shin guards, water bottles, and uniforms
- Video game equipment and videos
- Sewing and knitting supplies

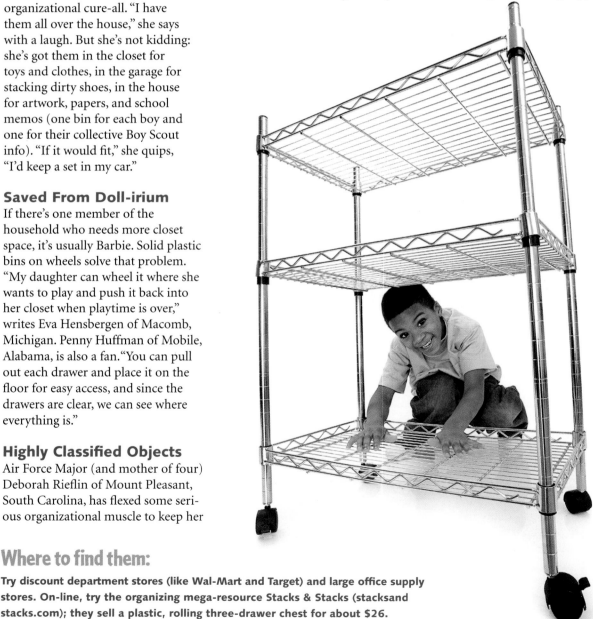

Where to find them:

Try discount department stores (like Wal-Mart and Target) and large office supply stores. On-line, try the organizing mega-resource Stacks & Stacks (stacksandstacks.com); they sell a plastic, rolling three-drawer chest for about $26.

First-class Projects

"My husband and I both work, so it's hard for us to do lots of volunteering at the schools," says Deb Garbenis of Peabody, Massachusetts. "Instead, we try to create a big project with our children's classes at least once a year."

When their daughter, Adrianna, was learning about puppets and communication in preschool, the family designed and built a puppet theater for the class. For Christopher's first-grade class, father and son sawed, sanded, and organized the wooden parts, then treated the students to an afternoon of making pinewood derby cars.

The projects, says Deb, are "an ideal way to show our children that we are interested in their schoolwork, and not just at homework time — plus, we're creating something that lasts."

KID-FRIENDLY TIP
First Tool Kit

To encourage your kids to help out with simple woodworking projects, give them their very own tool kit and keep it near your workbench. Raid the hardware store for a beginner's collection of tools (hammer, nails, safety goggles, etcetera), then pack them into a small toolbox or tool belt. Stash a box with hunks of wood for impromptu projects. Last, post and review a list of safety rules and let the construction begin.

FAMILYFUN SUCCESS STORY
Homemade Memories

"My mom and dad have made their house a kid haven — a place where memories get made for my children, Sarah, 11, and Nathan, seven. The fun happens down in the basement, where my father built a workbench for each child, complete with drawers, a vise, and a variety of child-safe tools. Grandpa also supplied all sorts of recyclables, glue, wood, paint, and all the wonderful old hinges and nails he's been collecting for 70 years. Grandma donated buttons, yarn, and fabric remnants to the stash of materials.

"The kids love it down there — there's a big old potbellied woodstove — and they disappear for hours at a time, each working away at his or her own bench, with Grandpa available to drill holes or cut pieces of wood. Some- times all three work together on a big project; sometimes Grandpa and the kids each work on their own projects. There's nothing artificial or overplanned about the time the kids spend down there with their grandpa. It's a kind of togetherness that just happens naturally, and it spans the generations."

— Janet Bricault
West Boylston, Massachussetts

Garage

ORGANIZE IT

The Great Garage Cleanup

Has your two-car garage become a no-car disaster zone? Park the junk elsewhere and put your cars back where they belong. Following these steps will help you tackle the chore.

1. First, clear out the driveway and drag all the junk out. Drag out the trash barrels too — you're going to need 'em.

2. After everything is outside, throw away all the trash. Be merciless. Get rid of flattened balls, broken inline skates, and that old tattered sofa.

3. Sort everything that's left into categories — tools, recreational items, paint cans, garden gear, and so on.

4. If certain items seem more logically stored elsewhere, relocate them. If not, decide how much room they will occupy, and how best to store them neatly.

5. Choose a storage location in the garage that makes sense. For example, the lawn mower and rake might be placed near the front for easy access when the garage is open. Shelving should be set up near the door to the house for tools, gardening, and sports equipment. The bikes might be placed on hooks in the back.

6. Store children's playthings in easy to open (and easy to close — parents can dream, can't they?) storage bins.

7. For a neater looking garage, store things off the floor. Hang tools and shovels on wall pegs and use shelves for bins and toolboxes.

8. Paints, cleaning supplies, and sharp tools should be placed inside a locking cabinet to protect curious kids.

TIPS AND TECHNIQUES
Tag Sale Tips

Selling off years of corduroy overalls, stuffed animals, and playthings is not easy. It requires a delicate balance between tossing enough to really empty your house and saving enough to soothe your nostalgia. Here's a practical plan for your next garage sale:

Keep the best, sell the rest. Save heirlooms you'll be able to pass on, such as hand-knit baby sweaters and favorite hardcover children's books. Be ruthless about getting rid of children's outgrown playthings, clothing, and so on, but stop short of selling items you'll really miss (you can always have another tag sale).

Plan it well, price to sell. Check with your town hall to see if you need a garage sale permit. Keep it short — two or three hours at the most. And place an ad in the classifieds of the local newspaper using all capital letters. Price reasonably, not to get rich. You'll make some money, help those who cannot afford to buy baby things retail, and unclutter your attic and basement.

Storing Sports Gear

Balls, sticks, bats, helmets, shin guards, shoulder pads, cleats, rackets — the list goes on and on. If you aren't careful, sports gear will turn your house into a dysfunctional locker room. To prevent lost equipment and late-for-practice meltdowns, devise storage solutions that are easy and convenient for kids on the way in or out the door.

Check Your Cleats at the Door

Look for an attractive and sturdy box or wicker hamper to station in the foyer, right inside the door, to stow equipment for the current in-season sport. With any luck, the kids will soon realize this store-all is the place to keep bicycle helmets, swimming bags, soccer cleats, and shin guards.

The Bargain Basement

Turn a section of your basement or attic into a used sporting goods store devoted to equipment that doesn't quite fit someone yet or is out of season.

Roll Out the Tarp

For outdoor equipment like playground balls, wagons, street hockey sticks, and Wiffle ball bats, the good news is they can take a few nights left out on the lawn. The bad news is they usually end up spending the entire summer there. If you want to keep using your garage for — gasp — a car, find a little-used space in your yard and construct a small toy corral from leftover building supplies (such as picket fencing, lattice, or scrap wood). For a neat look, cover your corral with a weatherproof tarp, affixing it securely to one side and angling it slightly to shed rainwater.

Keep It in Cans

Place a lineup of garbage cans (the extralarge size) in the garage to hold all kinds of sporting equipment. Organize and label by balls, shape (sticks, bats, and so on), sport (all soccer equipment in one can), or child (Travis's stuff in the blue can, Ashley's in the gray one).

CLUTTER BUSTER

Ball Bin

Covered in balls of different sizes and colors — small yellow tennis balls, large rainbow beach balls, red rubber game balls — the backyard can start to resemble some kind of overgrown Easter egg hunt. Make the most of your kids' gathering urges with a rolling shopping cart they can push and fill. When all the balls are collected, they can be rolled right into the garage and stored in the cart until game time.

FAMILYFUN SUCCESS STORY

Don't Even Think of Parking Here

If in-boxes and planning calendars appeal to your family, here's another simple idea playfully borrowed from the business world: the reserved bicycle-parking spot. Inside his family's garage, *FamilyFun* executive editor Jonathan Adolph outlined a chalk parking space for each of his two kids' bikes, labeling the spots with the owner's name as if the kids were senior VPs. "They know just where to park and like doing it," he says. "And I get to pull into the garage without worrying about squashing something."

CHAPTER EIGHT

Backyard Projects

With our step-by-step instructions, you can surprise your child with his very own picnic table, sandbox, or secret treehouse

Whatever its size, a backyard is like a sweet, green invitation — to kids, birds, pets, neighbors. It is the one room at your house where the doors are always wide open. It may not possess all the traditional elements of a room (walls and ceiling, for instance), but when the weather turns balmy, it's everybody's favorite place to hang out.

But like any other room, the backyard can be made even better with the application of a little creativity and a dash of sweat equity. Don't be daunted if you aren't the handyman type, though. We offer plenty of projects that can be completed without any fancy materials (the Two-room Fort on pages 168–171, for example, can be made out of a cardboard box and a bunch of sticks). We've also included more ambitious projects for those who want to make a family keepsake that money just can't buy, such as the portable picnic table on pages 144–147 and the clubhouse on pages 162–165.

Yards of Fun, page 153

Whatever project you choose, your kids will always remember how they got to help make and decorate it, and how excited they were when it was finished.

Tailor projects to your young helpers. Kids are full of energy and enthusiasm— especially at the start of a long project — so why not harness it? Some of the projects, like the Clothesline Theater on page 154, are designed to be completed almost entirely by supervised children. Others will lend themselves to more limited assistance. Look over the directions carefully with your children, and pick out the steps best suited to their skills: this may be sanding a board, nailing or screwing pieces of wood together, or painting a finished item.

Have everything you need on hand. There's nothing more frustrating than starting a project only to spend the rest of the day making repeated trips to the hardware store. Consult our material and tool lists, gather up what you already have, then set out with a shopping list to pick up anything else you might require.

Some of these projects — the sandbox on pages 148–151, for example — are long-term investments in time and money; consider buying the best-quality materials you can afford.

Take your time. You don't want to rush or cut corners, so give yourself plenty of time to set up and finish a project safely. Precautions might include safety goggles for woodworking, masks for heavy-duty sanding, and adequate ventilation for projects involving finishes or paints.

Consider the space on hand. Despite the backyard theme of this chapter, many of its projects are adaptable to differently configured spaces: you might build a smaller sandbox for a rooftop, hang chimes outside an urban bedroom, or mount a bird feeder on an apartment windowsill.

Backyard Essentials

Cover the kid-friendly basics, and your yard is sure to be a paradise for the pint-sized. Consider buying or making the following:

◆ **A swing.** This can be as simple as a tire suspended safely from a tree (see page 153) or as intricate as a canopied fort with a slide, swings, and a climbing wall. Either way, give it a periodic once-over for safety, checking for frayed ropes, loose bolts, or rusted-out chain.

◆ **A sandbox.** We offer directions for making a large one (pages 148–151), but sand is inviting in all containers, even a wheelbarrow or a plastic box. Whatever your container, be sure it's lidded (think rain; think cats), and fill it with play-quality sand. Keep sand toys — shovels, dump trucks, sieves, and the like — in a nearby lidded bin.

◆ **A picnic table (see pages 144–147)** for picnic lunches and outdoor tea parties.

◆ Other necessities will depend on your kids and your space: kiddie pools, sunny garden plots, croquet sets, and soccer goals might be the choices for your family. Or, if you live in an apartment, you may want to keep a grab-and-go tote bag by the door, filled with sidewalk chalk, balls, jump ropes — whatever you need for an afternoon in the park.

Silvery Wind Chime

I t's a breeze to craft this elegant homemade wind chime. The task of pounding the spoons flat is a job your kids will relish. Real silver or silver-plated spoons are required, and they can often be found sold in singles at thrift stores or tag sales. Choose utensils with thinner handles (about ¹⁄₁₆- inch thick), as they will be easier to flatten and drill.

MATERIALS

- **Brick**
- **2 old dish towels**
- **Hammer**
- **Wide rubber band**
- **4 spoons and 1 fork**
- **Spring clamp, about 5 inches long**
- **Scrap piece of wood**
- **Safety goggles**
- **Drill with ¹⁄₈-inch bit for drilling metal**
- **Needle-nose pliers**
- **Ruler**
- **Fishing line**
- **Beads**

Set the brick on the ground and place a folded dish towel on top of it. Fold the second towel (or just a piece of the towel, depending on how bulky it is) and wrap it around the striking end of the hammerhead. Use the rubber band to secure it. Now you can show your child how to flatten the spoons and fork.

Place a piece of silverware on the covered brick and pound it with the hammer. After a while, turn over the utensil and pound it from the opposite side. (Occasionally, as holes wear through the cloth covering the hammer, you'll need to unband it, refold the square, and reattach it.)

Once your child has pounded flat the remaining pieces, it's time to drill holes in the utensil handles (a parent's job). One at a time, tightly clamp each utensil to the piece of wood. Wearing safety goggles, drill a hole ½ inch down from the end of the handle.

Use the pliers to separate the tines of the fork and twist each of them into a small closed loop at the tip (another job for parents). Meanwhile, your child can thread a 7-inch length of fishing line through the hole in each spoon and knot the line around the handle. Next, she can thread several beads onto each strand and knot the line above the beads as well. Leaving 4 inches of line above the top beads, tie the spoons to the loops in the fork tines. Finally, attach fishing line to the fork handle and string on a few beads. Securely tie a loop in the end of the strand and the wind chime is ready to hang.

Just-my-size Table

"We live in a small house that is full of furniture and short on storage. So a few years ago when our daughter, Charlotte, now five, needed a play table for our deck, we were glad to hit upon an easy, inexpensive space-saving solution.

After discovering an old folding card table at a yard sale, we covered the top with Con-Tact paper, trimmed the legs to 16 inches, and added rubber feet. Suddenly we had the perfect art/tea party/game center that quickly disappears behind a dresser when not in use."

— **Missy Foran**
Santa Cruz, California

Portable Picnic Table

Fashioned from just a single sheet of plywood, this kid-size picnic table is a cinch to disassemble, making it easy to store and transport. If you know how to use a jigsaw, you can make it in a weekend.

MATERIALS

1 4- by 8-foot sheet of ³/₄-inch AC plywood

12 1¹/₄-inch wood screws

Primer and exterior paint

Tape measure, straightedge or carpenter's square, coffee can with 4-inch diameter, safety goggles, leather work gloves, jigsaw, 100-grit sandpaper, vibrator sander or sanding block, file, electric drill, paintbrush

Note: Getting the 4- by 8-foot sheet of plywood home from the lumberyard can be challenging. Rather than wrestle with it whole, have the yard cut three pieces from it:

1 24- by 48-inch piece (call it Section A) for the tabletop

1 44¹/₄- by 48-inch piece (Section B) for the legs, tabletop support and cleats, and carrying clips

1 27- by 48-inch piece (Section C) for the seats and seat supports

If you want to save sawing time later, you can also have the yard cut Sections A and B, plus the two 8³/₄- by 48-inch seats and the two 4³/₄-inch by 48-inch seat supports.

Section A

1. Round the tabletop's four cor-

ners by tracing around the coffee can and then cutting along the curves (shaded in red).

2. The football-shaped handle is a plus if you plan to carry your table often; otherwise, it can be omitted. Mark the handle with the coffee can (as shown below right), centering it horizontally on the board, then drill a ³/₈-inch starter hole within the football. Make smooth cuts so the handle will be comfortable to grip.

Tips for Cutting, Sanding, and Painting Plywood

1. Once you've drawn the straight cut lines, use the coffee can as a template to round off most of the corners, lay out the handles, and shape the feet. Use a dime to round off the slots in the table legs, as shown on the diagram for Section B (page 146).

2. Wear safety goggles so you can watch the blade and your guidelines. Try to make smooth, continuous cuts to minimize sanding later. Wear leather work gloves to avoid getting splinters.

3. The most important cuts will be the ³/₄-inch-wide slots for the interlocking joints. See the Tip in step 3 on page 146 for an easy way to keep the measurements and cuts as precise as possible. During assembly, you may have to use the jigsaw or file to widen some of the slots for a smooth fit.

4. Use a jigsaw equipped with a sharp wood blade that will allow you to make both straight and curved cuts. Support the plywood on a stable work surface, cut slowly, and let the blade do its work.

5. After you've cut your pieces, sand and round over all of the edges using 100-grit sandpaper, preferably on a sanding block or vibrator sander. Pay particular attention to the tabletop, seat edges, and handle cutouts.

6. When it's time to paint your picnic table, first apply a coat of quality exterior primer, then finish with two coats of exterior paint.

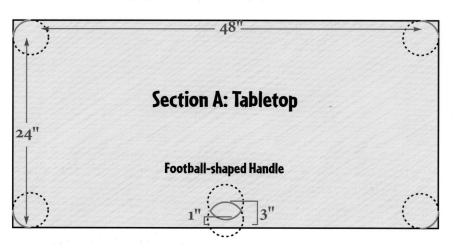

48"

24"

Section A: Tabletop

Football-shaped Handle

1"　3"

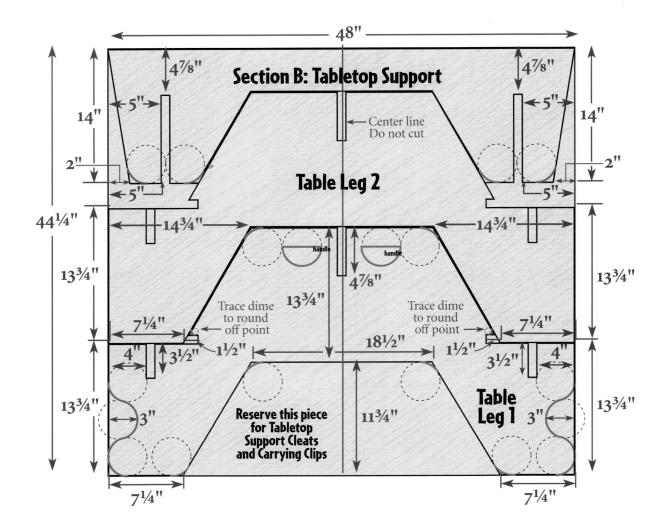

Section B: Tabletop Support

48"

4⅞"

5"

14"

2"

5"

Center line
Do not cut

Table Leg 2

44¼"

14¾"

14¾"

13¾"

handle

handle

13¾"

4⅞"

13¾"

Trace dime
to round
off point

Trace dime
to round
off point

7¼"

7¼"

4"

3½"

1½"

18½"

1½"

3½"

4"

13¾"

3"

Reserve this piece
for Tabletop
Support Cleats
and Carrying Clips

11¾"

Table
Leg 1

3"

13¾"

7¼"

7¼"

Section B

1. Draw a line down the middle of the board (2 feet from each side) — this is not a cut line, but will serve as a handy reference point for marking the pieces. Mark the cutting lines, as shown, again tracing around the coffee can. Darken the cut lines as indicated (in red) to create the curved edges and semicircle handles.

2. Cut out the piece of wood reserved for the tabletop support cleats and carrying clips. Mark and cut out the cleats as shown in the diagram below.

3. Mark the slots on table leg 1 and the tabletop support. **Tip:** After marking the length of the slot along its outside edge, mark the width (¾ inch) by setting one of the cleats on edge and using its thickness as a guide, as shown at right. When you cut out the slots, try to stay directly on the pencil lines so the openings won't

be too tight or too loose. You can also drill a ⅜-inch hole at the deepest point of each slot to make it easier to turn the blade and clean out the corners.

4. Cut out table leg 1 and use it as a template for table leg 2. Again, use the cleat to make sure the width of the slots is exact. Finally, cut out table leg 2 and the tabletop support.

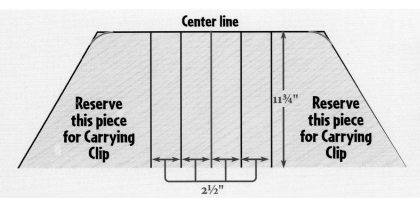

Center line

Reserve
this piece
for Carrying
Clip

11¾"

Reserve
this piece
for Carrying
Clip

2½"

Tabletop Support Cleats

Measure and mark the four tabletop support cleats from the center line (here, also a cut line) and cut them out. Reserve the end pieces for the carrying clips (see Making and Using the Carrying Clips at right).

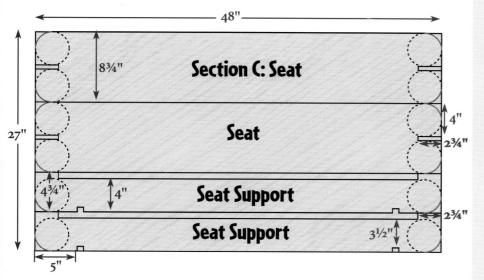

Section C: Seat

48"

27"

8¾"

Seat

4"

2¾"

4¾"

4"

Seat Support

2¾"

Seat Support

3½"

5"

Section C

1. If the lumberyard didn't do it for you, mark and cut the two seat pieces and two seat supports, as shown.

2. Use the coffee can to round off the corners where indicated. Then use a cleat to mark the width of the various slots (see Tip on page 146).

Attaching the Tabletop Support Cleats

1. Flip the tabletop so the underside is facing up. Fit together the table legs and tabletop support (see Assembling the Table, step 1, at right), then center the assembly upside down on the tabletop, as shown at right.

2. To ensure a snug final fit, position the cleats so that each pair sand-

wiches the tabletop support and the short ends butt up against the inside of the table leg. Screw each cleat in place with three screws (predrilling may be necessary).

Making and Using the Carrying Clips

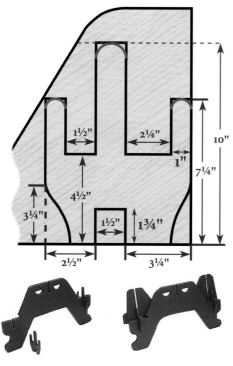

1½" 2¼"

1"

10"

7¼"

4½"

3¼"

3¼"

1½" 1¾"

2½" 3¼"

1. Draw a carrying clip on one of the two pieces of wood reserved for the clips. Cut out the clip and use it as a template for the second clip.

2. Place both legs together, aligning the seat support slots. Insert the bottom slot of each clip into a pair of seat support slots, with the clips oriented in the same direction. You should now have two sets of hooks upon which to hang all but the tabletop.

3. On the wider hooks, place the tabletop support (flat edge down), one seat, and one seat support (which locks onto the carrying clips). On the narrower hooks, place the other seat and seat support. Use the half-circle handles to carry the clipped pieces (and the football handle to carry the tabletop). Note that if you tilt the assembly, pieces could slide out.

Backyard Projects

Assembling the Table

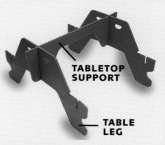

TABLETOP SUPPORT

TABLE LEG

1. Holding the two table legs upright, slide on the tabletop support, lining up the slots on the bottom of the support with those on the top of each table leg.

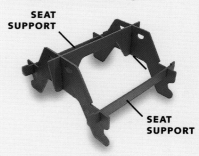

SEAT SUPPORT

SEAT SUPPORT

2. Slide on the two seat supports, inserting the slots into the table legs.

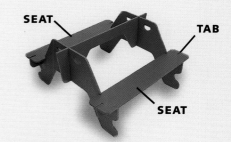

SEAT

TAB

SEAT

3. Fit the seats over the seat supports, tucking each seat's inside edge into the slots on the table legs and placing the end slots over the seat support tabs.

TABLETOP

4. Position the tabletop so the tabletop support fits into the channel created by the cleats.

Play Zones

Cutting the Lumber

Cut the following pieces from the lumber list at left — or ask if your lumberyard will make the straight cuts for you. Be sure to wear a mask and safety goggles when you're sawing any wood.

Wood for Sandbox
From 2 by 12 by 10's
- **External frame boards (cut two); see diagram A**
- **Internal frame boards (cut two); see diagram B**

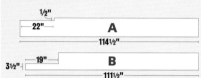

- **Internal frame ends (cut two 60-inch boards)**

From 2 by 12 by 8's
- **Toy box endpiece (cut one 79$^1/_2$-inch board)**
- **Blocks (cut two 8-inch boards)**
- **Seats (cut two 92$^1/_2$-inch boards)**

From 2 by 4 by 8
- **Lid storage endpiece (cut one 79$^1/_2$-inch board)**

From $^5/_4$ by 6 by 14's
- **Lid storage end seat boards (cut four 82$^1/_2$-inch boards)**
- **Battens (cut seven 22-inch boards)**

From $^5/_4$ by 6 by 10's
- **Toy box cover boards (cut four 60-inch boards)**

Wood for Lid Panels
From $^5/_4$ by 6 by 16's
- **Lid boards (cut twelve 64-inch boards and one 64- by 4-inch board)**
- **Short lid battens (cut four 16$^1/_4$-inch boards)**
- **Long lid battens (cut three 20$^1/_4$-inch boards)**

From $^5/_4$ by 6 by 8
- **Additional short lid battens (cut five 16$^1/_4$-inch boards)**

WEEKEND PROJECT

Build-your-own Sandbox

I t's sturdy, comfortable, and roomy enough for a summer's worth of play. Here's how your family can make your own 7- by 10-foot sandbox.

MATERIALS
Supplies
- **1 pound of 1$^1/_2$-inch square-head screws**
- **1 pound of 3-inch square-head screws**
- **3 heavy-duty 8-inch strap hinges**
- **1 6- by 8-foot plastic tarp (to line bottom of sandbox)**

Lumber
- **5 2-inch by 12-inch by 10-foot pressure treated boards**
- **3 2-inch by 12-inch by 8-foot pressure treated boards**
- **1 2-inch by 4-inch by 8-foot pressure treated board**
- **3 $^5/_4$-inch by 6-inch by 14-foot cedar boards**
- **2 $^5/_4$-inch by 6-inch by 10-foot cedar boards**

Optional lid
- **5 $^5/_4$-inch by 6-inch by 16-foot cedar boards**
- **1 $^5/_4$-inch by 6-inch by 8-foot cedar board**
- **1 pound of 1$^1/_2$-inch square-head screws**

Tools

Spade shovel, circular saw, carpenter's level, carpenter's square, drill with square screw attachment, rubber mallet, tape measure, dust mask, safety goggles, chisel, paintbrush (optional)

1. Once you've chosen your site, mark off a rectangle (7 feet by 9 feet 10 inches), then use the shovel to remove the grass and 1 inch of the topsoil. The

external frame board

lid storage end

internal frame board

toy box endpiece

2

block

lid storage endpiece

4

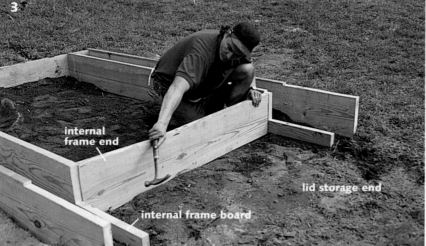

internal frame end

internal frame board

lid storage end

3

sandbox, whose final outside dimensions are 6 feet 8 inches by 9 feet 6½ inches, will be held in place by Mother Earth. If you need drainage, dig down 2 more inches and put down some gravel. Make sure the ground is level by laying down a board and checking it with a carpenter's level.

2. Set the two external frame boards into the dirt with the notch cuts at one end (this will be the lid storage end). Set the toy box endpiece in place at the other end. (The endpiece needs to be ½ inch lower than the internal and external frame boards. Don't cut it to make it lower; just dig it ½ inch deeper in the ground.) Square the frame using the square and check that it's level. Screw the toy box end of the frame together using 3-inch screws. Set the internal frame boards in place, as shown, leaving 8 inches in between each one and the external frame boards. Square them, then screw to the endpiece with 3-inch screws.

3. Using a rubber mallet or hammer, tap the two internal frame ends in place — one at the toy box end, 19 inches in from the toy box endpiece, and one at the lid storage end, flush with the L-shaped cut in the internal frame board. Lower these boards by digging them into the dirt an extra ½ inch. Screw in place with 3-inch screws.

4. Place the lid storage endpiece into the open end of the sandbox and

fasten with the 3-inch screws. Tap the two blocks into place at the lid storage end, to keep raccoons and kids from crawling underneath. These boards sit 1 inch in from the L-shaped cut in the internal frame boards and are set into the dirt ½ inch lower. Screw in with 3-inch screws. Recheck the levels and squareness of the box. Measure across the two diagonals between the far corners. If your box is square, the diagonals should be equal. Tap the frame with the mallet to make changes. To level the box, pry up the boards, push a few handfuls of dirt underneath, and tamp the boards down.

5. Place the two seats down and screw in place with 3-inch screws.

6. Assemble the toy box cover in what's called board-and-batten style. Line up the four toy box cover boards and lay three toy box battens across them. Place a batten 2 inches from each end of the boards and one in the center. Screw the battens on with 1½-

seat

lid storage end

toy box end

seat

5

boards

battens

inch screws, holding the boards together as you go. Screw the strap hinges onto the battens of the toy box cover. The hinge should open with the pin on the outside of the box. Chisel three ⅛-inch-deep by 3-inch-wide notches in the toy box end board that match the hinge spacing. Have two helpers hold the lid up, and screw the other half of the hinge on the box.

7. To build the seat for the lid storage end of the sandbox, again use board-and-batten style, with the four lid-end seat pieces as "boards" and the remaining four lid battens as "battens." This time, screw the seat together so that two of the battens are on the very ends and the other two are spaced evenly. Screw the seat onto the frame with 1½-inch screws.

8. To make the wooden panels, first look over the lumber you'll need (see Cutting the Lumber, page 149). The four panels are built in board-

and-batten style. Note that one of the panels is wider than the other three. For each of the narrower panels, use three of the lid boards battened by three of the short lid battens. For the fourth panel, use three lid boards, plus the extra 4-inch-wide lid board, and the three long lid battens. Space the battens evenly and about ¼ inch from the sides of the panels and 2 inches in from the ends. Screw in place with 1½-inch screws.

9. If desired, apply urethane or paint to the exposed surfaces. Put the tarp in the bottom of the box and poke 50 drainage holes in it (this keeps the dirt and sand from mixing and lets water drain.)

10. Fill the box with sand. The top-of-the-line (and priciest) stuff you can find is washed play sand, which is clean, weed-free, and a nice grade for building castles. You'll need about 30 bags for this box.

From Driveway to Playground

"Years ago, I began painting game areas on our backyard driveway, starting with a free-throw line for the basketball hoop, then hopscotch and four-square courts, all of which have had a lot of happy use. Next, my husband created a driveway tetherball court. To hold the pole, he sank a pipe sleeve into the middle of the driveway (level with the concrete surface), which allows the pole to be easily removed when we need to park there. Because I love to swing as much as our four kids, he also welded us a custom swing set and monkey bars and hung a climbing rope from the branch of a tree.

"As our kids' interests have changed, we've added new items, like a punching bag and an 8-foot skateboarding rail cemented securely into the ground alongside the driveway. With a little effort, we've created a playground that the kids can enjoy any time, not just at recess."

— Tamara Barnett
Bakersfield, California

FamilyFun **Home**

Terrific Tire Swing

An old tire, some rope or chain, a tall tree — could anything be more classic? The backyard tire swing has been entertaining kids pretty much since backyards were invented. Here's how to set one up right.

MATERIALS

- **Beltless, light truck tire**
- **Nylon or Dacron rope or ³/₁₆-inch playground chain**
- **Drill**
- **2¹/₂-inch drop-forged eyebolts**
- **3 washers**
- **4 nuts**
- **2 3-inch fender washers**
- **¹/₄-inch quick links**
- **Mulch or wood chips**

kellykennedy.com

If possible, find a used, beltless, light truck tire or old tractor tire (try a junkyard or tire store). Avoid steel-belted tires, whose sharp cords might eventually work their way out of the rubber sheathing.

Drill holes in the bottom of the tire so rainwater can drain.

Choose a healthy hardwood tree such as oak, walnut, sugar maple, ash, or cherry. (Beech, while strong, has delicate roots that resent trampling.) Make sure the branch is straight, forming an L-shape, not a V, against the trunk, and strong — at least 8 inches in diameter where you attach the swing. It should be 9 to 12 feet off the ground (the higher the branch, the farther you'll swing). If you don't have a large enough tree, you can retrofit a wooden swing set for either a vertical or a horizontal tire swing. Complete tire swing kits are available from CedarWorks Playsets (800-GO-CEDAR; www.cedarworks.com), or you can make your own with hardware from PlaysetParts.com (www.playsetparts.com).

The best way to suspend the tire (for both the swinger and the tree) is with a length of ³/₁₆-inch playground chain. Drill a ½-inch hole through the center of the branch, then insert a ½-inch drop-forged eyebolt through the hole, securing it on top with a washer and two nuts. (If you use rope, choose nylon or Dacron. Polypropylene and hemp don't weather well, and polypropylene can also slip too easily through small hands.)

Drill a ½-inch hole through the top of the tire. Thread a nut, washer, and 3-inch fender washer on another ½-inch eyebolt, slip it through the tire, and thread on another fender washer, washer, and nut. Secure the chain to the two eyebolts with ¼-inch quick links.

Spread a circle of mulch or wood chips around the trunk to protect tree roots and cushion falls.

TIPS AND TECHNIQUES

Yards of Fun

Here's some classic play gear for your backyard:

Tree Trolley
String the cable between two strong trees (or other support), and let kids fly. To order: Highlights Catalog (800-422-6202) or Back to Basics (800-356-5360).

Bocce

A cross between croquet (without mallets) and bowling (without pins). To order: HearthSong (800-325-2502) or www.lawn-toys.com.

Tetherball
Tons of fierce ball-slapping action in a tiny space. To order: www.onlinesports.com.

Clothesline Theater

This simple theater sets the stage for hours of backyard fun. To make one, string up two parallel lengths of polypropylene clothesline 6 feet apart. Paint scenery on a background sheet, as we've done — or pin on scenery cut from or painted on craft paper — then use clothespins to attach the sheet to the line farthest from the audience. For the curtains, suspend two sheets from the front clothesline using 1¼-inch binder clips hung at 1-foot intervals. The clothesline should go through the clips' triangular centers, thus allowing kids to slide the curtains open and closed for dramatic effect.

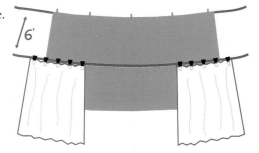

MAKE-IT-YOURSELF
Soccer Goal

For about $30 in materials (and an hour or so of time), you can build this versatile sports goal, just right for games of backyard soccer or driveway street hockey.

MATERIALS

2 10-foot lengths of 1^1/$_2$-inch PVC pipe

6 matching elbow connectors

Street hockey–size replacement net (we used a Mylec brand net, with sleeves that slide over the posts — about $15 from Hockey Giant; www.hockey giant.com)

Hacksaw or fine-tooth saw

Using the saw, cut one pipe into two 51-inch lengths, leaving 18 inches of scrap. Cut the other pipe into two 40-inch lengths and two 20-inch lengths. Then simply assemble the net as shown, sliding on the sleeves of the netting as you go.

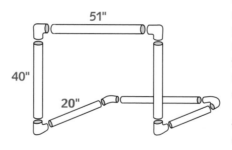

51"

40"

20"

Plywood Goalie

Caleb Leto, age 12, of the Pinellas Park, Florida, Hawks soccer team has such a strong kick that his daily backyard practice sessions were doing serious damage to his family's wooden fence.

Yes, a soccer net kickback might have helped, but they were too small for Caleb's needs (and they're expensive, too). So to save the wood without stifling Caleb's desire to practice, dad Carlo attached a plywood backboard to the front of the fence, securing the pieces with brackets and rods. Caleb painted on a soccer goalkeeper for inspiration.

"Caleb had knocked out about five or six slats in the fence before Carlo came up with this idea," says mom Marsha. "Now the fence is safe, and Caleb can kick the ball as hard as he wants."

Backyard Skating Rink

How can you have the perfect skating ice right outside your door? Just follow the Dahle family's practical plan for an ice rink, then add (lots of) water. To be sure, building a rink requires a chunk of money (as much as $600) and time (a day or so to set it up in winter, another to take it down in the spring). It also requires a level site and, of course, a cooperative climate. But thanks to the Dahles' design — a modular system of predrilled steel stakes, boards, and a plastic liner — what it doesn't require is a lot of construction know-how.

MATERIALS

Tools
- **Measuring tape**
- **Line level**
- **Sledgehammer**
- **String**

For the Dahles' Rink (36 by 70 feet, some walls 20 inches high)
- **22 2-inch by 10-inch by 10-foot spruce boards**
- **12 2-inch by 8-inch by 10-foot spruce boards**
- **6-millimeter polyethylene plastic (1 roll, 100- by 40-foot) available at lumberyards,**

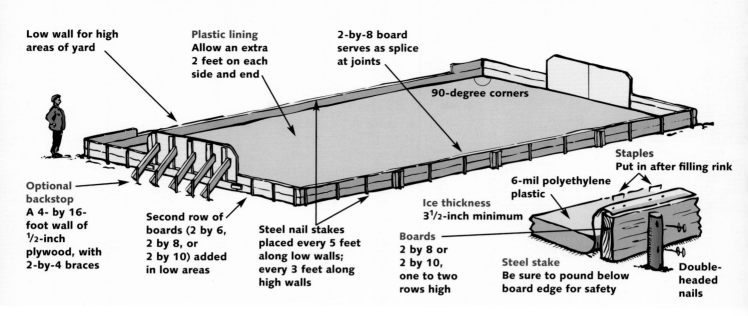

Low wall for high areas of yard

Plastic lining
Allow an extra 2 feet on each side and end

2-by-8 board serves as splice at joints

90-degree corners

Optional backstop
A 4- by 16-foot wall of ½-inch plywood, with 2-by-4 braces

Second row of boards (2 by 6, 2 by 8, or 2 by 10) added in low areas

Steel nail stakes placed every 5 feet along low walls; every 3 feet along high walls

Ice thickness 3½-inch minimum

Boards 2 by 8 or 2 by 10, one to two rows high

6-mil polyethylene plastic

Staples
Put in after filling rink

Steel stake
Be sure to pound below board edge for safety

Double-headed nails

home centers, or masonry or concrete supply stores

60 steel nail stakes (various lengths), available at masonry or concrete supply stores

2 pounds of 10d duplex (double-headed) nails, for splices

2 pounds of 6d duplex nails, for staking

For a smaller version (25 by 50 feet, single 8-inch wall)

18 2-inch by 8-inch by 10-foot spruce boards

6-millimeter polyethylene plastic (1 roll, 100- by 30-foot)

36 steel nail stakes (24-inch)

2 pounds 10d duplex nails

2 pounds 6d duplex nail

Optional backstop

4 4-foot by 8-foot sheets ½-inch CDX plywood

4 1-inch by 10-inch by 8-foot rough-sawn pine boards

10 2-inch by 4-inch by 8-foot studs, for brace

1. Testing Your Rink Site

Before You Begin

A backyard rink requires a large flat area, ideally in the shade and within reach of a garden hose. So before you do anything (like announce to the kids that you're going to make them their own skating rink!), check your yard's slope with a line level, a fluid-filled tube that hangs on a string (about $3 at hardware stores).

Determining the Slope

At your site's highest point, pound in a stake or large nail and tie on a length of string about 3½ inches off the ground, the height of your future ice surface **(A)**. Carry the string's other end to a low spot, hang on the line level, and raise or lower the string until the bubble indicates the string is level. Measure the distance from the string to the ground **(B)**. Repeat throughout the site. Ideally, the measurements at the lowest point shouldn't exceed 9½ inches (the height of a 2 by 10).

What If Your Site Is Too Sloped?

If the measurement is more than 9½ inches but less than 1 foot, you can add a second tier of lumber (2 by 6's, 2 by 8's, 2 by 10's, for example) on your lowest side. These double-high walls, however, require additional bracing and add to the price tag.

Getting It Square

Once you've determined that your site is level enough for a rink, you're ready to build. The Dahles usually set up theirs in late December, after the ground has frozen. The first step is to measure out the rink's dimensions and pound in the corner stakes. (**Tip:** Check to see if your rink's corners are square by measuring across the diagonals. They should be roughly the same measurement.) Now you're ready to begin erecting the frame, which is done one side at a time by first setting guidelines, then sledgehammering a row of stakes, then nailing on the boards.

2. Framing Up

A Corner, Guidelines, Then Stakes

First, nail or screw together two boards to form a corner **(C)** and place it in position. String guidelines from the end of one of the boards to the

C

D

Laying the Boards

After the first side is staked, begin laying in the boards **(F)** and nailing them to the stakes with 6d nails. Where the ends of the boards meet, use 10d nails or screws to affix a predrilled 1-foot section of 2 by 8 to the back side of the joint, as a splice **(G)**. Then drive in an additional stake at each splice (so with 10-foot boards, there's now a stake every 5 feet). For sides that are two boards high, use two stakes per board length in addition to those at the splices (one roughly every 3 feet). After staking and framing one end and side, continue with the remaining side **(H)** and then the far end. Since lumber lengths are irregular, you'll probably have to cut the last boards to complete the frame. At each corner, set stakes 3 inches in from the edge. All nails should be duplex, or double-headed **(I)**, which can be easily removed at the end of the season.

3. Laying In the Plastic Lining

For a lining material, the Dahles use one sheet of 6-mil polyethylene

next corner post **(D)** along the perimeter. Using your guidelines, sledgehammer in a row of steel stakes, measuring so that one stake will fall at the midpoint of each 10-foot board **(E)**. Note: The stakes, which come in varying lengths up to 36 inches, should be driven in at least 12 inches and (for safety reasons) far enough so that they do not poke over the top of the frame. You'll need longer stakes for walls that have to be two boards high.

plastic, measuring 100 by 40 feet. Splicing smaller pieces just doesn't work, Richard says. After the frame is set, the Dahles spread the plastic, covering the ground and running the liner up and over the boards on all sides **(J)**. It's important to maintain plenty of slack in the plastic until the water is in place. In the family's first rink, they wrapped the liner tightly under the frame and stapled it to the outside. The water pressure was so great it soon ripped the plastic away from the boards.

To avoid that, the Dahles now minimize the stapling until after the rink is filled and the water and plastic have settled. The plastic is set inside the frame and tacked in place with just a few staples, making sure holes won't be left below the waterline if the plastic tears. (If you do get a hole below the water-line, repair it by using silicone caulk to glue a plastic patch to the area.) Even

E

F

G

H

I

J

with the best care, however, the liner becomes brittle and has to be replaced every year, Richard notes.

4. Just Add (Lots of) Water

Filling a rink the size of the Dahles' to a minimum depth of 3½ inches requires about 12,000 gallons of water. Doing the job with a garden hose takes several days. The Dahles opt for a tanker truck delivery, which takes less than an hour but costs about $300. As the water flows in, make sure the plastic doesn't get caught and tear on the edges of the frame.

5. Ice Care

Once the rink freezes, the work goes on. After a snowstorm or a long skating session, the rink's surface needs to be cleaned. To keep the ice in top shape, Rian and his friends scrape it with shovels aligned like snowplows. Then Ann comes out with the garden hose and lets it run until an even coat of water covers the surface (later storing the hose where it won't freeze). If the weather gets too warm, the Dahles don't sweat it; they let the ice soften knowing that the next deep freeze will bring it right back.

6. Smooth Skating

With the rink so close to the house and thus so easily maintained, nearly every morning brings another day of perfect skating. Rian, who's on a traveling hockey team, has played as far away as Moscow. But there's no place he prefers more than his home ice, where he and his friends can show off their skills and still get rinkside hot chocolate service. As for Mom and Dad, they find that a family spin around the ice is the ideal way to end a winter day.

The Puck Stops Here

Because the Dahles' rink is used largely for hockey, the family installs plywood backstops at each end to keep flying pucks in the rink. The Dahles' backstops also serve as sections of the rink's frame, joined to the 2-by-10 wall with splices and staked, as with the other walls. (If you omit the backstops, simply continue the 2-by-10 walls.) Each backstop consists of two 4- by 8-foot sheets of ½-inch plywood (corners cut for safety), a 1-by-10 baseboard brace (nailed to the back of the plywood with roofing nails), and a series of angled 2-by-4 braces nailed to vertical 2 by 4's on the backstop and secured with staked, as shown. The plastic lining is stapled to the backstop's front and trimmed after the ice freezes. While not a necessity, the backstops allow for a more freewheeling game — and let players practice without worrying about hitting the neighbors.

Backyard Forts

A Sweet Place

Every child wants her own playhouse: a shady quiet spot for holding tea parties, playing games, and hosting neighborhood friends. But if you don't have time to build a playhouse of your dreams, here's a homespun one you can pull off in an afternoon. The frame is made out of scrap lumber, and the walls and roof are fabric, attached with a staple gun.

MATERIALS

Lumber

11 2-inch by 4-inch by 8-foot boards

Cut to the following lengths:

8 at 48 inches (crosspieces)

4 at 41 inches (crosspiece reinforcements)

4 at 48 inches (uprights)

4 at 33 inches (roof supports)

1 at 51 inches (roof beam)

Tools

Hand or circular saw

Tape measure

Hammer

Square

Staple gun

Supplies

2 pounds of 3-inch galvanized nails

5 yards of water-resistant nylon fabric, 60 inches wide

1. Construct four reinforced crosspieces for the frame. For each, lay a crosspiece on your work surface. Then stack a crosspiece reinforcement on top of it, creating a 3½-inch notch at each end. Nail the two together.

2. To build the side of the frame, lay flat two uprights, 4 feet apart. Set a reinforced crosspiece with the reinforcement facing down across the top and bottom of the uprights. Square off each corner and nail together. Build the second side the same way.

3. Stand the two sides 4 feet apart with reinforcements facing inward (sawhorses or chairs will hold the walls up). Set unreinforced crosspieces on the ground between the two sidewalls, completing a square frame.

Nail these bottom front and back crosspieces to both sides of the wall.

4. Nail unreinforced top crosspieces into place, 1 inch below the top of the side walls (this leaves a space to nail the roof supports). You now have a cube.

5. Cut both ends of the roof supports at 45-degree angles (the top edge of the support will measure 33 inches; the bottom, 26 inches). **Tip:** Measure a 3½-inch square at either end of the four roof supports. Draw a diagonal line from corner to corner. Cut along the diagonal.

6. Nail roof supports at each end of the top crosspieces. There will be a 1½-inch gap between the two for the roof beam.

7. Place the roof beam between the top ends of the roof supports and nail it in place.

8. With a staple gun, attach water-resistant nylon fabric to the frame. Decorate with banners. (**Note:** The playhouse is much easier to erect with a partner.)

A Child's Clubhouse

Like puppies, kids get territorial at a very young age. As soon as they can navigate the backyard on their own, most kids begin staking their claim to secret nooks on your property. Here, they find a refuge from a world where grown-ups call the shots. But soon will come the day when the open air is no longer enough. Your kids and their friends will need shelter from the elements with four walls and a roof over their heads; they will need that essential piece of childhood real estate known as the clubhouse.

Our clubhouse design, with lattice walls and a colorful canvas roof, can be built in under ten hours. The lattice will enable your kids to attach a variety of neat "extras" to the playhouse using nothing more complicated than a series of S-hooks.

FamilyFun **Home**

MATERIALS

Lumber

- **2** 4-inch by 4-inch by 10-foot boards, each cut into two 60 inch pieces; label each **(A)**
- **2** 4-inch by 4-inch by 8-foot boards, each cut to 84 inches; label each **(B)**
- **4** 2-inch by 4-inch by 12-foot boards, each cut into one 82½-inch piece; label two **(C)** and two **(D)**; and then into one 55-inch piece **(F)**
- **1** 2-inch by 4-inch by 12-foot board cut into one 82½-inch piece; label **(D)**; and one 43-inch piece; label **(E)**
- **1** 2-inch by 4-inch by 8-foot board cut into two 45-inch pieces; label **(G)**
- **2** 2-inch by 2-inch by 8-foot boards, each cut to 55 inches; label each **(H)** Or, if 2 by 2's are not available: 1 1-inch by 3-inch by 10-foot board cut into two 55-inch pieces
- **1** 1-inch by 3-inch by 8-foot board cut into two 48-inch pieces **(J)**
- **5** 8-foot long lattice channels, each cut into two 48-inch pieces
- **3** 4- by 8-foot plastic lattice panels cut to fit openings between posts (you'll need three pieces approximately 36 inches by 48 inches and two pieces approximately 45 inches by 48 inches)

Supplies

- **1** 48-inch-wide by 10-foot-long sheet of canvas (or any outdoor water-resistant fabric)
- **2** pounds of 12d galvanized common nails
- **1** pound of 6d galvanized box nails
- **1** pound of 2½-inch galvanized screws (optional)

Tools

Tape measure
Circular saw
Hammer
Rubber mallet
Nail set
Cordless screwdriver or variable speed drill (optional)

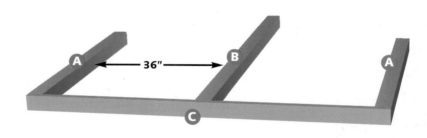

1. Begin front wall assembly by nailing plate board **(C)** to the bottom of corner posts **(A)**. Place center post **(B)** in the middle of plate board **(C)** and nail through **(C)** into the bottom of **(B)**. Repeat Step 1 to build back wall assembly. **NOTE:** Unless specified, all nails are 12d. (You can substitute screws for nails.)

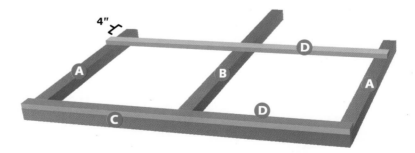

2A. For back wall, nail bottom rail **(D)** to corner posts **(A)** and center post **(B)**, flush with edge of bottom plate **(C)**. Nail top rail **(D)** to corner posts **(A)** and center post **(B)**, placing it 4 inches from top of corner posts **(A)**.

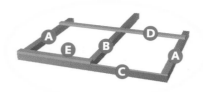

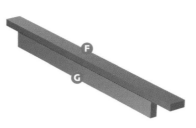

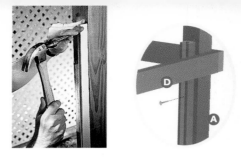

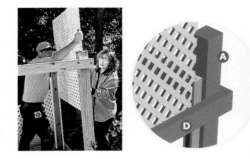

2B. For front wall, nail bottom rail **(E)** to corner post **(A)** and center post **(B)**, flush with bottom plate **(C)**. Nail top rail **(D)** to corner posts **(A)** and center post **(B)**.

3. Nail bottom side rail **(F)** to plate board **(G)**, forming an upside-down "L" and leaving a 5-inch space at each end. Repeat for other side.

6. Use 6d galvanized box nails to attach lattice channels to the inside of the corner posts **(A)**. Use a nail set to drive nail heads flush with inside track of channel.

4. Flip over the back wall so that top and bottom rails **(D)** are facing down. Nail top side rail **(F)** to corner post **(A)** where top rail **(D)** intersects. Nail bottom side rail assembly **(F)** and **(G)** to corner post **(A)** where bottom rail **(D)** intersects.

7. Measure openings between posts and cut lattice panels to fit. Slide lattice panels into channels between posts. (You may want to spray a lubricant, such as silicone, to ease the process.) When panel is as low as it will go, tap it with a rubber mallet for a secure fit.

8. Nail ridge poles **(H)** to sides of center posts **(B)**. (The poles will extend 1½ inches on each end.)

5. Tilt up back wall so side rails **(F)** are horizontal. Attach front wall assembly by nailing through side rails into corner posts **(A)**.

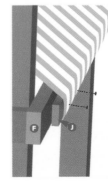

9. Drape canvas over top of ridge poles and fasten to side strips **(J)** by wrapping canvas around the strips and then nailing them to the top side rails **(F)** with 6d box nails (or use screws for easy removal or cleaning).

▲ For their eyes only: Secret (read: non-parental) messages can be posted on an interior "message center" — otherwise known as a plastic wipe-off board. To hang it, we attached two large butterfly clips (backward, so the board would lie flat), through which we looped medium-size S-hooks.

▲ Sign up here: A piece of scrap lumber becomes a mini billboard with some waterproof paint and two medium-size eye hooks screwed into each end (use S-hooks to hang the sign on the lattice).

◄ You've got mail: A small plastic crate becomes a mailbox with a little imagination and some indelible markers.

Unfurl the fun: Whether store-bought or homemade, a flag is the perfect finishing touch (page 163).

BUILD-IT-YOURSELF
Backyard Tepee

Just like the traditional Native American tepee that inspired it, this backyard shelter can be assembled and dismantled in a jiffy. Made with PVC pipe poles and a canvas tarp, it's weatherproof, fairly inexpensive (we paid $35 for supplies at our local home center), and provides a fun, shady playspace on a sunny day.

MATERIALS

- 9- by 12-foot canvas tarp or drop cloth
- Measuring tape
- Colored marker
- White cotton rope
- 10 8-foot-long white PVC pipes, ¾ inch in diameter (you can cut longer PVC pipes to length with a hacksaw)
- 2 chopsticks or similar strips of wood

1. Fold the tarp in half so that it forms a 9- by 6-foot rectangle. Measure in 1 foot along the fold and mark the spot. Then cut a 6-foot length of rope. Have your child hold one end of the rope at the marked spot while you tie the opposite end around the colored marker. Step away from your child until the line is taut and move the rope in an arc, marking a line on the canvas as you go. Cut the tarp along the line and then cut out a 12- by 6-inch rectangle to the left of the marked spot at the top corner of the tepee.

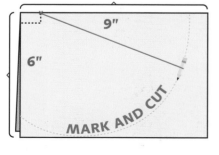

2. Now you're ready to assemble the tepee. Loosely tie together three of the PVC pipes 2 feet down from the tops with a piece of rope.

3. Next, stand them up like a tripod. Lean the remaining poles against the tripod so that they are evenly spaced.

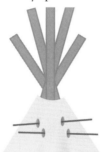

4. Drape the cut canvas around the tepee frame, overlapping the top a bit. Make two sets of holes through both layers of the overlapped portion and thread the chopsticks through them to hold the canvas in place.

5. To secure the lower edge of the canvas to the frame, first snip a small hole about 1 inch in from one of the tarp's bottom corners. Loop a short length of rope through the hole, as shown, and tie the ends around the base of one pole (this pole will become part of the doorway).

6. Now gently stretch the canvas around the PVC frame so that the canvas extends past the first pole to create a door flap. Snip a small hole near the lower edge of the canvas where it falls on the remaining poles and tie it in place using the same method as before.

FAMILYFUN SUCCESS STORY
Game Table

When her daughters were younger, Jane Quinlan of Brunswick, Maine, ran a home-based day-care center. She had a small picnic table made for her charges to eat, draw, and play at. One day, she thought of having a table with built-in game boards. So she had another table built, and upon delivery Jane designed the tabletop games and painted the alphabet and numbers to run along the sides.

Meanwhile, daughters Meaghan, then 12, and Emily, ten, painted the backgammon and checker boards and sponge-painted squares on the benches. Dad Gregory added four to five coats of polyurethane to protect the table. Although Jane's day-care business is no more, the family's new table gets plenty of use by the girls.

As Jane says, "We have created some delightful memories as we reflect on how much fun it was to work on such a wonderful art project together." And her daughters are tickled as well — now they don't always have to halt a game for dinner.

Backyard Projects

Two-room Fort

To kids, few things are as captivating as an honest-to-goodness fort. They might call it the clubhouse, the hideaway, or any of a thousand secret names, but it's all the same — a place built by them, for them, using easy-to-find materials, a few tools, and lots of imagination. If they need inspiration for building their own undercover place, show them our two-room fort. It can be made out of sticks, rocks, rope, a refrigerator box, and a little creativity.

Building the Box Fort

The cardboard half of our fort offers a room with a view, courtesy of the simple awninged windows. The door is wide open, but you'll still need to say the secret password to get in. Just whisper it through the special hole.

MATERIALS
Utility knife
Sticks
Grass or leaves
Markers (for signs)
Large cardboard box (ask at appliance stores)

1. Lay the box on its side and with a utility knife (a parent's job) cut three sides of a flap for a door and for windows, leaving the top side for a hinge. Prop open the windows and door with sticks, as shown.

2. Cut a password hole near the door and identify it with an appropriate sign, like Say Password Here.

3. For a camouflaged look, place a layer of grass clippings, hay, weeds, or brush on top of the box. In the fall, try burying the box with leaves, starting around the bottom and piling the leaves in a heap over the entire fort.

Adding a Lean-to

The lean-to half of our fort is spacious and shady, with a rustic roof that affords plenty of ventilation. For safety's sake, be sure to properly secure your support sticks and not use anything heavy or sharp for sheathing.

MATERIALS

Sticks

Rope

Rocks

Brush and various sheathing materials

1. Find two trees, 8 or so feet apart, and at least 4 inches in diameter. Lash a cross pole between them parallel to the ground. (See the lashing instructions on the next page.)

2. Lean a row of sturdy sticks against the cross pole at about a 60-degree angle. If necessary, cut the sticks to the proper length (a parent should help with any sharp tools).

3. Create side walls with shorter sticks. Anchor the sticks in place with a perimeter of heavy rocks.

4. Further secure the frame by weaving and tying lengths of scrap rope to connect the various supports.

5. Lay on whatever sheathing material you have on hand, such as old tarpaulins, scrap lumber, hay, or cardboard. Again, avoid sharp or heavy items.

6. Continue placing on layers of sheathing until the lean-to is covered (keep a few spots open for doors and windows). Decorate with signs.

How to Lash a Cross Pole to a Tree

1. **Tie the rope to the tree with a clove hitch, placing it around the tree and over itself, then around the tree again and back under itself.**

2. **Pull the clove hitch tight. Place the cross pole directly above the hitch. (Ask a friend to help hold it.)**

3. **Begin weaving the rope around the junction: over the cross pole, back behind the tree, over the pole, behind the tree, and so on.**

4. **Continue weaving until the cross pole is firmly bound to the tree.**

5. **Tighten the lash by looping the rope several times between the pole and tree, as shown, and pulling tight.**

6. **Tie off the rope and tuck the ends into the lashing.**

Windows

Walls

Decorations

Security

Windows
Cover windows with curtains made from old towels or scraps of cloth.

Walls
Hang original drawings and posters, even an unbreakable mirror, on the walls.

Decorations
Decorate with pottery, flowers, collected stones, shells, and leaves.

Security
Cut a spy hole in the wall so your kids can keep a lookout with a periscope or binoculars.

Storing Your Top-secret Stuff

What would a fort be without treasures — and clever places to hide them in? Here are some ways to safeguard your prized possessions.

Floor safe: Dig a shallow hole in the fort's floor and line it with plastic (see photograph, left). Place your treasures inside, then lay a board across the hole. Cover the board with a carpet scrap, rug, hay, or pine needles.

Wall safe: Hang an old cereal box on the wall (with a door cut in its front), then cover it with a poster, cloth, or piece of art.

Table safe: Turn a box or crate upside down and place valuables beneath. Cover the box with an old sheet and use it as a table.

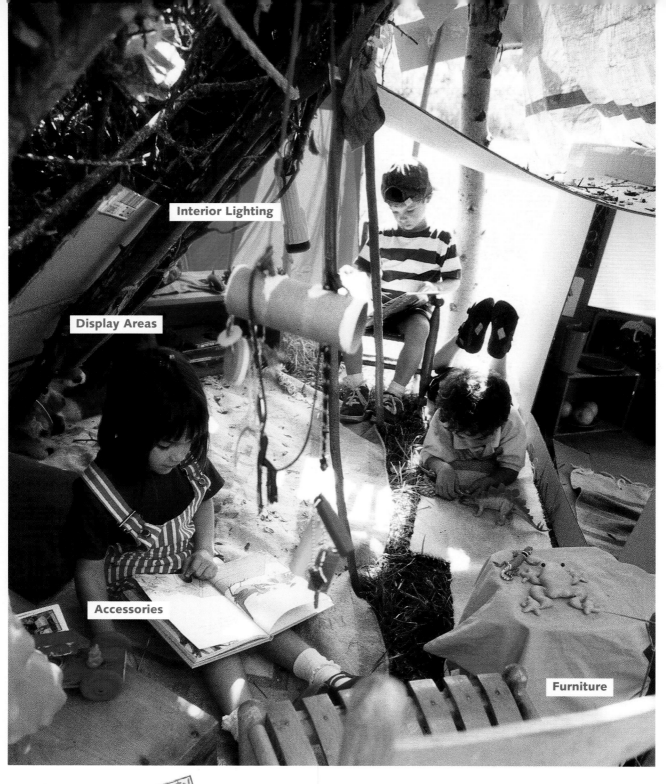

Interior Lighting

Display Areas

Accessories

Furniture

Finishing Touches

Signs **Put up Welcome or Private signs with the fort's official name. Tip: Hang them on sticks poked through the fort's wall.**

Interior Lighting **Hang a flashlight from the ceiling with a piece of string for reading stories at night.**

Display Areas **Set up grocery store boxes or wooden crates for tables and shelves to hold your stuff. Stumps and milk crates can** also serve in a pinch.

Alarm System **Tie several jingle bells to a length of string and hang it across the fort's entrance.**

Bead Curtain **Hang strings of beads from the top of the door, creating a shimmering curtain across the entrance.**

Accessories **Stock your fort with "necessary" items, such as a battery-operated cassette player or radio, old dishes, pots and pans, a tin-can tele-** phone, stuffed animals, toys, and books.

Furniture **Always keep an eye out for discarded household furniture that will fit inside your fort: chairs, card tables, even bookcases or shelves. Old tires make good chairs, as do large pieces of firewood set on end.**

Mail and Messages **Make a mailbox or slot for letters. Put up a cork bulletin board for news of club meetings or important messages.**

Backyard Birds

Bird Feeder

One of the first signs of spring is the sight and song of birds returning from warmer climates where they've wintered. A thoughtful way to welcome them back is to hang a tray feeder (a style many types of birds will eat from) filled with a mix of black oil sunflower seeds and millet.

MATERIALS

- 1- by 3-inch (actual measurement is ³/₄ by 2¹/₂ inches) pine board, 4 feet long
- Drill with ⁵/₆₄- and ¹/₄-inch bits
- Hammer
- 5d galvanized box nails
- 10-inch square of aluminum screening (sold in most hardware stores)
- Copper upholstery tacks
- Pair of rawhide laces, each 36 inches long

Cut the pine board into two 10¹/₂-inch lengths and two 9-inch lengths. Stand the shorter pieces on end and set one of the longer pieces on top of them (like a table), so that the ends are flush, as shown. Use the ⁵/₆₄-inch bit to predrill holes, then nail the pieces together. Flip over the assembly and nail the other long piece in place (again predrilling the holes) to form a square frame.

Tack the screen to the bottom edges of the frame, as shown. Finally, use the ¹/₄-inch bit to drill a pair of holes in two opposite sides. Thread a lace through the holes in each side, knot the ends, and the feeder is ready to hang.

Birding Basket

The sudden arrival of a colorful new visitor at a backyard bird feeder can be just the thrill that turns a kid on to the wonders of the natural world. Set up a birding basket — equipped with binoculars, guidebooks, and a birding log — and he'll be ready for bird-watching at the drop of a feather. The National Audubon Society suggests that you furnish your basket with compact, rubber-coated binoculars; a good guidebook, such as the group's own *First Field Guide: Birds* by Scott Weidensaul (Scholastic, Inc.; $9 paperback); and a blank journal, pen, and coloring pencils. The journal can be used for sketching and keeping track of the birds you see — their shapes, colors, and sizes, and whether they chirp or sing.

Indoor Bird Blind

For some genuinely "cheep" thrills, try this easy-to-assemble windowsill bird blind. It's just a cardboard box with strategically placed peepholes (for eyes or binoculars) and a pocket to hold field guides, sketching paper, and a bird-watching log.

1. **To accommodate your child's head and shoulders**, use a craft knife to cut the box to a depth of about 6 inches on the top. The sides can remain deeper — about 10 inches or so. For the pocket, cut a rectangle from the scrap cardboard, bend the sides, and secure it with masking tape to the inside walls of the box, as shown on the left-hand side.

2. **Set the box in the window** to determine the best place for your viewing holes (we added two sets, one level with the feeder and the other closer to the nearby bushes, where birds tend to congregate before and after a meal). Place the box bottom side down and trace around your binoculars' lenses, then cut out the traced holes with a craft knife.

3. **Secure the blind to the window** with masking tape. For extra support, place it on a table.

4. **Store pens and pencils in the coffee can**; slip your field guide, sketching paper, and a birding log into the cardboard pocket; and tuck a clock and binoculars next to the coffee can. When your birding is done, the blind can serve as your supply storage box.

Terra-cotta Birdbath

Believe it or not, even in the summertime, a fresh, clean source of water can be hard for birds to come by. That's why a birdbath is a practical device for attracting all kinds of species, such as catbirds, wrens, waxwings, even screech owls. Here's one that couldn't be simpler to put together.

MATERIALS

- **2 unglazed clay pot trays, one 8¼ inches in diameter and one 12¼ inches in diameter**
- **Unglazed clay pot, 6 inches in diameter**
- **Permanent enamel satin-finish paint (we recommend Delta Ceram-Decor's PermEnamel air-drying nontoxic paint)**
- **Paintbrushes**
- **Clear satin-finish enamel glaze**

First, invert the smaller clay tray and the pot on a newspaper-covered surface so your child can paint a decorative design on the stand. (Don't paint the larger tray, though, as the unpainted surface will provide a better grip for visiting birds.) Let the paint dry thoroughly. For added durability, seal the paint with a coat of clear satin glaze.

To assemble the birdbath, center the inverted pot on the tray base, then set the larger tray right side up atop the pot and fill it with no more than 3 inches of water.

Squirrel Café

Just as we humans enjoy a good bite to eat at our favorite summer roadside diner, so can the bushy-tailed travelers in your neck of the woods — if your family opens up one of these easy-to-build squirrel cafés. It's a great craft for beginner wood-workers. Once you've constructed it, stock up on dried corn on the cob (sold at most garden centers), and you're in business.

MATERIALS

- **3-foot-long 1- by 3-inch (actual measurement is ³⁄₄- by 2¹⁄₂-inch) pine board**
- **5-foot-long 1- by 4-inch (actual measurement is ³⁄₄- by 3¹⁄₂-inch) pine board**
- **Ruler**
- **Handsaw**
- **Drill with ⁵⁄₆₄-inch twist bit**
- **Hammer**
- **1 pound of 5d galvanized box nails**
- **1 12d galvanized box nail**
- **Indoor/outdoor latex paints, polyurethane, and paintbrushes**
- **Dried ear of corn**

1. Help your child measure, mark, and label the two boards as shown and then cut out the pieces with a hand-saw. As you assemble the café, we rec-ommend predrilling holes before your child nails the pieces together.

2. Begin with the chairs. For each one, stand a leg **(A)** on end and center a seat **(B)** on top of it so that the two pieces resemble a T and the backs are flush. Nail through B into A. Now attach the chair back **(C)** by centering it along the back of the A/B assembly with the bottom of A and C flush. Nail through C into the A/B assembly.

3. Next, make the table. Stand the table leg **(D)** on end and cen-ter the floor **(F)** on top of it. Nail through F into D, making sure the nail goes into the solid part of the leg. Now nail the 12d nail through the center of the tabletop **(E)**. This will be used to attach the corn to the table once the café's built. Then flip over E (the spike will be pointing up out of the wood) and nail it, positioned diagonally, to the top of D.

4. To assem-ble the café, turn the chairs upside down and facing each other so that they are resting on the very tops of the seat backs. Have your child turn the floor/table assembly upside down and set it on top of the chair bottoms so that the ends of the floor are flush with the backs of the chairs. Nail the floor to the chair bottoms.

5. Measure and mark 8 inches up from the bottom of the back wall **(G)**. Align the bot-tom of the café floor with this mark and nail through G into the edge of the adjacent chair and the floor. Center the angle brace **(H)** under the floor and against G. Nail H to the floor and to G. For added stability, drive another nail through the back of G into the end of H. Finally, drill two nail holes in G, one ¹⁄₂ inch down from the top and another ¹⁄₂ inch up from the bottom, to use for nailing up the feeder.

6. To spruce up your café before put-ting it up, use indoor/outdoor latex paint to add a tablecloth and seat covers. For extra durability, once the paint is dry, brush on a top coat of polyure-thane. Finally, attach the corn by pushing the bottom of the ear onto the nail.

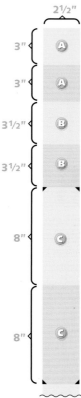

One-board Birdhouse

You can say it's for the birds, but this little lodge — built from a single board — is a rewarding starter project for young carpenters. Predrill the nail holes, and it's even more of a cinch for a child to put together.

MATERIALS

- **6-foot-long 1- by 6-inch red cedar board**
- **Ruler**
- **Handsaw**
- **6-penny stainless-steel ring shanked siding nails or galvanized box nails**
- **1 stainless-steel 1⅝-inch trim screw**
- **2 galvanized eye hooks**

1. Start by using a pencil and ruler to mark the cut lines onto the cedar board, as shown. Then help your child cut out the pieces with a handsaw.

2. Mark and cut triangular entrance and perch openings in front pieces **A** and **B** (here's the proper width of the entrance in inches for the type of bird you hope to attract: bluebird 1½; Great Crested Flycatcher 1¾; nuthatch 1⅜ ; Redheaded Woodpecker 2 inches.) Then fit the peg end into the perch cutout in front **A**, drill a nail hole, and tack it in place.

3. Nail a short end of roof **C** to a short end of roof **D**.

4. Next, use two nails to attach back **E** to side **G** and one nail (positioned near the top) to attach back **F** to side **H** (which will pivot).

Note: The sides are shorter than the backs to allow for ventilation.

5. Push together the long edges of back pieces **E** and **F**, set the roof on top, and use four nails to tack the roof to the back side.

6. Attach the floor by nailing through the back of the house into one of the floor's 5-inch edges.

7. Lay the front pieces in place atop the side walls and nail them to the side pieces. Again, use only one nail in front **B**, positioning it directly opposite the nail in back **F**. Attach the lower corner of front **B** to the side with a screw (this will let you clean the house seasonally by removing the screw and pivoting the side upward on the nails). Nail the edge of the roof to the tops of front **A** and **B**.

8. Finally, hang the finished birdhouse (according to the specifications that follow) from galvanized eye hooks screwed into the roof. Or tack a wooden "chimney" to the back and securely nail it to a post. Adjust the height above ground in feet to attract the birds for whom you made the opening in the front: bluebird 3 to 6; Great Crested Flycatcher 8 to 20; nuthatch 5 to 15; Redheaded Woodpecker 10 to 20 feet.

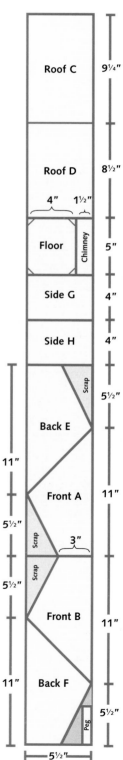

1 packet of gourd seeds (birdhouse or large bottle variety)
Garden fencing for trellising (optional)
Black plastic mulch (optional)
Balanced (10-10-10) fertilizer
Electric drill with various bits
Wire for hanging
Acrylic paints (optional)
Satin polyurethane (optional)

Growing the gourd: Allow each plant 10 to 15 square feet of garden space; you can get away with a little less if you trellis your plants. For each plant you plan to grow (one will suffice for this project), plant a half dozen seeds, following the directions on the seed packet. Before planting, mix some fertilizer into the soil, then reapply it monthly during the growing season. Keep seeds and plants well watered.

Drying the gourd: Harvest your gourd before the first frost, taking care to cut rather than twist the stem. Ideally, the fruit will have attained a diameter of 6 or more inches. Wash the gourd carefully to remove any dirt or debris. As an extra safeguard against rot, some experts recommend dipping gourds in a solution of 1 part bleach to 10 parts water. Drill a small hole through the gourd's neck, insert a hanging wire, and suspend the fruit in a dry, well-ventilated space until the seeds rattle around inside the shell (about four weeks but sometimes longer). Once the gourd is dry, any surface mold or fungus can be removed with steel wool, or left on for a more rustic look.

Making the birdhouse: Drill a 2-inch-diameter hole in the side of the gourd for the birds' front door. Remove the dried seeds and fibers. Drill two ¼-inch holes about 1½ inches up from the bottom of the gourd for ventilation and drainage. For a more colorful look, paint the gourd in the motif of your choice, then finish with two coats of satin polyurethane. Hang the birdhouse in a sheltered area at least 6 feet from the ground.

GARDEN PROJECT

Gourd Birdhouse

Gourds prove that nature has a sense of humor: their wild markings, eye-popping colors, and space-alien shapes transform the late-summer garden into a natural amusement park. If you've considered growing gourds but wondered what in the world to do with them, this project will answer your question — and

please the birds in the process. One gardening note: large gourds such as the birdhouse or bottle variety can take up to 130 days to mature. In areas with shorter growing seasons, ask at your garden center about black plastic mulch, row covers, and other season-extending devices and techniques.

Bat Roost

If your family is interested in attracting mosquito-munching residents to your yard, try offering them a place to roost: this simple bat house made out of a piece of pine board.

MATERIALS

- **8-foot-long 1 by 10-inch pine board**
- **Carpenter's rule**
- **Handsaw**
- **Small piece of fiberglass screening**
- **Handful of 2-inch common nails**

Measure and mark the board as shown in the diagram at right, using a carpenter's rule to draw the lines. Saw the wood into pieces.

To give the bat something to cling to inside the house, stretch the fiberglass screening across the back piece and tack it in place. Use scissors to trim the screen flush with the wood edges. Then, assemble and nail together the house pieces as shown.

Nail the house to the side of a shed or tree, facing east and about 15 feet from the ground. You may have to wait at least a year for a tenant to move in, or you may have to try a new location.

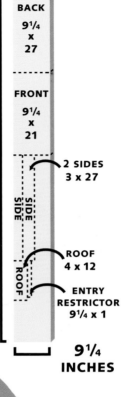

8 FEET

BACK
9¼
x
27

FRONT
9¼
x
21

SIDE
SIDE

ROOF
ROOF

2 SIDES
3 x 27

ROOF
4 x 12

ENTRY
RESTRICTOR
9¼ x 1

9¼
INCHES

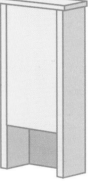

Bird's-eye View

"A few years ago, my husband built a large bird-feeding platform just outside our sunroom window. My daughter, Cassidy, then age five, and I visited our local nature center and picked up several copies of a pamphlet identifying backyard birds. I had these guides laminated so that we could use them as place mats. We also set up Cassidy's old baby monitor outside near the feeder, keeping the speaker inside so we could hear the birds' various cries and calls. We were then able to enjoy breakfast each morning while watching, listening to, and identifying the birds as they dined outside."

— Julie Slover,
Rogersville, Missouri

Backyard Projects

CHAPTER NINE

Gardening With Kids

Garden projects your kids will dig, from growing a sunflower fort to planting a butterfly garden

Witness a seven-year-old gathering wildflowers or a preschooler intently probing the vegetable bed for worms, and you can see the special relationship kids have with gardens. Here may be the most kid-friendly environment on earth — a place where dirt and water aren't off-limits, where surprises lurk beneath every leaf, and where all you need to succeed is a seed, some soil, and a smattering of sun.

But that doesn't mean you can hand your four-year-old a hoe and expect him to gleefully weed the flower border. What kids like most about gardening isn't the quotidian stuff — the watering, fertilizing, and all those other chores that demand regular attention — but the garden's magic: how you can stick a tiny seed in the ground and end up with a vine full of tomatoes or a ten-foot sunflower.

The garden projects in this chapter tap into that sense of wonder. From growing a cucumber in a bottle (page 184) to planting a friendly scarecrow (page 182), we

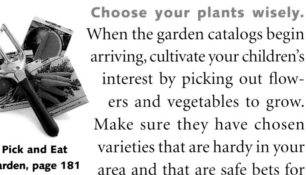

Pick and Eat Garden, page 181

hope each project will not only make your garden a more enchanting place to spend time together, but will also spark a love of growing things that lasts a lifetime.

So as you head out to your garden this year, don't forget to take your kids along. But before you get down and dirty, review these garden basics.

Choose your plants wisely. When the garden catalogs begin arriving, cultivate your children's interest by picking out flowers and vegetables to grow. Make sure they have chosen varieties that are hardy in your area and that are safe bets for beginners to grow successfully. Generally, kids have the easiest time handling large seeds (gourds and watermelon, for instance) and like the quick reward of early risers (radishes and cucumbers). If you want more instant gratification, buy starter plants at a garden store or farmer's market (put them in the ground, and — presto! — you have a garden).

Give kids a little space. Let your child test her green thumb with a garden of her own. Even a small patch or a window box can be enough to grow fresh flowers and vegetables. If you already have a garden, let her cordon off a corner with small stakes and string or rows of pebbles. Or give her space in the yard for a specific garden project, such as growing the sunflower sunroom on page 189.

Teach kids how to be good gardeners. Help your child develop a sense of responsibility for her garden by giving her simple kid chores in the family garden, such as watering, decorating garden signs, cutting flowers, and, of course, giving garden tours to friends and neighbors. If she has her own plot, explain that you will be there to help her, but like a pet, the garden will be her responsibility. Although you will shoulder some of the work, it is important for kids to exercise stewardship for their green, growing things.

Start a family garden book. In a three-ring binder, keep all your important gardening notes — and memories — to refer to year after year. Start with the basic garden plans from each year (plans can be made on graph paper with a pencil, correctly noting the proportions of the plot and labeling the plants). Keep records of the perennials in your garden and when they bloom. You can also cut out pictures and cultivating instructions from garden catalogs — or keep actual seed packets — and slip them into the binder. Your kids can add diaries of their plant's growth, drawings, photographs, and even some flowers, pressed and dried.

Gardening Essentials

Caring for a garden is a labor of love. But to make sure your labor pays off, review our tips.

- **Tools.** To encourage budding gardeners, invest in kid-size gardening tools.
- **Climate.** Discuss with your child each plant's compatibility with your climate and soil, and show her a plant hardiness map. Talk about the amount of water, sunshine, fertilizer, or compost you'll need for your plants.
- **Soil.** In the springtime, test the soil by squeezing a handful. If it crumbles, rather than packs together, it's ready to till. Preparing the soil is mainly a grown-up job. If you don't know the details, look for a garden reference book at your local library.
- **Weeding.** Teach your child to differentiate weeds from plants and demonstrate how to pull up weeds by the roots.
- **Watering.** Water the garden during dry spells with a hose, sprinkler, or can, being sure to moisten the soil thoroughly so the plants' roots can drink their fill. Concentrate on watering the dirt, not the leaves. This is best done in the cool evening.

Vegetable Gardening

Pick and Eat Garden

Garden projects satisfy our hunger for fun, but what about real hunger? For that, we recommend a pick-and-eat garden, a fast-food spot that may actually get kids to eat their vegetables. Look for varieties that can go from vine to mouth with just a quick wash with the garden hose. Some top picks:

Peas. Try the compact varieties that don't require trellising, like Sugar Ann or Improved Laxton's Progress.

Pole beans. Kentucky Wonder and Kentucky Blue are both dependable varieties that produce long, tender, stringless beans. Create a tepee of bamboo stakes for them to climb.

Cherry tomatoes. Try Super Sweet 100 because they're easy for

small hands to harvest. Ask for seedlings at your local garden center. Plant in cages or stake.

Radishes. Kids may find them spicy to eat, but few crops grow faster. Plus, it's fun to yank them from the earth. Try the Easter Egg II variety.

Strawberries. Being perennials, these are a more long-term investment. But what sweet dividends. Try

the Alpine or ever-bearing variety.

Cucumbers. Grow slicers, such as Sweet Success, for snacking and making tea sandwiches, or try picklers, such as Country Fair.

Peppers. Kids love bell peppers, which start off green, then change to red when fully ripened.

Pizza Garden

What's the recipe for the perfect kid-friendly garden? Pizza! Here's how to plant your favorite pizza ingredients in a wooden barrel.

MATERIALS

Large stone

Small gravel pieces or stone

Half whiskey barrel (available at garden supply stores)

About 65 pounds of potting soil

5 pounds of compost

Seedlings (basil, oregano, tomato)

Wooden spoon and acrylic paints

Place the large stone over the top of the barrel's drainage hole and then make a layer of gravel or stone 1 to 2 inches deep in the bottom of the barrel. Fill the barrel with a mixture of potting soil and compost to within 3 inches of the rim.

Transplant your pizza ingredient seedlings to the barrel (we used basil, oregano, and tomato, but you could also try peppers, garlic, or eggplant, depending on your crew's choice of pizza toppings). Stake the tomatoes, if necessary.

Set your barrel in a sunny spot and water regularly.

For a pizza garden sign, decorate

the wooden spatula with acrylic paints. Allow the paints to dry, then place the handle several inches deep in the soil.

center of the plot to a depth of about 12 inches. To form the frame for the skirt, push the garden stakes into the soil in a circle about 2 feet out from the center pole, slanting them inward, and at a depth of 10 to 12 inches. There should be a roughly equal distance between each stake. Gather the eight garden stakes together tepee style around the center stake and lash them in place securely with garden wire.

3. For the arms, position the 48-inch stake horizontally about 10 to 12 inches down from the top of the center stake and lash together the two with garden wire, crisscrossing the wire around both stakes until the horizontal stake doesn't wobble. Slip the shirt onto Mrs. Green Beans's arms and button it to the top. Tie the scarf around her waist.

4. To make a resting spot for the head, cut two sticks to about 5 inches long, then lash them on each side of the center pole, about 4 inches from the top. Using the craft foam and glue, create a face on one side of the terra-cotta pot. When the glue is dry, fill the pot nearly to the top with potting soil, then add the plants and water well. Place the flowerpot head onto the center stake by slipping the hole in the pot's bottom over the stake.

5. Plant three to six bean seeds around each garden stake according to the package directions. When the seedlings are 2 to 3 inches high, thin them to one plant per pole. In a few weeks' time, the young plants will begin to twine their way around the stakes, forming Mrs. Green Beans's skirt. If the vines eventually get too high, you can trim them or train them to grow back down through the skirt.

GARDEN NOVELTY

Mrs. Green Beans

With her bean-vine skirt and hair that really grows, this garden giant is a scarecrow that your kids will fall in love with. Plant your seeds at the end of May (or whenever the time is right where you live), and you'll see a full skirt of foliage by mid-July. Not only is she attractive, Mrs. Green Beans also offers the bonus of a three-month harvest.

MATERIALS

Spading fork or hand cultivator
Fertilizer (check with your garden
    store for recommendations)
2 garden stakes, one 48 inches high
    and one at least 72 inches high
    (you can also use straight
    branches)
8 72-inch garden stakes

Garden wire
Button-down shirt and scarf
2 sticks, each at least 5 inches long
Craft foam and Elmer's Stix All glue
8-inch-diameter terra-cotta pot
Potting soil
2 to 3 prestarted plants with showy
    foliage, such as dusty miller or
    gazania
1 package of pole bean seeds (we
    used Blue Lake)

1. For this project, you'll need a sunny patch of earth that's about 4 feet square. Loosen the soil to a depth of 8 to 12 inches with a spading fork or hand cultivator and add fertilizer. (If possible, fertilize 2 to 3 days before planting seeds.)

2. Drive the taller stake into the

Trash Can Potatoes

Harvesting potatoes is a little
like hunting for Easter eggs: toss
aside the withered vines, reach
down into the soil, and see what the
Spud Bunny's left for you. And as if
searching for treasure elbow deep in
dirt weren't reward enough, this
project offers kids a lesson in the
importance of soil — in this case, a
magical mixture of compost and sand
that almost guarantees a bumper crop.

MATERIALS

Drill
Metal trash can
Sand
Compost
Fertilizer
Seed potatoes

Drill or cut 6½-inch-diameter
holes in the bottom of the trash can (a
parent's job). Set the can in a sunny
outdoor location and fill it 1 foot deep
with a mixture of 1 part sand to 3 parts
compost (potatoes like their soil rich
but light and airy, and they don't like
to sit in water, which is where the sand
comes in). Mix in the fertilizer.

Place the seed potatoes on top of
the soil, each about 6 inches in from
the edge of the can, with at least one
of the eyes (the bumpy protrusions)

facing up. Cover the potatoes with
another 6 to 8 inches of compost–
sand mixture, then water well.

Keep the soil evenly moist. When
the vines are about 2 weeks old, cover
all but the top inch with additional
compost and sand. Continue burying
the vines every 2 weeks until they've
reached the top of the can, then let
them grow. When the vines wither in
the fall, gently pull them up, roll up
your sleeves, and start hunting!

CONTAINER GARDENING
Tomato-in-a-tire Planter

If your family loves the taste of fresh
tomatoes, but you just don't have
the space, time, or inclination to prepare an entire garden bed, here's a
great solution. Lay an old, scrubbed-
out tire on its sidewall and then fill
the center with loose, airy soil. Drive
a garden stake through the soil-filled
center and into the ground. Then
plant your tomato seedlings. The tire
will keep the soil moist and warm
while your tomato plant grows.

Cuke in a Bottle

Show your kids how to have fun in the garden with this horticultural sleight of hand. Their friends will be in a pickle wondering how they managed to squeeze a big vegetable through a skinny bottle neck.

MATERIALS

1 packet of cucumber seeds
12-ounce or 1-liter plastic soda bottle, with cap
Vinegar
Pickling spices (optional)

When the soil is warm (late May to early June in most areas), sow your seeds in small hills, four to five per hill. When the seedlings are about 3 inches high, thin to two to three plants per hill. Cukes like full sun and room to sprawl, but you can save space by growing them on a fence or trellis. Make sure they receive at least an inch of water a week.

After the first yellow blossoms have appeared, start searching for tiny young cucumbers. Choose one at the bottom of the plant; the upper leaves will provide shade and keep the cuke from "cooking" in the bottle. Gently slip the bottle over the baby cucumber. Save the bottle cap and, for best results, shade the bottle slightly with a sheet of newspaper secured with a few rocks.

Once the cuke reaches a suitably impressive size, snip it off the vine and fill the bottle with vinegar (it acts as a preservative). Add pickling spices for that authentic deli look and replace the cap. As tempting as the pickle may be, it should not be eaten (how would you get it out, anyway?). Instead, keep it in the fridge — taking it out regularly to confound your friends and neighbors.

Tattooed Pumpkins

Pumpkins, by their very nature, are magical: from one tiny seed, you can produce a vine of gargantuan proportions, with flowers and fruit to match. To extend the charm a bit, try this project that allows you to create one-of-a-kind personalized pumpkins as easily as writing your name.

MATERIALS

1 packet of pumpkin seeds (we used Jack-o'-Lantern)
Church-key-type can opener (or slim metal skewer)

Plant the seeds according to the packet directions. When the pumpkins just start to show orange streaks, your child can use a can opener or skewer to gently etch his name into the rind. Try not to go much deeper than about ⅛ inch or you could hurt the pumpkin. Your child can personalize his pumpkins in other ways too, from drawing on a jack-o'-lantern face to scratching in his favorite sports logos. Be sure to leave the etched side up to help prevent rot. As the pumpkin gets bigger and ripens, the etching will become a tan scar.

Gardening With Kids

Flower Gardening

Child's Flower Garden

Giving your child his own flower garden offers just the right balance of big dreams and little tasks. A small garden of annual flowers is easy to take care of, and he will learn many skills as he nurtures seedlings and cuts bouquets for the kitchen table.

Creating a Plot
The ideal plot for a child's annuals is something like your kids: small and special. You and your child can section off a corner of a larger garden, build a flower box, or dig completely new beds. In any case, a sunny plot of 16 square feet or even smaller will do fine. A traditional rectangle is a cinch to dig and will have clearly marked, straight beds that are easy to weed. A border garden works nicely if it is narrow enough for kids to reach to the back without stepping on flowers in the front. A circular design accommodates a fanciful border, pie-slice flower beds, and a perfect birdbath spot. Designate clear paths through your garden by spreading sweet-smelling cedar chips or lining them with stones. Besides being irresistible to kids, pathways keep eager gardeners from trampling new shoots.

Choosing What to Grow
With a plot plan in mind, sit your family down with a pile of seed catalogs and gardening books. Your child is likely to be entranced by rosebushes and splashy perennials, but steer him toward bright, cheerful, easy-to-grow annuals, such as **cosmos, marigolds, zinnias, nasturtiums, pansies, sunflowers, and snap-dragons**. These low-maintenance flowers produce beautiful blossoms until summer's end, so they are more likely to give your child sustained satisfaction.

Planting the Flowers
Whether you start plants from seeds or seedlings depends on your budget, your kids' ages, and your patience. If you and your child decide to plant seeds outside, choose those that germinate easily. Starting with seedlings is more expensive, but you often can see exactly what the color scheme will look like as you lay out your garden. Regardless, be sure to plant taller flowers in the back of your garden and shorter ones in the front.

Cutting the Flowers
Regularly cutting flowers and removing spent blossoms is healthy for plants — and in many cases makes them bloom more profusely. Clip stems with a sharp knife (parents only) or a good pair of clippers, and always cut on a slant. Cut flowers last longest if kept in cool water in a cool room.

Plant a Theme Garden

Marigold heart: Say "I love you" to the garden — with marigolds, that is. In a sunny spot, sketch out a large heart in the soil. Place marigold seeds (we like Burpee's Jaguar, but any of the smaller varieties will do) within the lines of the sketch at about 3-inch intervals. Water and wait for your valentine from Mother Nature.

Surprise your senses: Herb gardens don't just look great; they smell, taste, feel, and even sound good. Consider lavender or sweet alyssum for your nose, mint for your taste buds, woolly lamb's ears for your fingers, and money plant for your ears (when the seed heads dry, they rattle).

Pansy plot: Pansies thrive even in chilly weather. Plant starters in early spring, and within days — really — they will bloom in every color of your child's crayon box. Look for pansies, violas, or Johnny-jump-ups, the thimble-size varieties.

Bulb garden: This fall, plant bulbs (tulips, hyacinths, crocuses, daffodils, and snowdrops) for spring blossoms. Plant bulbs 4 to 8 inches deep in a sunny area — then wait for spring to arrive.

Sunflower Scrapbook

If you think your kids grow quickly, you haven't planted any sunflowers recently. Their dizzying ascent from tiny seedling to garden giant is nothing short of miraculous. For proof, try measuring your child against a sunflower this summer: with the two standing side by side, take a photo every couple of weeks, noting the height of both child and plant. For big, dependable plants, we especially like Mammoth sunflowers, which can grow up to 12 feet high.

At the end of the summer, you can memorialize your photos, and corresponding measurements, in a sunflower scrapbook. (You can even embellish the book with your child's crayoned sunflower portraits, along with pressed petals from the real thing.) When the heads are dry, let the plants stand for a few weeks to feed the birds.

A Sunroom

You don't need a hammer and nails, or even wood, to build this pretty house — just a handful of sunflower seeds.

Any time after the last frost is prime growing season. Use a mix of Mammoth sunflower seeds (for height) and Teddy Bear or Dwarf sunflower seeds (to fill in the walls). Following package directions for planting, set the seeds in a horseshoe shape. Choose a sunny plot where the soil is dry and drains well (sunflowers can take the heat but will suffer from overwatering).

While waiting for the seeds to sprout (it takes 2 to 3 weeks in warm temperatures), spruce up the grounds around the house site, laying a stone walkway to its door or making a Welcome sign.

Growing Sunflowers

These beauties attract butterflies and produce seeds to feed the birds. Mammoths can grow 12 feet tall and shade other crops, so plant seeds on your garden plot's north side and tie the stems to bamboo poles. Dwarf sunflowers are a nice alternative for window boxes.

Fairy Chair

Why not give your garden fairies a pretty place to perch? Plant morning glory seeds under an old chair and watch them fully bloom.

MATERIALS

An old chair, preferably one that's past its prime (only fairies will sit in it) but sturdy enough to survive the elements
Exterior paint in one or more colors
Paintbrushes
1 packet of morning glory seeds

Give your chair one or two base coats of paint (we chose lavender for both its magical properties and the way it complements green). If you like, you can accent the chair with other colors.

When the paint is dry, place the chair in the garden where it will receive full to partial sun. Make sure there's loosened garden soil around the legs of the chair.

A few inches out from each chair leg, plant three to six morning glory seeds, following the directions on the seed packet. When the morning glories just start to twine, thin them down to one or two plants per chair leg.

Water the plants regularly, especially in full sun — and keep an eye out for fairy footprints.

GARDEN NOVELTY
Moon Garden

Just like some people, there are flowers that work the night shift. That is, they open up after dark. Here are a couple of varieties you and your kids can plant in your yard that will add a soft glow and sweet fragrance to your summer evenings.

Pink Evening Primrose: This quick-spreading perennial has 2-inch blossoms that range from soft pink to white. It likes partial shade or full sun and blooms through July.

Moonflower: Cousin to the morning glory, this large-faced white perennial flower has a pleasant lemony scent and opens at dusk (although the vine thrives in full sun). It can grow 10 or more feet long, making it a prime candidate to plant against a fence or trellis.

FamilyFun **Home**

QUICK GARDEN PROJECT
Doorstep Garden

Welcome guests on your front steps with flowers — favorite annuals planted in an old boot.

Remove the lace from the boot or loosen it enough to allow the tongue to be pulled forward, as shown. Fill the bottom of the boot with a layer of pebbles or aquarium gravel to provide drainage. Then pack in a 2-inch layer of potting soil or loam.

Now fit in the root base of a small bunch of annual flowers (pansies, marigolds, or impatiens work well for this project). Gently pack more soil around and on top of the roots.

Remember to water the flowers regularly (unlike those that are planted in the ground, these blooms cannot draw moisture from the surrounding soil).

WEEKEND PROJECT
Very Special Seeds

Seed-saving is the perfect nature science activity. Kids will find the process of turning this year's blossoms into next year's seeds endlessly fascinating. To add to the fun, use markers and crayons to create your own personalized seed packets.

Among the flowers that are the most reliable to grow and easiest to harvest are morning glory, cornflower, cosmos, impatiens, marigold, sunflower, and zinnia. Start collecting your seeds in late August or any time you spy mature seed heads.

MATERIALS

Flowers that are going to seed
Clippers or scissors
Bowl or paper bag
Small manila envelopes
Photographs of your flowers
Crayons and markers
Plastic storage container with lid

To harvest the seeds, pull or clip the seed heads from the plant, holding a bowl or paper bag underneath (if you're saving more than one variety, mark the container to avoid mix-ups).

Indoors, open the seed heads over newspaper, discarding the chaff (the seed coverings and other debris). Let the seeds dry on the newspaper in a cool, well-ventilated space for 2 to 3 weeks. (We've sometimes skipped this step, and most of our seeds sprouted anyway.)

Meanwhile, decorate your envelopes with photographs of the mature flowers, noting the flower's name and the year grown with markers and crayons.

Pour in the seeds, seal the envelopes, and place them in a plastic container with a lid. Store your seeds in a cool, dry place like your refrigerator or the basement.

Butterfly Garden

In the flower garden in Stephen Swimburne's Vermont yard (shown here), the butterflies have arrived: monarchs on the zinnias. White admirals on the purple coneflowers. Fritillaries on the black-eyed Susans. Stephen and his daughters Hayley and Devon attracted these gentle visitors by planting precisely the types of nectar-producing flowers that butterflies love. To plant your own butterfly garden, follow these tips from Stephen and his family.

Find a site: The first step is to find a site for your butterfly garden, ideally one that receives at least 6 hours of sun a day and offers shelter from the wind. You don't need acres of land for a butterfly garden. Stephen's plot was a modest 5 by 10 feet in his front yard, beside a protective picket fence. A nearby row of shrubs or evergreen trees, or even a rock, also could have served as a wind block.

Choose your flowers: Find out what butterflies live in your area (look in a guidebook at your library or nature center). This will help you determine what flowers you should grow. Then, using a garden book, pick the nectar-producing flowers most likely to attract those butterflies, as well as the flowers that will grow well

FamilyFun **Home**

in your region. In Stephen's New England garden, he planted five annuals (ageratum, impatiens, marigold, zinnia, and cosmos) and five perennials (coreopsis, butterfly weed, purple coneflower, black-eyed Susan, and bee balm). Many other plants could have worked equally well, but this selection gave him fast-growing flowers in a range of colors and heights and guaranteed that something would be in bloom throughout the growing seasons. **Tip:** Choose plants with the nectar needs of adult butterflies in mind; butterfly larvae, or caterpillars,

eat the leaves and seeds of other plants and herbs, such as milkweed, pussy willow, violets, and dill. Grow these as well and you may encourage visiting butterflies to breed and lay eggs.

Planting the garden: Once you know what flowers you will be growing, draw up a plan with the proper flower spacing (your gardening book will have this information). Till the soil with a garden fork. Stephen added peat moss, creating a loose, fluffy soil for the tender roots of his young plants. Plant short flowers up front and tall ones in the back. This design works visually and keeps both low-feeding and high-feeding butterflies happy.

Maintaining the garden: Give the ground a daily soaking. The butterflies suck the wet soil for salts and fluids, a behavior known as puddling. Generally, butterflies are attracted to large masses of color. So try planting groups of flowers rather than single plants. And keep your butterfly garden pesticide-free.

LEARNING AT HOME
Butterfly Cuisine

A quartet of summer visitors: 1. A monarch uses its long proboscis like a drinking straw to suck nectar from a zinnia, perhaps fueling up for its 2,000-mile migration to its winter home in Mexico. 2. A white admiral gathers the nectar of a purple coneflower. It also eats rotting fruit, dung, tree sap, and carrion. 3. A fritillary also enjoys the nectar of purple coneflowers. 4. A Milbert's tortoiseshell stops on a marigold. These wide-ranging butterflies overwinter as adults in hollow trees or log piles. While the average life span of butterflies is just a few weeks, the tortoiseshell may live 5 months or longer.

Planting Trees

Grow a Kid-size Tree

This spring, help your child plant a tree that's as tall as he is and then compare growth spurts as future spring seasons pass. (You may want to snap photos of the duo — the tree and child — each spring for family history's sake.) For information on which trees grow best in your area, contact your local garden center or visit The National Arbor Day Foundation's website (www.arborday.org).

MATERIALS

Tree seedling (from a local garden center)
Shovel and rake
Garden hose or large bucket
Peat moss or compost
Mulch

1. When buying your tree seedling, be sure it appears healthy, with branches spreading evenly from a single stem. The buds should be full and green inside. Most important, it must have a compact, abundant root system. Watch out for any abrasions, or discolorations on the trunk that could mean an injury, and be sure the bark on the trunk and branches is not shriveled.

2. At home, you should try to get the seedling in the ground as soon as possible. Most sites need some preparation before you plant the seedling. If you have rich, loose soil, all you need to do is dig a hole 6 inches wider than the spread of the roots. In many places, however, the soil will be heavy and compacted or composed of thick clay. In this case, you will need to dig a hole two or three times as wide as the root ball. This will give the roots room to grow out around the tree. The hole should not be any deeper than the root system. Make sure the sides of the hole are rough; roots can't penetrate a smooth wall. Roughing up the sides is a good job for small hands using a trowel or stick.

3. Place your tree gently into the hole and let it rest at the same ground level as it grew at the nursery. Make sure the bare trunk is not below ground level and that all roots are covered. If necessary, adjust the level by taking out or adding soil under the roots. For container-grown trees, carefully cut away the container. When planting a bare-rooted tree or a container-grown seedling whose roots have started growing around the container in a circle, you need to untangle the roots delicately and spread them out in the hole. Burlap does not need to be taken off balled roots, but the string and any plastic covering must be removed.

4. If you have extra-thick soil or heavy clay, a good trick is to mix peat moss or compost into your soil pile before you begin filling in the hole. In any case, as you fill the hole around the roots with soil, tamp down the dirt every few shovelfuls and give it an occasional complete watering. Continue alternating filling and tamping until the ground is level and the tree is standing straight. If the tree does not stand upright on its own, loose stake lines can be used with wide straps around the trunk, but these must be removed within 6 months to a year.

5. Give the tree one more thorough soaking. Add about 2 to 3 inches of mulch over the planting area, but don't mulch the area right next to the trunk. Now stand back and admire the new life you have added to the earth.

Family Trees

Mother's Day Tree: A flowering tree, such as a magnolia or dogwood, makes a lasting Mother's or Father's Day gift. If you time it right, you will have blossoms for your celebrations year after year.

New House: When you move into a new house, plant a seedling tree — and watch the tree grow along with the memories in your new home. Someday, the tree may even become a cherished climbing tree for your children's children.

Birthday Tree: Welcome a new baby into the world by planting a strong oak tree during his or her birthday month. As your newborn grows, the fragile seedling will grow into a mature tree.

FAMILYFUN SUCCESS STORY

Tiny Trees

"Last year, my daughters, Julia, then age seven, and Olivia, then four, grew their own tiny Christmas trees. We soaked pinecones in water for a few minutes, then packed them with potting soil — and plenty of grass seed. We placed the pinecones in plastic containers with a bit of water, set them in the sun, and sprayed them daily with a plant mister. After two weeks, we had mini green trees."

— Beth Powanda
Santa Cruz, California

Water Gardening

Lily's Pond

Lily, the daughter of *FamilyFun* contributor Leslie Garisto Pfaff, is a natural in the garden. And because the only thing she enjoys more than being covered in compost is being up to her knees in a pond, Leslie devised an inspired project to engage not just Lily but also the entire family: a water garden, complete with lilies (what else?), floating plants and fish and, of course, water. All you need to create your own water garden like Lily's pond is a watertight container, water plants from a local nursery, and an adventurous spirit. **Safety note:** Parents of younger children should keep in mind the potential hazards of open water.

MATERIALS

- **Half whiskey barrel (or similar container)**
- **5- by 5-foot EPDM or other synthetic tub liner**
- **Staple gun**
- **Hammer**
- **Water plants (see page 199)**
- **Terra-cotta or plastic pots (8-inch pots for the parrot's feather, dwarf taro, and dwarf sweet flag; a 12-inch pot for the lily)**
- **Topsoil**
- **Granular 5-10-5 garden fertilizer**
- **Pebbles or sand**
- **5 to 8 bricks**
- **12 to 20 broken quarry stones (or other decorative pond edging)**
- **Goldfish, snails, tadpoles**
- **Wood and chicken wire for nightly cover (optional)**

1. Begin your project by visiting an aquatic nursery to choose water plants. (You can also shop via catalog; see Water Garden Resource Guide, page 199). For a small water garden, choose

plants that don't mind tight quarters. Also, pick plants that are functional as well as good-looking (see Guide to Water Plants, page 199). Leslie recommends oxygen-producing parrot's feather, floating fairy moss, and duckweed; for so-called marginals, she likes decorative dwarf taro and grasslike sweet flag. And because Leslie couldn't imagine a pond without a lily, she chose the variety Mary Patricia.

2. Dig a hole for your whiskey barrel in a level patch of ground that gets at least 4 to 6 hours of full sun a day

(water lilies, especially, are sun lovers). Leave a 1-inch gap around the sides. If you don't have a suitable bit of ground, you can set the container on a sunny porch or patio.

3. Line your barrel with synthetic rubber sheeting (available at many large garden centers) to make it watertight. Our barrel required a 5- by 5-foot section of sheeting. Set the liner in the container and trim the excess, leaving at least 6 inches overhanging the top. Fold over and staple the liner into position with a staple gun, trying

to minimize the size of any unsightly folds. Then, tap the staples with a hammer. **Tip:** Hold the liner in place by partially filling the barrel with water. After trimming and stapling the liner, bail out the barrel to move it to its final location.

4. Sink the lined container into the hole and fill it with water that has been warmed in a clean trash can for 48 hours. This waiting period helps rid the water of chlorine — a must if you plan to stock your pond with fish. Use some of the newly dug soil as backfill to close the gaps around the barrel.

5. Transplant the plants from their nursery packaging into terra-cotta pots. Because conventional potting soil is too light and porous for aquatic plants, use heavy topsoil, mixing in granular 5-10-5 garden fertilizer (1 tablespoon for lilies, 1 teaspoon per pot for the others). You can also pot the parrot's feather, just to keep it anchored neatly (it can also float). With oxygenating plants, however, there's no need to add fertilizer.

6. Mulch the top of each pot with a half inch of pebbles (you can also use sand) to keep the topsoil in the pots and out of the pond water.

7. Slowly sink each pot into the pond, tilting all slightly to allow air to escape and keep the topsoil from muddying the water. Set any water lilies right on the bottom of the barrel; the other plants can be placed on stacked bricks so the pot rims are just 2 inches below the surface. Toss the floating duckweed and fairy moss into the pond.

8. To give the pond a finished look, line the edge with broken quarry stones (available at garden centers). You can also use bricks, slate, or anything else that appeals to you and suits your overall landscape.

9. Release the goldfish, tadpoles, and snails (voracious bottom feeders that will vacuum away unwanted organic matter) into their new home. Once your garden is up and running, keep an eye out for dragonflies skimming and hovering about the surface and tiny snails on the underside of lily pads.

10. The only real maintenance required for the pond is topping off the water weekly to compensate for evaporation, monthly fertilizing of the lily and marginals (easy-to-use tablets are available at aquatic nurseries), mucking out the prolific duckweed — a delightfully yucky chore that a kid will likely perform enthusiastically — and feeding the fish (which could actually survive on mosquito eggs and duckweed). To deter nocturnal marauders like raccoons who could feast on your fish, you may want to devise a wood-and-chicken-wire cage to set over the pond at night (weight it with bricks). Finally, unless you live in a warm climate, you'll have to empty the pond before the first frost, but many of its plants can overwinter indoors, and others are inexpensive enough to be purchased anew in the spring.

Dwarf taro

Parrot's feather

Water lily

Duckweed

Dwarf variegated
sweet flag
(not visible)

Fairy moss (underwater)

Guide to Water Plants

To promote a healthy ecosystem, be sure to stock your pond with at least one oxygen-producing plant (to keep the fish happy and stagnation at bay) and some floating varieties (to shade the water from algae-inducing sunlight). Only about 25 percent of the water's surface should remain uncovered. Here are the plants we chose.

Water lily: The flowery centerpiece of our water garden. All you need is one plant, a small- to medium-size variety, in any color you'd like.

Duckweed: A shade-producing floater that also provides an ample source of food for the pond's goldfish.

Parrot's feather: An ethereal-looking oxygenator with delicate foliage.

Fairy moss: Another shade-producing floater — with a magical name.

Dwarf taro: Nicknamed elephant's ear (for obvious reasons), this so-called marginal provides a sense of height in the garden.

Dwarf variegated sweet flag: Another decorative denizen of the water's edge, with pretty, grasslike foliage.

Water Garden Resource Guide

Catalogs: The following suppliers offer a range of water garden accessories: Waterford Gardens (201-327-0721), Lilypons (800-365-5459), and Van Ness Water Gardens (800-205-2425).

Books: For more information on water gardening, check out *The American Horticultural Society Complete Guide to Water Gardening* by Peter Robinson (DK Publishing) and *Water Gardening in Containers: Small Ponds Indoors & Out* by C. Greg Speichert and Helen Nash (Sterling Publishers).

Garden Crafts

DECORATE IT
Garden Stones

This clever craft not only dresses up your garden (and helps you ID all the newly sprouted seedlings in your vegetable patch), it also finally offers a way to use that annual crop of garden rocks.

MATERIALS

Smooth rocks in various shapes and sizes

Waterproof acrylic paints and paintbrushes

First, rinse the rocks to remove any dirt and let them dry. Apply a base coat of acrylic paint to the top and sides of each rock. We painted our rocks to match the colors of the vegetables themselves.

When the base coat is dry, your child can decorate the rocks with the name of the appropriate flower or vegetable. In addition to row markers, we also created some purely decorative rocks (for example, a "welcome to my garden" rock). For flourishes and lettering, we especially liked the look of black paint. When the paint is dry, place your rocks in the garden.

PAINTING PROJECT
Garden Apron

Cultivating a green thumb takes practice, patience, and a few handy accessories, like this personalized apron your child can wear to keep all her garden tools within reach.

Buy a canvas carpenter's apron at your local hardware store. While you're there, pick up a pair of cotton gloves to use for weeding. At home, your child can decorate the set with fabric paints. Brush on a garden design, such as a row of bright yellow sunflowers or a bunch of carrots. Or slice an onion and a pepper into halves, dip them in the paint, and embellish the set with vegetable prints. Fill the pockets with seed packets, a garden trowel, and a plastic misting bottle. Use pinch-style clothespins to clip the gloves to the front of the apron when they're not being worn.

FamilyFun **Home**

Stepping-stones

This garden path offers a concrete method of preserving your most precious harvest: happy memories. Each family member gets to decorate his or her own stone, inserting personal (nonperishable) mementos: seashells, pet rocks, small toys, impressions of a favorite leaf, free-form "tiles" made from a broken flowerpot — if you can step on it, you can preserve it.

If you've never worked with concrete before, don't be daunted. Mixing mortar, in fact, is a lot like preparing cookie dough. **Safety note:** Concrete contains portland cement, a potentially caustic substance, so the job of mixing the stuff is strictly for grown-ups. After making handprints, be sure to wash with soap and water.

MATERIALS

12-inch-diameter cardboard building form and small handsaw (optional)
Spade
Small stones or gravel
Concrete mortar mix such as Quikrete (a 60-pound bag will yield 3 stones)
Mixing tub or bucket
Hoe
Trowel
Scrap of wood
Mementos
Craft knife

Making the molds: For round stepping-stones, use the handsaw to cut a 2½-inch-wide section from the building form. In the area where you'll be setting the path, dig a hole just large enough to accommodate the form and set it into the ground, firming the soil around it. Alternatively, you can create a free-form stone by simply digging a hole in the shape you desire, roughly 2½ inches deep. Once the mold is complete, place a 1-inch layer of pebbles, small stones, or gravel in the bottom.

Mixing the concrete: Following the directions on the bag, combine the concrete with water in a mixing tub and stir them together with a hoe. It's ready to pour when the mix doesn't fall off a hoe held nearly parallel to the ground. Use the hoe and a trowel, if

necessary, to scoop the concrete into each form (photo 1). Smooth the surface with a scrap of wood.

Adding mementos: When your fingertip leaves a lasting impression in the mixture (usually after 1 to 2 hours), you can start customizing.

Using a stick or pebbles, write your name and the date, make impressions (of your hand, a favorite toy, a prize begonia), and add your mementos (photo 2). Let the stones cure for several days. If your winters are severe, cover the stones with a cloth and mist them with water several times a day for 3 or 4 days to keep them from cracking. Remove the cardboard forms with a craft knife.

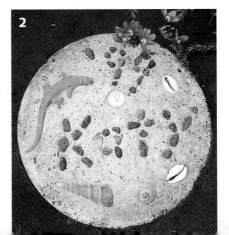

them well watered. You'll need two to three good-size plants to give you enough dried nip to fill the mouse. (If you're worried about neighborhood cat burglars, you can sow seeds or plant starters in plastic pots and haul them in at night once the plants get going.)

When the first tiny flower buds appear, pull the entire catnip plant out of the soil. Cut off the roots, then tie the stems together with a rubber band or raffia. Hang the bundles upside down to dry in a cool, well-ventilated, cat-free area. The catnip is ready to use when the leaves crunch between your fingers.

Making the mouse:

1. Using scissors, cut off the toe section of the child's sock up to the heel, as shown. Also cut two mouse

ear shapes from the felt scraps and cut a teardrop shape from the plastic stock, all as shown.

2. Then insert the plastic teardrop into the sock (it serves to hold the mouse's shape) and fill the sock with the dry, crumbled catnip leaf. Turn back the sock's edge and, with the cotton yarn and darning needle, lay a

running stitch around the opening, as shown. Draw the yarn tight to close the opening.

3. Tie off the cotton yarn, leaving the extra for the tail. Sew on the felt ears and create embroidery floss whiskers, as shown.

MAKE-IT-YOURSELF

Catnip Mouse

If the only catnip your kids have ever seen comes in a cardboard box, they'll be amazed at its lush, green garden incarnation. With this project, kids can use their homegrown plant to make their beloved cat a present that will leave him feline groovy.

MATERIALS

For filling

- **1 packet of catnip seeds, or 2 or 3 catnip starter plants**
- **13-inch plastic pots and enough potting mix to fill (optional)**

Rubber bands or raffia

For mouse

- **1 child's sock**
- **Felt scraps**
- **Plastic from milk or detergent jug**
- **Cotton yarn**
- **Darning needle**
- **Black embroidery floss**

Growing the catnip:

Sow a dozen or so seeds (or plant your starters) in a sunny spot and keep

Tin Man

Every vegetable garden needs a scarecrow — and this heavy-metal-faced guard is well equipped to ruffle some feathers. The jangly hands and face are made with kitchen supplies.

MATERIALS

- 7-foot-long 2- by 3-inch wooden stud
- 3-foot-long ³/₄-inch dowel
- 1-foot-long ³/₄-inch dowel
- Large brass hooks
- Twine
- Metal spatula, measuring spoons (3 sets), coffeepot, saucepans (2), and colander
- Safety pins
- Blue jeans, suspenders, flappy shirt, and bandanna
- Drill and metal washers (optional)
- Wire

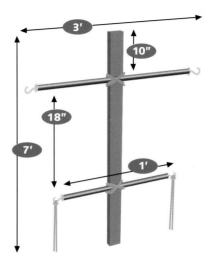

Set one end of the 7-foot-long wooden stud 18 inches into the ground. Next, screw large brass hooks into the ends of both dowels.

With the twine, tie the longer dowel to the stud 10 inches from the top, as shown. Hang metal spatula "forearms" from the hooks **(A)** and use safety pins to attach metal measuring spoon "fingers" to the spatulas **(B)**. Tie on the shorter dowel 18 inches below the top one. Loop leg-length pieces of twine around the hooks on the short dowel.

Dress the scarecrow in jeans, using suspenders to hang them from the "shoulder" dowel. Thread the twine through the legs and tie saucepan "boots" to the ends **(C)**. Button on a flappy shirt.

For a head, fit an inverted metal coffeepot atop the stud. Drill holes in its side and screw on metal washers for eyes. Tie a bandanna around the "neck." Cap it all off by using wire to firmly fasten a metal colander hat to the coffeepot handle and then attach measuring spoons for hair **(D)**.

Garden Web Site

In a contest for top gardener, we vote for the spider. Who else can eat its weight in bugs and decorate the garden in the process? Have your kids attract a few arachnid artists to your garden with this easy-to-make web frame.

MATERIALS

Handsaw
1 **¼- by 1½-inch wood furring**
    strip, at least 70 inches long
Sandpaper
Wood glue
Wire cutters
20-gauge copper wire (often sold
    in small 50-foot spools in
    hardware stores)
Hammer
1 **1½-inch nail**
1 **1- by 2-inch wooden stake,**
    at least 3 feet long
Acrylic paint and paintbrush

1. Saw the wood strip into four 13-inch pieces, two 7½-inch pieces, and two ¾-inch pieces (parents only). Sand any rough edges.

2. Lay the four 13-inch pieces in a square, allowing the edges to overlap at each corner by about ½ inch. Secure the corners with wood glue.

3. Using the wire cutters, cut four 30-inch lengths of copper wire. When the glue has dried, wrap one length of wire around each corner joint, forming an *X* pattern on the front of the wooden frame, as shown in the finished sign. Trim off any excess wire with the wire cutters.

4. To form a cozy nook for your spider to hide in, place the two 7½-inch strips diagonally across one corner of the square so that one strip is on the front of the frame and the other on the back; the tips should extend at least ¼ inch beyond the edges of the frame. To level the strips across the overlapping wood of the corner, slide a ¾-inch shim under each diagonal strip. Glue all the strips in place and let dry.

5. Using the wire cutters, cut two 24-inch lengths of copper wire. When the glue on the spider nook has dried, wrap the edges with wire as shown in the finished sign, trimming off any extra with the cutters.

6. Hammer the nail into the top of the stake until it protrudes about ¼ inch. Glue the stake to the back of the Web Site at the center of the bottom slat, making sure to position it so that the top of the nail is just level with the inside edge of the wooden frame. Let the glue dry.

7. Cut a 36-inch length of wire and use it to wrap the frame to the stake, as shown below, looping the wire tightly around the nail.

Paint the words "Web Site" on the front of the frame or decorate the frame with a suitably spidery motif. When the paint

is dry, you can take your Web Site out into the garden. Choose a spot among the flowers or vegetables that you can get to easily without trampling anything. Then insert the stake 3 to 6 inches into the soil until it's steady.

Like bakers and jazz musicians, most spiders do their best work at night, so mornings — especially dewy ones — are the perfect time for web observation.

Toad Abode

Your kids will dig this: a single toad, with flicks of its long, sticky tongue, can gobble up to 20,000 slugs, grubs, potato beetles, and other garden pests in a single year. So how can you lure a few toads to hang out around your plot? By setting up an easy-to-make, shady retreat for the helpful creatures.

Pick a spot in your garden that is protected from wind and where the soil is moist. Have your child dig a shallow depression in the earth. Then, lay a terra-cotta flowerpot on its side and fill the pot with enough dirt to partially bury it, as pictured below.

To create an even more favorable environment, place some rocks in a wide, shallow container and fill it with water (let tap water first sit outside for two days to rid it of chlorine).

Once some toads have settled in, do not disturb their home, but do listen after dark for sounds of the happy croakers.

Garden Soap

This gritty cornmeal bar makes cleaning up after a day in the garden a cinch. Plus, your kids will enjoy shaping soap on a rope.

MATERIALS

Raffia or string
²⁄₃ cup of grated bar soap
²⁄₃ cup of cornmeal
2 tablespoons warm water
2 tablespoons baby oil
Essential oil (optional)

To make one bar, braid raffia or string into a 2-foot length (or simply use a 2-foot piece of rope), then tie together the ends to form a loop.

In a mixing bowl, combine the grated bar soap with the cornmeal. Add the warm water and baby oil. You can scent your soap by adding a few drops of essential oil (found at some craft and health stores). Use your hands to combine the ingredients until the mixture makes a stiff dough. (**Tip:** If the mixture is too dry, add more water, a teaspoon at a time.)

Shape the dough around the knotted end of the rope loop, packing it firmly. Allow the soap to dry completely before using, about 7 to 10 days.

Gardening With Kids

Indoor Gardening

Sweet Potatoes

Chances are, you sprouted sweet potatoes yourself as a kid. Although they can take up to a month to sprout, your patience will be rewarded with vividly moldering tubers. Sweet potatoes are routinely sprayed with a chemical that inhibits sprouting — a boon to shippers and grocers but a nuisance to kitchen gardeners. For faster sprouting, choose potatoes that have not been sprayed or have already started to sprout. Starting at this stage, you should see lush, vinelike plants in a matter of weeks.

MATERIALS
1 sweet potato
Glass jar
Wooden toothpicks
Potting mix
Terra-cotta flowerpot for eventual transplanting (choose a size that accommodates your tuber with room left over)

Planting technique: Pierce the middle of the sweet potato with two toothpicks, one on each side, and suspend it over the jar. Fill the jar almost to the top with lukewarm water and set it on a bright windowsill. Make sure that the pointier, root end of the potato faces downward. (Your potato will sprout if placed upside down, but it will take several weeks longer than its companions to send out roots.)

Days to sprouting: Seven to 14. The first thing you'll notice are little whiskery rootlets growing under the water. Be patient: in a week or two you should see some tiny red sprouts at the top, which will soon open into small, red-veined green leaves. Then watch out! Your sweet potato will turn into a growing machine, churning out masses of ivylike foliage at a prodigious rate.

Long-term care: When growth is about 6 to 8 inches high, it's time to transplant to a more permanent con-

KID-FRIENDLY PROJECT
Kitchen Jungle

Nothing makes a home more fun to live in than an adventure in gardening in the great indoors. But before you go out and buy expensive houseplants, ask your kids to help you sprout kitchen scraps into bright green plants. Carrots, sweet potatoes, and even oranges will happily sprout on almost any bright windowsill. And it is the element of surprise — what will we get? when will it arrive? — that makes growing a kitchen jungle so fascinating for everyone in the family.

Planting technique: Remove any greens, then cut the carrots about 2 inches down from the crowns. Fill the bowl about 1½ inches deep with pebbles, then push in the crowns until they're firmly anchored. Fill the bowl almost to the brim with lukewarm water and set it on a sunny windowsill.

Days to sprouting: Three to 6 — the most satisfying thing about sprouting carrots is their eagerness to regrow those leafy tops.

Long-term care: Aside from having their water topped up when needed (usually every other day once the plants start growing), carrots require no maintenance. When the plants begin to look tired, simply discard them and start over again.

Citrus Plants

Citrus plants are slow to grow, but even when small they're appealing, with glossy, oversize leaves topping slender "trunks." And given a modest amount of TLC, they can develop into lovely indoor trees, attaining a height of nearly 10 feet and producing a yearly display of delicate white blossoms and even fruit of their own.

MATERIALS

Peat pots
Soil-less potting mix
Citrus fruit (for best results, use juice oranges or tangerines, which are more likely to contain seeds)
Ziplock bags
Houseplant fertilizer
5-inch terra-cotta pots (for later transplanting)

Planting technique: Fill each peat pot almost to the top with the soil-less potting mix, then add water until the mix is moist throughout. In each pot, press three or four seeds of the same type about ¼ inch into the mix, making sure that they're well covered. Slip each pot into a ziplock bag, labeling it to avoid confusion. If possible, place the bags near a source of heat (the radiator in winter or a warm corner in summer). As soon as sprouts appear, remove the pot from the bag and set it on a sunny windowsill.

Days to sprouting: On average, citrus seeds take about 14 days to sprout. Ours were a bit slower, the first appearing after 3 weeks or so, and the most sluggish taking a good month before making their debut. Try not to lose patience (though after 6 weeks, you might unearth a few seeds to make sure that they haven't rotted).

Long-term care: When the plants have produced two sets of leaves, choose the strongest seedling in the pot and remove the others. This is also the time to start feeding with a soluble houseplant fertilizer diluted to half strength. Continue to keep your citrus plant moist. When roots begin to protrude through the peat pots, transplant the entire pot and seedling into the terra-cotta container (the plant's roots thus remain undisturbed; the peat pot eventually degrades).

tainer. Fill the flowerpot about a third of the way up with potting mix, then place the tuber on top of the mix and fill in around it. If at all possible, cover the tuber completely with mix to discourage rotting. Water often enough to keep the mix lightly moist.

Carrot Crowns

While you're waiting for everything else to get going, your carrot crowns will already be sending up lacy green foliage. Although the plants last only a few months, they're so quick to sprout that you can easily have them year-round.

MATERIALS

A shallow bowl (about 2 or 3 inches deep)
Pebbles or glass marbles
Water
3 or 4 carrots (preferably the kind sold with greens)

Mosaic Flowerpot

These flowerpots let you preserve treasured, but broken, pottery, loose charms, and pretty shells. The process is easy enough for even the littlest hands.

MATERIALS

Pieces of broken pottery, tiles, beads, marbles, beach glass, shells, or charms

Ceramic tile grout (available at hardware stores)

Plastic knife

Terra-cotta flowerpot

Sponge

Cover your work area with newspaper. Before your child starts decorating his pot, sort through the pottery pieces and discard any that have sharp edges (a parent's job).

Help your child spread a heavy layer of tile grout onto the flowerpot with the plastic knife. Now he can press the tile pieces into the wet grout. When he's finished making his design, help him spread a bit more grout between the pieces, so that most of the broken edges are covered. After the pot is dry, wipe off any grout film with a damp sponge.

Tip: If you don't have broken pottery, place chipped, leftover tiles in a clear plastic bag (this way you can see what you're smashing) and break them with a hammer. Another good source for broken tiles is your local tile or hardware store; many will give you broken display tiles for free.

FAMILYFUN SUCCESS STORY
Garden Gift

"At the end of the school year, the twelve girls in Girl Scout Troop #886 wanted to give a thank-you gift to their three leaders. I purchased three large terra-cotta pots, and using masking tape and paper, I covered the parts of the pots not being painted. The girls then painted a wide, white strip around each pot and divided the strip into thirteen sections, one for each girl plus one for the troop number and year. Each Scout painted a flower on each pot and initialed it. Then I sprayed the pots with a sealer, and the girls filled them with annual flowers and presented them to their leaders."

— Susan Lill
Upper Saddle River, New Jersey

Tiny Terrarium

A terrarium can teach kids a lot about tropical ecosystems — such as how water recycles itself and, in the process, supplies plants with the moisture they need to survive. Plus, the sight of green leaves can be a real boost in midwinter.

To make one, first you'll need to pick up several plants at a local nursery, florist, or garden center. Some good choices are small ivies, palms, pilea (also known as the aluminum plant), or even African violets. You'll also need to buy small bags of stone, horticulture charcoal, and potting soil.

At home, help your child layer ½ inch of stone, ½ inch of charcoal, and 1½ inches of potting soil in a widemouthed clear jar (a large pickle or mayonnaise jar works well). Next, arrange and plant the greenery in the potting soil. If your child desires, she can also add pieces of wood, pretty pebbles, or other decorative items.

Now have your child moisten (not drench) the soil and cap the jar. Place the terrarium in a well-lit place, but not in direct hot sunlight, and keep a good eye on it for the first couple of days. If water beads up on the inside of the glass, uncap the jar and let it dry out. Then add less water than the first time and recap the jar. If beading doesn't reoccur, water the plants occasionally with a mister (once every 2 to 4 weeks should suffice).

LEARNING AT HOME
Planting Peanuts

Did you know that a peanut isn't really a nut? It's related to the pea family. When the plant's bright yellow flowers fade, the stalks curve into the soil, where the seeds (peanuts) form in a pod or shell. If your family wants to try growing one, start with a raw (not roasted), shelled peanut, plant it about 1 inch deep in a pot of sandy soil, and water it well. Place the pot in a warm, sunny spot, and before long, round leaves and strong stalks should emerge.

FAMILYFUN SUCCESS STORY
Mini Greenhouses

"Each spring, my kids love starting seeds indoors. To make the process easier, I first collect a few clear parfait or sundae cups from our fast-food restaurant visits. Next, I buy peat pellets at a local gardening center, and we place one in the bottom of each cup, adding water according to the pellet instructions.

The kids enjoy watching them expand as they soak up the water like a sponge. After the pellets swell, we make a hole in each with a pencil and drop in two or three seeds. We then place the covers on the cups, put them in a sunny window, and add water as needed to keep everything moist. This is a quick and clean way to teach kids about growing seeds and to get them involved in gardening."
— Chevelle Kelly
New Bedford, Massachusetts

Desert in a Box

Maybe it's their space-alien appearance, or the way they evoke the Wild West, or the fact that they thrive with virtually no care. Whatever the reason, kids love cacti. This group planting technique lets kids have their own patch of desert, even if your climate is more arctic than Arizonan.

We started with a plastic drawer organizer filled with a 50/50 mixture of potting soil and builder's sand (you can also use premixed cactus soil). We selected a variety of miniature cacti (look for them in garden centers and florist's shops), transplanted them into the soil mix using salad tongs, and lightly watered them in. We then added a thin layer of gravel (from the pots the cacti came in), along with some desert decorations: a steer skull crafted from modeling clay, a guardian lizard (from a local craft shop), a plastic cowboy, and a road marker made from craft sticks. To keep your cacti happy, water them once a month until the soil is damp to the touch but not soggy.

CREATIVE SOLUTION
Found Art Gardening

These whimsical planters — and even the greenery inside them — can all be scavenged from around the house.

The Pot: An outgrown rain boot

The Plant: A pineapple top

Start with a layer of pebbles, then add potting soil nearly to the top of the boot. Chop the crown off the pineapple. Remove all the fruit, cut small slices in the bottom to expose the bumpy root buds, and set the pineapple crown aside for a week to dry. Plant it firmly in the boot and water so the soil remains slightly damp but never soggy.

The Pots: Toy teacups

The Plants: Grass

Mix some sand with premixed potting soil, fill each cup nearly to the rim, and spread grass seed evenly over the top. Use a mister to keep the seed moist. When the grass is up, water it lightly but frequently using a teapot.

The Pot: Toy dump truck

The Plants: Carrot tops

Layer the truck's bed with pebbles, cut the tops off the carrots (organic or any with greens, but snip off the greens), and gently work them into the pebbles. Cover the pebbles with water. In about a week, you'll see tiny buds, which will soon open into ferny foliage.

Gardening With Kids

MAKE-IT-YOURSELF
Popcorn in a Picket Planter

If your idea of the perfect garden is a drift of lush greenery nestled inside a picket fence, you don't need to wait till summer to get it. This picket planter with popcorn plants is as easy to make as popcorn itself.

The planter's base is a wooden clementine box. We glued a line of wooden clothespins to the top edge, and wooden beads atop the corner posts and the adjacent clothespins. Once the glue was dry, we gave the planter two coats of paint (we used latex semigloss wall paint). We set plastic seedling trays — easily removed for watering — inside the box and filled each to an inch from the top with potting soil. We then sprinkled on popcorn kernels (not the microwave kind) and covered them with another half inch of soil. We kept the soil moist, and our corn was up in about a week. The greenery lasted for several weeks more.

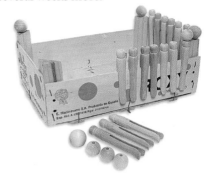

Home Resources

Organizing Ideas

1 2 3 SORT IT
www.123sortit.com

This award-winning on-line resource features the latest techniques and tools to help your family get organized. There are several useful links, tips, and a fun interactive approach. Click on "Residential Organizing" to find ideas for organizing your attic, bathrooms, kids' bedrooms, kitchen, and laundry room.

Organized Home
www.organizedhome.com

If you want to declutter your home, check out this website. Here, you'll find storage solutions and practical product reviews as well as chore checklists and a free printable household planner.

Storage Resources

The Container Store
www.thecontainerstore.com

Besides selling storage and organizational products, The Container Store offers a free custom plan to assist you in designing a workable storage space in your home — including custom-fit shelving and racks for organizing your child's closet. To find a store near you, click on the store locator.

Organize-it
800-210-7712
www.organizes-it.com

This Michigan store designs and installs storage systems to fit in any area of the house — closets, garages, pantries, utility rooms, basements, you name it. If you don't live nearby, you can purchase one of its do-it-yourself kits through its catalog (order the catalog — or view the extensive storage product line — on the store's website).

Rubbermaid
888-895-2110
www.rubbermaid.com

Rubbermaid is known for its supertight seals on its plastic storage containers — the company claims that they won't open unless you open it. Rubbermaid also offers a full range of home organization products for kitchens, baths, and your backyard. It even has insulated containers for family picnics. Click on "store locator" to find stores that sell Rubbermaid products within 30 miles from your home.

Stacks and Stacks
800-761-5222
www.stacksandstacks.com

This website offers a wide variety of bins, boxes, crates, and stackers for organizing all the odds and ends in your family home. Stack and Stacks also carries heavy-duty equipment, such as refrigerators, steam cleaners, and dehumidifiers, as well as kitchen appliances like juicers and smoothie makers. There are only three stores, all located in California, but you can request a catalog on line.

Family Home Furnishings

Ikea
800-434-4532
www.ikea.com

This global home furnishing store features items for every room in the house, from couches for your family room to cabinetry for your kitchens and baths. For kids' rooms, it has reasonably priced bunk beds, cribs, and kid-size tables and chairs. (The Project Table and chairs on page 45 cost $29.95 unpainted at Ikea). Many of the products require assembly, which keeps the prices low. Visit the website to find a store in your area, request a catalog, or place an order.

Pottery Barn Kids
www.potterybarnkids.com
800-922-9934

Pottery Barn Kids sells stylish furnishings (kids' desks, art tables, and fort beds) and accessories (comfy bedding, gingham lamps) for children's bedrooms and nurseries. It also features playful shower curtains and bath mats for kids' bathrooms. You can find a store in your area, request a catalog, or order the products on the website — and search for products by child's gender, age, and price range.

RugsUSA
877-784-7872
www.rugsusa.com

Click on "Children Rugs," to find a variety of sports, interactive, educational, and colorfully themed rugs for kids' rooms. You can also search for different types of rugs to complement other rooms in your family home. The choices are endless!

Target
www.target.com

This mass merchandiser sells an abundance of family home items, such as home décor selections, kitchenware, furniture, bins and other organizers, and laundry room supplies. For kids, it has playful bedroom furnishings and decorations, such as themed bedding sets, lamps, rugs, artwork, and attractive toy storage containers. For the other rooms in the home, it has an endless supply of affordable, fashionable furniture, from wall mirrors and bookshelves to coffee and end tables. To find a store close to you, click the "store locator."

Home Decorating Ideas
Creating Home Decor
www.creatinghomedecor.com
Do-it-yourselfers and avid crafters will find this website a great resource for home projects. It features decorator secrets, tips and hints, painting question and answers, sewing patterns, and seasonal art projects. Check out their calculators, too, before you redecorate your rooms to estimate the cost of all that wallpaper and paint.

Home and Garden Television
www.hgtv.com
Tune into the popular cable station, HGTV, to find ideas for decorating, renovating, or organizing your home. If you like an idea featured on one of the episodes, you can find the directions on hgtv.com. You'll also find home calculators, message boards, and an extensive archive of home and garden projects. The site is simple to follow: just click on your favorite topics — Decorating, Remodeling, Gardening, At Home, or Crafts. While you're there, you may also want to check out the HGTV Store for home and garden gear. Or find out when your favorite home shows air on HGTV.

Homestore
www.homestore.com
At first blush, homestore.com looks like a site solely dedicated to home buying, but root around because it's much more! Its decorating section gives ideas for themed children's bedrooms, plus reveals just exactly what

feng shui is and how it will help your family live in harmony; its gardening pages give basic tips on weeding and soil preparation, as well as specific information on how to grow different fruits and fruit trees in your yard. On the home improvement pages, you'll find everything from dressing up your driveway and snow-shoveling safety tips to how to care for wood and upholstery. There are also calculators that help you determine paint, wallpaper, and drywall needs for your home projects.

Home Improvement
Build.com
www.build.com
This excellent site will make your home improvement job easier. It contains a well-organized list of home improvement links and should be your first stop on the do-it-yourself information highway.

Handyman.com
www.handyman.com
This website offers a home improvement project library from *Family Handyman* magazine, home plans for dog houses and backyard playhouses, product and tool information, as well as homeowners advice on home projects. Be sure to check out the interactive estimators, project calculators, and special project visualizers. These tools will help you estimate the potential cost of a project, determine the materials you would need, and help you envision what the finished design will look like. Handyman.com can also assist you in finding the right contractors.

Hometime
www.hometime.com
By the producers of the PBS television show, this website is loaded with how-to articles, photos, user forums, and information on ordering instructional videos for home improvement projects.

FamilyFun.com

If you are looking to take on a fun home improvement project, check out FamilyFun.com's Home & Garden solution center. Here, you'll find all of our best projects for sprucing up your home and yard, from planning and preparing your child's first garden to building the ultimate loft bed for your child's bedroom. Here are some highlights:

◆ **Solutions: Backyard & Gardening, Get Organized, Build-it-Yourself, Design and Decoration**

◆ **Home & Garden Tools: the Home Project Finder, Weekend Project Guide, and The Garden Center**

◆ **Message boards: Come share your ideas about kids' bedroom decorations, clutter busters, and more, with other parents**

◆ **Checklists: Garden Supplies and Tools, Home Safety Basics, Kitchen Drawer Tools**

www.familyfun.com/homeandgarden

Household Tips

Michigan State University Extension
Home Maintenance and Repair

www.msue.msu.edu/imp/mod02/master02.html

This website is all business. Put together by Michigan State University, it has a plethora of household tips listed alphabetically on a site without a hint of a design. But don't let the dullness of the design deter you from checking out the know-how on issues such as preventing mildew, removing cheese from a carpet, cleaning ceramic tile walls, and repairing dents on wood furniture.

Tipking.com

www.tipking.com

This website is like a virtual grandma. It knows everything, from how to sew the perfect hem to how to rid yourself of hiccups. The 700 subjects range from Christmas Tips and Get Organized to Handyman and Car Care. Many of the entries are written by tipking.com readers.

Paint Supplies

Benjamin Moore

800-826-2623

benjaminmoore.com

Benjamin Moore & Co. carries a complete line of high-quality exterior and interior finishes and primers, industrial coatings, and sundries. In addition to its wall paints line, there are also special F/X paints including glitter, glow-in-the-dark, and chalkboard paints. It also manufactures Crayola brand interior paints. On its website, check out project ideas, as well as color selections. Click on "retail store locator" at the top of the page under "where to buy" for a retailer nearest you.

Sherwin-Williams

800-474-3794

sherwinwilliams.com

Available exclusively through Sherwin-Williams stores, this company sells quality paints and stains, a large wallpaper selection, and all the tools you'll need for painting projects. From its home page, click on "about Sherwin-Williams" to find a site map. Be sure to take advantage of the on-line painting and coatings, which has definitions of terms and phrases frequently used in the wonderful world of painting.

Home Office

Office Depot

888-463-3768

www.officedepot.com

Although Office Depot is primarily a resource for small businesses, it also serves as a practical source for any home office or computer area. Here, you'll find telephone and self-stick pads for your message area, family calendars, school supplies for the kids, and much more. You can also buy bookcases and shelving or carts and stands for your computer, kitchen, or television. Use the store locator to find a store close by or sign up for a catalog.

Office Max

800-283-7674

www.officemax.com

Office Max also carries numerous desk accessories and office supplies that work well for the home. You can also look at furniture perfect for the computer area, multimedia accessories, laptops, and monitors. On their website, look under "specialty shops" to click on "art and framing." You'll discover great decorating tips and recommendations for lengthening or broadening rooms, adding space, or heightening low ceilings. Click on "store locator" to find a store near you.

Garden Supplies

Burpee

800-333-5808

www.burpee.com

Burpee seed company stocks hundreds of vegetable and herb varieties, flowers, perennials, shrubs and vines, and fruits. A full product line is available through its catalog, but its seeds are also sold at many hardware stores and garden centers across the country. On the website, you can order seeds — and use their garden wizard tool to help you find the best plan for your garden. Be sure to check out their vegetable recipes, quick garden and kitchen tips, nutrients guide, and accessories.

National Gardening Association

802-863-5251

www.garden.org

The website of the National Gardening Association focuses on home gardening from the beginner to the expert. Explore the website for FAQs, garden crafts and recipes, lawn and landscaping articles, garden care, growing guides, how-to projects, and a plant dictionary. You can also access the National Garden Association garden shop for two shopping sites — one for plants and bulbs, and the other for gardening products. Be sure to check out the children's area, kidsgardening.com, which features garden projects for the classroom and home, garden gifts kids can make, and a store for purchasing kids' gardening tools. All profits support the NGA's educational mission.

Kitchen & Bath

Bed Bath & Beyond

800-462-3966

www.bedbathbeyond.com

This chain store carries a large selection of bath and bedding items, storage and cleaning solutions, home décor options, as well as electronics, dining, and kitchen essentials.

Linens 'N Things
866-568-7378
www.linensandthings.com
This large retailer of home textiles, housewares, and home accessories carries high-quality, brand-name furnishings. You can shop for kids' bedding, towels, and pillows, plus organization essentials and seasonal décor.

Tools and Hardware

Ace Hardware
www.acehardware.com
Ace Hardware has over 5,000 retailers across the country. In its stores, you'll find a wide range of home improvement products, such as paint, lawn fertilizer, or just a simple welcome mat. If you have a leaky faucet or need a rooftop delivery, Ace also provides both everyday and specialty services. When visiting their website, be sure to check out Answers@Ace for solutions to hardware and home improvement questions and a glossary of hand and power tools.

Home Depot
800-553-3199
www.homedepot.com
The Home Depot carries just about everything for your home needs — lawn and garden equipment, hardware and power tools, building materials, kitchen and bath products, cleaning supplies, and so on. On its website, you can locate a store nearby. If you click on the Project Index, you'll find ideas with step-by-step instructions along with useful tips and safety alerts. Click on Home Depot Expo and you'll find home design ideas and inexpensive prices for home decorating.

Lowe's
800-445-6937
www.lowes.com
Lowe's Home Improvement Warehouse stocks a number of appliances, tools, and home décor, organizational, and household products and equipment. On its website, you can design a room, new closet, or storm door through an "interactive workshop" at the top of the page.

Wall-to-Wall Fun Materials

Paints and supplies for the creative kids' bedroom on page 78

Chalkboard Paint: To turn any surface into a usable chalkboard, coat it with chalkboard paint. Crayola Paints by Benjamin Moore (see page 214) makes black paint, and Klean-Strip makes green. The black is latex, relatively odorless going on, and easy to apply with a roller. The green is oil-based, smells strong, and should be thoroughly stirred before application. Both varieties need two coats and a drying period of about three days. Follow package directions.

Corkboard: Most hardware stores carry cork in a roll for about $2 a square foot. You can cut the cork with scissors, then attach it to a corrugated cardboard base with wood glue or carpet tape. Large cork pieces curl while drying, so you may have to hold them down with masking tape. If you need only a square of cork, a regular bulletin board will do the trick.

Glitter Paint: Also from Crayola, this paint is clear with glitter suspended in it. It can be tinted if you are going to cover a whole wall with blue glitter, for example, or you can just apply it over prepainted areas to give them a glittery accent. The glitter settles rapidly in the paint can, so stir often (putting a small amount in a cup makes it easier to keep well stirred).

Glow-in-the-dark Paint: Crayola Paints makes this product ($18 a quart), which you can have tinted at the store or use over existing paints to make them glow in the dark. The more you tint these paints the less they will glow, so unless you are tinting them with a light shade, it makes more sense to paint over existing hues. They won't cover up the color — they'll just give it a milky topcoat.

Magnetic Paint: This gray paint ($60 a gallon) called Magna-Paint isn't actually magnetic; it just contains bits of metal, and thus magnets stick to it. You can work the gray color into your designs or paint over it, though this may reduce the paint's magnetic powers. Either way, you'll need two to three coats and lots of ventilation. Any magnet will work, but ceramic and vinyl sheet ones hold best. Available by calling 800-663-5690.

Marker Board: At the hardware store, ask for white bath panel; then you can cut it into shapes using a jigsaw or handsaw. A 4- by 8-foot sheet costs approximately $20. You can also buy dry-erase boards at office stores. Either way, you must use dry-erase markers.

Wall Paint: Be sure to use a semigloss or eggshell paint for your background and accents. Both, especially the semigloss, are much more washable than flat paints — you can actually scrub off dirt or crayon marks.

Home Index

Art & Photography Credits

Dazzling Du...

Special thanks to the following *FamilyFun* magazine photographers, illustrators, and stylists for their excellent work:

PHOTOGRAPHERS

Susan Barr: 24

Robert Benson: Back Cover (top left , middle right), 16, 18, 19, 45, 51 (bottom), 85 (top), 103, 124, 130 (middle), 138, 148, 149, 150, 151 (top, middle), 156, 157, 158, 159

Michael Carroll: 90 (middle), 91 (top), 117 (2 middle left)

Steven Foster: 190 (bottom left)

Peter N. Fox: 142, 154, 155 (top left, bottom), 166, 168, 169, 170, 171, 172 (top), 174, 175, 191 (top left) 194

Andrew Greto: 7 (top), 9, 11, 20 (bottom), 23, 32 (left), 53, 55, 60, 63, 66, 67 (right), 69, 71 (left), 72 (top), 76, 77, 92, 100, 109, 110, 112 (top), 116, 117 (bottom right, 2 top left), 119 (bottom), 122 (top), 128, 129 (bottom), 130 (top), 141, 153, 181 (bottom), 204, 210, 211, 223 (top)

Jacqueline Hopkins: 75 (bottom)

Ed Judice: Cover, Back Cover (top right; bottom left, bottom right), 2, 6, 7 (middle), 8, 10, 12, 13, 15, 17, 20 (top), 21, 22, 26, 27(right, bottom), 28, 29, 30, 31, 32 (right), 33, 34, 35, 36, 37, 38, 39, 40, 41, 44, 46, 47, 48, 49, 50, 52, 54, 56, 57, 58, 59, 61, 62, 64, 65, 67 (left), 68, 70, 71 (right), 73, 74, 75 (top), 78, 79, 80, 82, 83 (top), 84, 85 (bottom), 86, 88, 89 (left), 90 (top, bottom), 91 (bottom,), 93 (top, middle), 94 (top), 95, 96 (bottom), 97 (right), 98, 99, 101, 102, 104, 105 (top, middle), 106 (top, bottom), 107, 108 (bottom), 111 (bottom), 113, 114, 115,117 (top right), 118, 119 (top), 120, 121, 123, 125, 127, 129 (top), 131, 132, 133, 134, 135 (top), 136, 137, 139 (bottom), 139 (bottom), 140, 143 (right), 144, 145, 147, 152, 162, 163, 164, 165, 172 (bottom), 173, 176, 178, 181 (top), 183 (top), 184, 186, 189, 191 (top right,

bottom), 201, 202, 203, 205 (top), 208 (top), 209, 222 (bottom), 224 (top)

Al Karevy: 180, 182, 185, 187, 188, 190 (top), 200 (top, bottom left)

Kelly Laduke: 155 (top right)

Andrew Lawson/ Garden Image: 190 (bottom right)

Brian Leatart: 205 (bottom)

Dorit Lombroso: 160, 161

Lightworks Photographic: 14, 81 (top)

Mike Malyszko: 43, 51(top), 108

Tom McWilliam: 42, 126, 196, 197, 198, 199, 206, 207

Shaffer/Smith Photography: 25, 87, 96 (top), 139 (top)

Team Russell: 7 (bottom), 179, 200 (bottom right)

Stephen R. Swinburne: 192, 193

Jeremy Woodhouse/ Getty Images/ Photodisc: 177

ILLUSTRATORS

Douglas Bantz: 15, 38, 54, 57, 73, 137, 145, 146, 147, 154, 155, 163, 164, 167, 174, 175, 183 (top)

John Bidwell: 157

Bradley Clark: 204

Linda Davick: 183 (bottom)

Moira Greto: 172

Kelly Kennedy: 153

Ron Peterson: 190

Kevin Rechin: 173 (top)

Kirsten Soderlind: 173 (bottom)

STYLISTS

Bonnie Anderson/ Team, Bonnie Aunchman-Goudreau, Kevin Ayer, Rebecca Bluh, Catherine Callahan, D.J. Carey, Susan Fox, Hugh Harline, Sarah Leddick, Marie Piraino, Abigail Reiser, Ruth Steinberg, Kimberly Stoney, Maryellen Sullivan, Amy Wickland, Lynn Zimmerman

**Picture Pals,
page 69**

Changeable Chair Upholstery, page 82

Also from FamilyFun magazine

◆ **FamilyFun magazine:** a creative guide to all the great things families can do together. Call 800-289-4849 for a subscription.

◆ **FamilyFun Cookbook:** a collection of more than 250 irresistible recipes for you and your kids, from healthy snacks to birthday cakes to dinners everyone in the family can enjoy (Disney Editions, $24.95).

◆ **FamilyFun Crafts:** a step-by-step guide to more than 500 of the best crafts and activities to do with your kids (Disney Editions, $24.95).

◆ **FamilyFun Parties:** a complete party planner featuring 100 celebrations for birthdays, holidays, and every day (Disney Editions, $24.95).

◆ **FamilyFun Cookies for Christmas:** a batch of 50 recipes for creative holiday treats (Disney Editions, $9.95).

◆ **FamilyFun Boredom Busters:** a collection of 365 crafts, activities, and games for every day of the year (Disney Editions, $24.95).

◆ **FamilyFun.com:** visit us at www.familyfun.com and search our extensive archives for games, crafts, recipes, travel destinations, and creative home ideas.